ART'S EMOTIONS

Art's Emotions

Ethics, Expression and Aesthetic Experience

Damien Freeman

ACUMEN

First published in 2012 by Acumen

Acumen Publishing Limited
4 Saddler Street
Durham
DH1 3NP
www.acumenpublishing.co.uk

ISBN: 978-1-84465-511-3 (hardcover)
ISBN: 978-1-84465-512-0 (paperback)

British Library Cataloguing-in-Publication Data
A catalogue record for this book is available
from the British Library.

Printed and bound in the UK by MPG Books Group.

To the memory of Peter Avery

Contents

Acknowledgements

At the Royal Wedding in 2011, the Bishop of London remarked, "As the reality of God has faded from so many lives in the West, there has been a corresponding inflation of expectations that personal relations alone will supply meaning and happiness in life." The occasion, and the sentiments expressed, would have appealed greatly to my friend, the late Peter Avery, an orientalist and Fellow of King's College, Cambridge, who had devoted his life to Persian poetry, and in particular to the works of Háfiz of Shíráz. As I was unbuttoning Peter's waistcoat after taking dinner in Hall at King's last night, it occurred to me that the present work's underlying idea, that art allows us to reconcile ourselves to the world in a way that personal relations cannot, was central to Peter's life as much as it was to his passionate study of Háfiz.

This book has its origin in a doctoral thesis written under the supervision of Professor Raymond Geuss, of the Faculty of Philosophy in the University of Cambridge, and the shadow supervision of Dr Hallvard Lillehammer, now of Churchill College, Cambridge. The extent to which I have succeeded in refining my chaotic thoughts into some sort of argument stands as testimony to my debt to Professor Geuss for forcing me at every turn to confront their initially inchoate nature. What will be less apparent is my debt to him for the forbearance with which he faced instalment after instalment of my "appalling prose". I am also indebted to Dr Lillehammer for his periodic assessment of the direction in which my work was developing, and for his suggestions and encouragement – not least for encouraging me to commence Chapter 1 in Aramaic, which he confirmed was possibly the only ancient language that Professor Geuss does not read. If so, it is certainly the only occasion on which both Jesus and I will have one up on Professor Geuss. Whereas I am grateful for the conscientiousness with which my supervisor and shadow supervisor discharged their obligations, my gratitude to Professor Derek Matravers, of Emmanuel College, Cambridge, is of another order. He was under no obligation to read my work, and I have benefited not only from the close attention he paid to the final draft, but from his insights into the popular overestimation of the value of happiness. This has reminded me of the persisting influence that Professor Richard Wollheim has had on both of us. It is an influence best summed up in Professor Wollheim's own words when explaining the influence that the aesthetes of the past had on him: "In one way I can clearly recognize [his] continuing influence: in an impatience I have after a little while with any form of culture that turns its back on history, or complexity, or melancholy."

We have Steven Gerrard to thank for the removal of the Aramaic and insertion of subheadings, which he assures me render the work eminently more appealing to discerning readers. But more importantly, we have him to thank for the very fact of publication. This is a fact only because of his commitment to publishing new authors – a rare and precious trait in contemporary publishers. In revising the manuscript for publication, I had the benefit of most perspicacious observations about the shortcomings of my PhD thesis in the reports of my examiners, Professor Malcolm Budd and Professor Sebastian Gardner, of University College, London. Once revised, Kate Williams undertook that most thankless task of attempting to iron out such flaws as have passed by the eyes of so many before her prior to publication.

But what would any of this matter, were it not for my mother? Would that I were able adequately to acknowledge my debt to her. Perhaps she knows it. I doubt it.

D. T. F.
Pembroke College, Cambridge

Is this so-called philosophy of art a mere intellectual exercise, or has it practical consequences bearing on the way in which we ought to approach the practice of art (whether as artists or as audience) and hence, because a philosophy of art is a theory as to the place of art in life as a whole, the practice of life?

R. G. Collingwood, *The Principles of Art*

Introduction

The three perfections

In China, art that combines poetry, calligraphy and painting is known as a work of the three perfections.[1] The three perfections have long been regarded as the highest arts on account of their expressive qualities, and Shih-t'ao (1642–1707) was regarded as a master of all three expressive arts.[2] His masterpiece, *Returning Home*,[3] is a book of twelve pairs of leaves, each consisting of a poem written in calligraphy on one leaf and a painting on the facing leaf.[4] A pair of leaves such as "Gathering Lotus Flowers" is conceived of as a single entity.[5] What makes this a single entity? What is the sense in which the poetry, calligraphy and painting are unified to form a whole? The curators at New York's Metropolitan Museum of Art would have us believe that this unity comes from the sense in which the three elements complement one another: the painting illustrates the poem; the calligraphy imitates the brushstrokes of the painting; and the poem is written in the calligraphy that imitates the painting that illustrates the poem.

This reading meets with several problems. It is not clear that the painting actually illustrates the poem: the poem speaks of fields of flowers and leaves, a boat gathering flowers, and bits of lotus floating on the water; whereas the painting is a simple line drawing – in the blank-outline style – of a single flower and several leaves. There is clearly some loose connection, but the painting is not an illustration; it is not an attempt to render into visual form the subject of the poem. And while it is possible to point out how the brushstrokes of the calligraphy resemble those of the painting, this is inconsistent with the history of the development of the three perfections. Painting was the last of the three arts to be elevated to the status of the perfections, and it acquired this status at the moment when painters mastered the ability to express their inner condition through their paintings in the way that poets and calligraphers had long been able to through their art forms.[6] So if there

1

is any imitation, we should be looking for how the painting technique imitates that of the calligraphy.

An alternative way of understanding the relationship between the elements of this work of the three perfections attends to each element's status as an expressive art in its own right. Each element expresses an emotional condition through a different artistic medium. I suggest that what gives unity to this work is not that each element complements the others by illustrating or imitating them, but that each in its own way expresses emotion. What gives unity to the work is that the expressive power of each of the poem, painting, and calligraphy operate in concert to offer a special experience of emotion. Shih-t'ao's achievement is to create this "harmonized" affective experience through his command of each of the three perfections.[7] This interpretation, I suggest, allows for a deeper understanding of the unity of *Returning Home* as a work of the three perfections, one that draws on its components' common status as expressive arts. If we are to understand it in this way, however, the natural question to ask is: what is this special emotional experience that we have when we engage with each of the three perfections?

An emotional experience of art

While there may be a number of possible readings of *Returning Home*, any satisfactory reading will have to provide an adequate account of the relationship between its three elements: the poem, calligraphy and painting. We might try to understand the relationship by studying the techniques that each element employs and how these have been manipulated by the artist so as to complement each other. We might try to understand why the critic employs similar language to describe each of the three elements and try to understand what is similar about the way he uses language in his response to each of the three elements. But neither of these endeavours would help us to understand what is fundamental to the genre. The genre is fundamentally an expressive one that brings together three expressive arts. We need to understand what it means for the three elements of the work to offer its audience a harmonized expressive experience.

The reading that I have offered of *Returning Home* maintains that what is fundamental to its unity is the way in which the experience of each of the poem, calligraphy and painting are "harmonized" in order to provide a special emotional experience. This places phenomenology at the core of an appreciation of the work. If the phenomenology of the experience of a work of three perfections is fundamental to understanding the genre of the three perfections, we need to understand what this special experience is and how to give an account of it.

What do our experiences of poetry, calligraphy and painting have in common that is distinctive and valuable about them as experiences of the expressive arts? There is something that the experience of reading a poem about a man in a boat has in common with the experience of looking at a painting of a lotus flower, but which is lacking in the experience of actually seeing a man in a boat. Understanding the expressiveness of the three perfections is a matter of understanding what our experience of the painting of the flower has in common with our experience of the poem about the man, and which distinguishes both of these from the experience of seeing the actual man. In other words, there is something about the emotional experience of art that differs from other emotional experiences, and it is this difference that we must analyse in the following chapters.

Understanding this special emotional experience is not merely the key to understanding the genre of the three perfections. It is also the key to understanding the philosophical problem of the expressiveness of art. The three perfections are each expressive arts, and what unifies a work that employs all three is the relationship between the expressiveness of each element. What is fundamental to understanding their expressiveness is the emotional experience that each offers. The philosophical problem presented by the expressiveness of art is fundamentally a question about the nature and significance of our emotional experience of art, and so it is this that we must investigate.

A distinctive experience of art

Given that we seek an account of the emotional experience of works of art, how ought we to go about giving this? There are two questions that we should want to ask about such an experience: what is distinctive about the emotional experience of art; and what is valuable about this distinctive experience?

We can determine what is distinctive about a particular kind of emotional experience by placing it in the wider context of our other emotional experiences. We begin with a survey of emotional experiences, and consider the sense in which they are similar and the sense in which they differ from one another. This enables us to determine the different kinds of emotional experience that are possible and the components of such experiences, so that we can identify which components account for the distinctiveness of each kind of experience. We can then determine the sense in which our emotional experience of art is continuous with our other emotional experiences, while also isolating what, if anything, distinguishes our experience of art from other emotional experiences.

This approach appears to be in sharp contrast to that adopted by John Dewey in *Art as Experience*.[8] Dewey wants us to see that aesthetic experience does not need to be conceived of as something fundamentally different from ordinary experience. In this way, he departs from the Kantian tradition, which seeks to characterize the aesthetic nature of aesthetic experience by pitting it against ordinary experience as a distinction between interested and disinterested attention to an object.[9] Dewey argues that aesthetic experience is not a variety of experience to be distinguished from ordinary or practical experience, but rather is distinguished by the way in which the affective and perceptual parts of the ordinary experience are unified in a way that they are ordinarily not unified.

What is interesting about Dewey's approach, for present purposes, is the sense in which ordinary experiences are thought to shed light on artistic experiences, and vice versa. Dewey regards all experience as having a uniform structure, and while aesthetic experience is continuous with ordinary or practical experience, what distinguishes it is the sense in which it is an exemplary instance of the ordinary experience. This suggests both a similarity and a difference between Dewey's approach and that which is developed below. Whereas Dewey argues that all experience has a uniform structure, we shall see that the emotional experiences of our ordinary life have different structures. The emotional experience of art is not continuous with the emotional experiences of ordinary life because it shares their same structure: how could it be when the other experiences do not all have the same structure? Rather, it is continuous with the other emotional experiences because it incorporates them into a single experience. So there is a distinctive way of experiencing emotion in art, but it is not a way that is additional to our ordinary experience of emotion. It is a matter of having an experience in which each of the ordinary ways of experiencing emotion are combined into a single way of experiencing emotion. Thus, just as Dewey emphasizes the sense in which aesthetic experience is to be understood in terms of ordinary experience, so we find that the emotional experience of art is to be understood in terms of the variety of other emotional experiences.

A valuable experience of art

Does the emotional experience of art have any particular value on account of its distinctiveness? In order to answer this question, we need to determine what would give value to such an experience. The measure of value that I shall suggest is relevant is what contribution, if any, such experiences make to human flourishing. Why would we prefer a life in which the emotional experience of art is a possibility to a life in which it is not? If the experience does have some special value, it will have to be a value that it has in virtue of what is distinctive about it. Given that the distinctiveness of the experience is derived from the way in which it combines ordinary experiences, it is this combining that will have to be shown to make a valuable contribution to the good life.

Just as we determined what is distinctive about the experience by comparing it with other experiences, we can now determine how this distinctive experience enriches our lives by asking why we should prefer this distinctive emotional experience to other kinds of emotional experience. So the way to understand the expressiveness of art is to understand the emotional experience it offers, and the way to understand what is distinctive and valuable about the emotional experience art offers is to understand this kind of experience in the context of the variety of other kinds of emotional experiences that are possible. We shall find that there is a contribution that the emotional experience of art makes to the good life that other emotional experiences cannot make. By combining other kinds of emotional experiences as aspects of a single emotional experience, the experience engages the agent's emotional condition more completely than the other experiences do. This, we shall see, meets a deep need for emotional engagement.

This approach to value is also very much within Dewey's tradition. Dewey regards value as serving some need that helps the organism to cope with its environment. For him, aesthetic experience is valuable because it engages the individual more fully than any other experience does. The emotional experience of art that we shall consider below, it will be argued, engages the perceiving agent's emotional condition more fully than any other emotional experience, and in this way it is able to allow for an experience that alleviates emotional isolation through emotional engagement with the world in which it perceives emotion. As in Dewey's aesthetics, the experience is valuable for the contribution that it makes to our practical life. This places it in sharp contrast to the Kantian tradition, which characterizes aesthetic experience as something separate from practical life.[10]

Overview of the argument

The account of the emotional experience of art developed in the following chapters moves through four distinct phases. First, we shall require an account of emotion that can be used to analyse our experience of art. Second, we shall consider illustrations of different kinds of experience that involve both perceiving emotion and the perceiver's own emotion. Third, we shall analyse the emotional experiences that have been illustrated, and in doing so we shall determine what is distinctive about the emotional experience of art. Finally, having developed an account of what is distinctive about the emotional experience of art, we shall enquire into the significance of the distinctive emotional experience of art.

So we begin by considering the nature of emotion. Chapter 1 opens with a discussion of an experience of fear, and the senses in which the experience involves both a phenomenological state of being in fear and a fear-disposition – or an impulse – that gives rise to various mental and bodily phenomena, including the phenomenological state. As we see in William James's classic account, a proper analysis of the experience should account for both of these components. Such an approach allows us to consider all the aspects of the non-artistic experience and ask whether they are present in the experience of a work of art, and if so, in what sense they are part of the experience. The theory that is developed to account for this is an account of emotion as an economy of mental dispositions and mental states, and this is contrasted with Jenefer Robinson's theory of emotion as a process.

The stage is then set for Chapter 2's account of experiences of emotion in the world. We have experiences of our own emotions, as discussed in Chapter 1; for example, we feel sad. We are also aware of the presence of emotion in the world around us, and we have experiences in which we perceive this; for example, we perceive somebody else to feel sad. More often than merely perceiving emotion in the world, however, we have an emotional experience of the perceived emotion; for example, we feel sadness, or pity, or joy, or nothing at all, when we perceive somebody else to feel sad. In such experiences, there is an interaction between the perceived emotion and the perceiver's own emotion. It is this interaction that we need to investigate. In doing so, we must consider how such investigations into perceptual properties relate to the debate about the reality of aesthetic properties that Frank Sibley's work has spawned, and which continues in response to Jerrold Levinson's defence of this position. But, primarily, understanding the interaction requires an account of how the perceiver comes to perceive a psychological property – such as emotion – in the world.

There are, I shall suggest, two ways in which we can perceive emotion in the world around us. First, we might conceive of what we perceive as a subject that possesses a psychology. In this case, our perception of emotion is the perception of the externalization of what the perceived subject is feeling. This is the sense in which a baby's cry externalizes or expresses how the baby feels. Second, we might not conceive of the object as possessing a genuine psychology, but we might conceive of it as being appropriate to project our own emotion onto. In this case, we can perceive the object to possess a projective emotional property. This is the sense in which Wordsworth might be thought to have perceived the daffodils to be jocund. In some cases, only one of these two forms of perception is possible; in other cases both are possible. The difference between perceiving externalized properties or projective properties, or both kinds of properties, gives rise to the variety of emotional interactions that we shall investigate.

Chapter 3 provides an account of the different experiences in which the perceived emotion and the perceiver's emotion can interact, and discusses the relevance of externalized or projective properties for such experiences. The first of these interactions – "infection" – is an experience in which the perception of an emotional property is attended by the perceiver's feeling an emotion identical to that which he perceives. The second kind of interaction is that of "communication", in which the perception of emotion is not attended by the perceiver's feeling the same emotion, but by his feeling some other emotion in response to that which he perceives. This is the experience that most commonly occurs in human interaction when, say, the perception of another person's fear is experienced by the perceiver with his own feeling of pity. The third kind of interaction is "articulation". In this case, the perceived emotion does not prompt the perceiver to feel the emotion he perceives or any other. Rather, it encourages him to comprehend for himself the nature of that emotion. The perception of an emotion does not necessitate that the perceiver comprehends it: to comprehend an emotion is something distinct from perceiving or feeling it. So we need an account of what it means to comprehend a feeling, and the experience in which a perceiver is prompted to do so.

These different interactions are treated as discrete experiences in Chapter 3. They might also, however, form aspects of a single experience. Chapter 4 provides an account of the kind of experience that combines all three interactions, an experience I call the plenary experience of emotion. It is at this point that a theory of artistic experience emerges. We find that, in the case of works of art, we can perceive both externalized properties and projective properties in the same object, whereas we can only perceive externalized properties or projective properties in other objects of perception. For this reason, all three interactions can form aspects of an experience of a work of art. This creates the possibility of a distinctive kind of emotional experience, one that only occurs when we engage with a work of art.

It is not enough, however, to identify a distinctive kind of experience, unless we can say what is valuable about that experience. In Chapter 5, we consider why the possibility of having a plenary experience of emotion makes a valuable contribution to human flourishing and, hence, why art, as the object of such an experience, is intrinsically valuable to us. It is the intrinsic value of the experience of art that is linked, by Malcolm Budd, to its artistic value. So the plenary experience of emotion will count as an artistic value if its value is shown to be intrinsic to the experience of the work of art.

Roger Scruton connects the idea of feeling at home in the world with the value of art through his account of beauty. I suggest that it might also be connected to art through the emotional experience offered by art. The argument developed in Chapter 2 makes use of the idea that, in addition to having our own emotions, we are able to perceive the presence of emotion in the world. In Chapter 5, certain consequences of these two capacities are investigated. In particular, it is argued that a creature capable of having an emotional response to the world needs to be able to respond to the emotions that he perceives in the world if he is to feel at home in the world. Failure to respond in this way will result in emotional isolation. The desire to escape emotional isolation provides the basis for understanding the value of the plenary experience of emotion.

The different interactions that form part of the plenary experience each involve an engagement with different parts of the emotional economy. Drawing on the idea of a characteristic mixture of activity and passivity that Naomi Eilan developed in relation to perception, and which Peter Goldie has suggested might be applied to emotion, Chapter 1 argues that, although we are either active or passive in respect of each part of this economy, the emotional economy can be understood in terms of its characteristic mixture of activity and passivity. Unlike the discrete experiences that involve a single interaction, the plenary experience is an engagement that involves both emotional activity and passivity. This engagement with the whole emotional economy enables us to escape emotional isolation. Because art alone offers us the plenary experience, it is uniquely positioned to offer us the requisite emotional engagement for escaping from emotional isolation. In this way, our emotional experience of art offers a unique contribution to the good life. In proposing such a link between the emotional experience of art and ethical life, it is necessary to consider how this claim relates to the relationship between art and morality as this has been understood by other theorists, such as Berys Gaut, in his work on the ethical criticism of art.

Wollheim's influence on the argument

The ideas and general philosophical approach of Richard Wollheim are frequently to be found beneath the surface of this argument.[11] There are four aspects of his philosophy that have exerted a profound influence on my own. First, his interest in art and emotion rejects any attempt to focus on linguistic concerns.[12] Rather, he characteristically begins his analysis by considering features of our experience. This is the second influence: a contemplation of some aspect of the phenomenology of an aesthetic or affective experience that the philosopher's intuitions suggest holds the key to explaining the experience.[13] Third, the explanation of the key aspect of the phenomenology of experience often involves having recourse to a depth psychology not commonly consulted in analytic philosophy.[14] For Wollheim, this means the hypotheses of Kleinian psychoanalysis. Within the more generous conception of mind accommodated by the depth psychology, Wollheim is able to explain highly sophisticated activities, such as aspects of artistic appreciation, in terms of much more basic – or archaic – mental functioning. This introduces the fourth influential aspect of his approach. Once features of the mind's primary activities are identified (whether these form part of the depth psychology or ordinary psychology), Wollheim seeks to show how aspects of the remarkable breadth of human experience can be explained in terms of the redeployment of more basic features of our primary experiences in ways that give rise to highly sophisticated secondary experiences.[15] So, for instance, projection is primarily a defence mechanism in psychoanalytic theory. But Wollheim attempts to demonstrate how it is possible for this capacity, once in place, to be redeployed in a way that accounts for our more sophisticated capacity for expressive perception.[16] While I do not always agree with the way in which Wollheim argues that mental functioning is redeployed, the idea that the features of ordinary experience can form the basis for more specialized experiences is at the core of my account of the ways in which we perceive emotional properties in works of art.

What makes this a legitimate philosophical approach is Wollheim's conception of the philosophical project and the nature of philosophical explanation. In the introduction to *On the Emotions*, Wollheim explains that his work is an exercise in applied philosophy, and he identifies three features that distinguish applied philosophy from pure philosophy.[17] First, whereas the method employed in pure philosophy is conceptual analysis understood as linguistic analysis, applied philosophy supplements linguistic analysis with whatever else will serve its needs, for example observation, experiment, common usage, and even traditional lore. Second, applied philosophy does not aim at conceptual necessity, but at the lower standard of theoretical necessity: it aims at giving an account of how things happen to be, rather than how they must be in all possible worlds. Finally, applied philosophy studies the more general features of this world or a fragment thereof, whereas pure philosophy is concerned with giving an account of things as they must be anywhere. Like Wollheim, I am inclined to think that the study of emotion, art and the deeper parts of the mind benefits from such an approach, and I conceive of this study as an exercise in applied philosophy. I shall not endeavour to argue why this is the best approach, but any headway that the project makes will stand as testimony to the value of studying the subjects in this way.

Art and human possibilities

This account of the plenary experience of emotion in art allows us to understand what is distinctive and valuable about our experience of *Returning Home*. The interpretation I have offered of *Returning Home* is not advanced as the only interpretation, nor even as the one Shih-t'ao necessarily intended. It is simply one possible interpretation of the work. There may be a number of different ways in which we can understand such a work, and these might all be valid interpretations.[18] In *Radical Hope*, Jonathan Lear asks what it would mean to find a way for one's thick ethical concepts to persist after the collapse of the civilization in which they were formed.[19] He discusses the way in which the last great chief of the Crow nation, Plenty Coups, was able to make use of two dreams he had as a child in order to "thin down" the Crow concept of courage and, in doing so, to develop a new concept of courage that was meaningful in a context in which the traditional life of hunting and warfare was no longer possible. In offering this interpretation of Plenty Coups's dream and its place in his life, Lear acknowledges that the account that he gives is not necessarily historically accurate: it might not have been how Plenty Coups actually interpreted his dream. But that does not affect Lear's project. His argument is that there is a way of understanding the dream and its significance for the Crow people that shows how it might have been possible for them to reinvent their ethical concepts after the collapse of their old way of life.[20] This, for Lear, shows us something about an important human possibility: the capacity that we all have to survive cultural devastation. It is in this spirit that I begin with *Returning Home*. I do not need to argue that the experience that I suggest we can have of the work is the one that the appropriately qualified Chinaman of taste actually has. Rather, my purpose is to demonstrate that there is a special experience that it is possible for him to have, and why it is important that this experience is possible.

There are a number of different ways in which we can experience a work of art such as *Returning Home*. These different experiences might all be valuable, perhaps for different reasons. Part of the value of a work of art might be that it is susceptible to being experienced in different ways. In investigating one possible experience, I do not suggest that it is more important than other ways of experiencing art. Rather, I hope to show why the emotional experience of art that I describe is one possibility, and why it is an important one. It is possible, I suggest, to perceive emotion in different ways, and these possibilities give rise to different ways in which we can engage with perceived emotion. The particular experience of art that I describe draws together these different ways in which we can experience emotion in the world.

So this is a study of the possibilities that our emotional nature holds for our interaction with the world, and of one possible experience that art offers on account of our capacity for these different emotional interactions. My account is not intended to explain what actually happens whenever we attend to a work of art. Rather, I have tried to explain what might happen, and why it is important for human flourishing that this is possible. It is, then, a study of human possibilities: of what we are capable of, and of how this enables works such as *Returning Home* to enrich our lives.

1

The emotional economy

Belshazzar the king made a great feast to a thousand of his lords, and drank wine before the thousand ... In the same hour came forth fingers of a man's hand, and wrote over against the candlestick upon the plaster of the wall of the king's palace; and the king saw the palm of the hand that wrote. Then the king's countenance was changed in him, and his thoughts affrighted him; and the joints of his loins were loosed, and his knees smote one against another.

(Daniel 5:1–6)

Fear

When Belshazzar saw the writing on the wall he was afraid. We are provided with an account of the object of his fear: the hand that appears mysteriously at the feast and writes on the wall. We are also given an account of the occurrent states that constitute the king's response to this stimulus: the change in his countenance, the thoughts that entered his mind, the feeling of his joints loosening, and the smiting of his knees against each other. We are told less about why he responds to the object in these particular ways. This is hardly surprising, as biblical narrative is largely concerned with action rather than emotion, and gives the audience a free hand to fill in the psychology of the characters.[1] So in this case we are left to speculate about what precipitated these responses in Belshazzar. Was it his attitude to the supernatural? His desire to retain power? His frustration at his own inability to read what the hand wrote? Was it simply the effect of the alcohol he had consumed? Was it an instinct? Or were they simply arbitrary responses that occurred for no particular reason?

What is clear is that such an experience of fear involves two aspects: Belshazzar's fear in the sense of the fear-state that he was in, and also his fear in the sense of the fear-disposition – the trigger that initiates these states as the appropriate responses to his perception of a supernatural hand writing on the wall. When we seek to provide an analysis of this illustration of an experience of fear, we need to analyse fear both as the occurrent states that constitute a response and as the disposition that initiates these states as a response to the object of fear. So a full account of a fear-experience would have to tell us about fear as the phenomenology of the fear-state and as the underlying fear-disposition that makes such states an appropriate response to the object.[2]

If, like Belshazzar, our ordinary experiences of fear involve both occurrent responses and dispositions that precipitate the responses, we can ask whether either or both aspects of the ordinary experience of fear might, in some sense, form part of other experiences that we have. When we turn to our experience of art, for instance, we might ask whether either or both of the two elements of the ordinary experience of fear can in some way lend a sense of fear to the experience of a painting such as Rembrandt's *Belshazzar's Feast*.[3] In this painting, Rembrandt captures the suddenness of the shocking vision through *chiaroscuro* and various other techniques that manipulate light and shadow to evoke a mood of shock, awe and fear.[4] If the work succeeds in expressing Belshazzar's fear, we might compare the components of an ordinary experience of fear, such as Belshazzar's, with those involved in the experience of fear that attends the experience of Rembrandt's work of art. In this way, we will be able to provide an account of what distinguishes the emotional experience of art from other emotional experiences.

Whereas Rembrandt seeks to offer us an experience of the moment of fear when the imminent destruction of an empire is anticipated, in *Guernica*,[5] Picasso offers us an experience of the moment of suffering felt in the immediate aftermath of the destruction of the Basques' ancient town and cultural centre by German bombers during the Spanish Civil War. This monumental painting does not attempt to depict a scene or narrate a story. It is simply an expression of suffering. Picasso does not refer directly to the town or the aeroplanes, the explosion, geography or time when this happened. He uses personal imagery of the girl, the bull and the horse to depict suffering. John Berger regards the painting as a protest even though there is no depiction of what it is a protest against:

> Where is the protest then?
> It is in what has happened to the bodies – to the hands, the soles of the feet, the horse's tongue, the mother's breasts, the eyes in the head. What has happened to them *in being painted* is the imaginative equivalent of what happened to them in sensation in

the flesh. We are made to feel their pain with our eyes. And pain is the protest of the body.

Just as Picasso abstracts sex from society and returns it to nature, so here he abstracts pain and fear from history and returns them to a protesting nature ... Picasso appeals to nothing more elevated than our instinct for survival.[6]

Berger speaks of the painting prompting us to feel pain *with our eyes*, and of the painting engaging with an instinct. At this point it is unclear to us what it would mean for us to perceive such emotion in the painting. But it seems clear that Berger takes for granted that this is what happens, and that in some way this perception engages with certain emotional states and instincts or dispositions. Exactly what it would mean for this to occur requires philosophical analysis.

We would want a philosophical account of our experience of art to explain what it means for Rembrandt to create an image in which the spectator sees fear, and for this to engage with the spectator's fear. And we would want the same analysis to account for how Picasso's very different painting can achieve a similar effect in which the spectator sees suffering and this engages with the spectator's suffering. Such an account would explain how the artists seek to engage either or both of the spectator's emotional states and emotional dispositions. The analysis of emotional experiences of art in terms of the engagement with emotional states and emotional dispositions enables us to compare the experience of looking at *Belshazzar's Feast* with that of looking at *Guernica* by identifying what they both aspire to, and evaluating which is more successful. Armed with this theory, we are able to explain why Picasso's picture might be regarded as more successful than Rembrandt's, if it is better able to engage with both our emotional states and dispositions. It also allows us to compare how fear-states and fear-dispositions attend our experience of looking at *Belshazzar's Feast* with how fear-states and fear-dispositions might have attended Belshazzar's own experience of the hand writing on the wall at the feast. Indeed, it shall be a recurrent theme of mine that we can only properly understand the emotional experience of art when our analysis allows us to compare the experience of *Belshazzar's Feast* with both other artistic and non-artistic experiences of emotion.

This suggests that what is required is an analysis of fear-experiences in terms of fear-states and fear-dispositions and an account of the different ways in which these mental states and mental dispositions attend artistic and non-artistic experiences. A quite distinct project would begin by asking which of the components of Belshazzar's fear-experience we should identify as the fear-emotion. Are we able to say whether his fear-emotion is more fundamentally the fear-state or the fear-disposition that gives rise to the fear-state? It might be thought that this is in need of resolution before we can study the relationship between art and emotion: first we determine what emotion is, and then we consider whether it is ever a component of our experience of art. Such conceptual analysis of emotion, however, might not benefit our study of art. So we must begin by considering not only what is the best way to theorize about emotion, but also which approach to emotion will most enhance our study of art.

Mental states and mental dispositions

How are we to theorize about the constituents of experiences such as Belshazzar's fear? Any explanation will have to account for both the disposition to respond to an object in a particular way and the particular responses to the object. There are several ways in which we might go about doing this. First, we might acknowledge that such experiences involve two distinct kinds of phenomena, and offer a discrete account of each of them. Second, we might argue that one of the components is more fundamental, and that the other component – and, indeed, the experience to which they both contribute – can be understood in terms of the first component. In this case, an analysis of emotion is really only concerned with understanding the fundamental concept. Third, we might argue that a proper analysis cannot explain the experience in terms of either one of the two concepts. Rather, both concepts need to be explained not independently, but as two components of a unified account of a broader psychological phenomenon; for example, Belshazzar's fear-disposition and fear-state need to be analysed as components of his fear-experience, rather than as discrete phenomena, one of which might be identified with the fear-emotion.

The contemporary literature on emotion in analytic philosophy is essentially a response to (which often includes a radical departure from) William James's analysis of emotion in *The Principles of Psychology*.[7] What was regarded as radical about James's approach to emotion is his definition of emotion in terms of our feeling of bodily changes rather than in terms of cognitive activity. Following James, the question of whether emotion is to be identified with somatic or cognitive states has occupied much of the recent philosophy of emotion. However, that is not my interest. What concerns me is the explanatory use James makes of dispositions and states in his account of emotional experiences such as fear.[8]

It is well to begin by asking which of the three approaches to analysis of states and dispositions sketched out at the beginning of this section James takes. Depending how one interprets the relationship between the two relevant chapters of the *Principles*, James might be interpreted as analysing emotion in any of these three ways. Critical attention has focused on Chapter 25, "The Emotions". This has led James's interpreters to locate his full analysis of a fear-experience in the analysis he offers of emotion in terms of the felt experience of a bodily state. On this reading, James argues that one component of the experience (the fear-state) is fundamental to the experience and all that is required is the proper analysis of this component. However, when we appreciate that the preceding Chapter 24, "Instinct", deals with another aspect of experiences such as fear (the fear-impulse), it becomes apparent that James might be read as identifying two components of the experience and offering a discrete analysis of each. If James does identify two components of the experience, we might then wonder whether a better interpretation would not involve reading the two chapters together as providing a unified account of two components of a certain kind of psychological experience, rather than as two discrete accounts of distinct psychological concepts.

When James is read as providing an account of two discrete psychological concepts, Chapter 24 is concerned with instinct as an impulse to action and Chapter 25 is concerned with emotion as the feeling of a bodily change. For James, instinct is the faculty of acting to produce ends without foresight of those ends, or without previous education. Instinct is a reflex action: an impulse. However, these impulses are not blind. An individual's early experience of the impulse creates expectations that either reinforce the impulse or inhibit it. In this way, action is a function of instinct as modified by the life that the individual leads, and the impulse can be seen to evolve over the course of an individual's life history. To suggest that impulses are reflexive is also misleading for another reason. Contrary instincts might act upon the same object, and the resulting conflict might block one of the instincts, thus diminishing the predictability of the reflex. Instincts can also be inhibited by habit. Partiality to the first specimen might make an agent unresponsive to subsequent specimens. Furthermore, some instincts are transitory and, having matured at a certain age, fade away unless a habit is formed. What all of this tells us is that the impulses that determine how we respond to situations are instinctual; but they also run a course that is influenced by the vicissitudes of the agent's life.

In Chapter 25, James provides his famous account of emotion as the feeling of bodily changes. He argues that "the bodily changes follow directly the perception of the exciting fact, and that our feeling of the same changes as they occur is the emotion".[9] In making this claim, his principal concern is to refute the commonsense intuition that bodily changes are consequences of emotions. Thus, although we think that we weep because we are sad, in fact we are sad because we weep. It is a fact, for James, that a pre-organized mechanism enables perceived or imagined objects to excite bodily changes, and every one of these changes is felt when it occurs. That these feelings are the emotions is thought to be apparent from the fact that, when we abstract the feelings of bodily symptoms from an emotion, we find that there is nothing left: there is no residue of "mind-stuff".[10] This theory of emotion has been submitted to close scrutiny over the last century. While there are some glaring errors (such as James's erroneous claim that all bodily changes are felt), the current neuroscience seems to suggest that James is correct in thinking that bodily changes precede our registration of an emotion.[11]

I introduced my initial illustration of fear as an example of a fear-experience. James's accounts of instinct and emotion might then be understood as two independent phenomena that are part of this particular kind of experience: the fearsome object excites the fear-instinct and the fear-emotion. Each of these components of the experience can be studied separately. The prevailing approach among James's interpreters, however, has not been to treat this as a study of "emotional experiences" (in which one asks "What are the components of an experience of fear?"), but to treat him as enquiring into the concept of emotion (in which one asks "What is the essence of the concept of fear?"). When read in this way, what matters is that he identifies emotion with the feeling of a bodily change, and this is regarded as a definition of emotion. By interpreting Chapter 25 as a definition of emotion, the disposition identified in the previous chapter ceases to feature in an account of what constitutes an emotion. The impulse might be causally responsible for the experience of an emotion at a particular point in time, but it is not relevant to understanding what an emotion is. When James is read in this way, the issue becomes one of whether he has correctly identified the emotion with the feeling of the somatic state, and, if not, what modification needs to be made to the account in Chapter 25 in order to identify the emotion correctly. Whereas my first reading of James regards the project as analysing a kind of psychological experience that involves two discrete psychological concepts, this second reading understands the project as one in the conceptual analysis of emotion.

Both of these interpretations assume that the two chapters are to be treated discretely (either as studies of discrete aspects of a particular kind of experience, or as studies of discrete concepts). The question is whether the subject of one or both chapters is relevant to the issue for which we seek an account. An alternative approach, however, is to read the two chapters as providing a sustained account of the same issue. Wollheim argues that the correct way to understand James is to read the two chapters as providing a single theory of the concept of emotion.[12] He maintains that we should really understand the impulse identified by James in Chapter 24 as providing the emotion's dispositional context, and the felt state in Chapter 25 as the feeling state in which the emotional disposition manifests itself. James's error lies in his terminology: Wollheim maintains that James should have called the felt state described in Chapter 25 "feeling" rather than "emotion", and he could then have called the impulse discussed in Chapter 24 by the more accurate term "emotion", rather than the misleading term "instinct". When we read Chapter 25 in isolation, as James's interpreters have done, Wollheim believes that we get a distorted picture of James's concept of emotion. Wollheim's own theory of emotion identifies it with a mental disposition rather than a mental state, so it suits him to argue that, when James is read accurately, he too identifies emotion with a mental disposition and feeling with a mental state.

Whether or not we subscribe to Wollheim's own theory of emotion as a mental disposition, I suggest that there is still good reason to read the two chapters together. It is clear that, for James, a fear-experience must be analysed in terms of a fear-impulse that disposes the subject to respond in a particular way to a perceived, imagined or remembered object, and in terms of a fear-state that the subject is caused to feel on account of the fear-disposition.[13] If our primary concern is in understanding the ontology of the fear-emotion, it matters that we can resolve whether to identify the fear-emotion with the fear-state or the fear-disposition. If, however, our primary concern is to offer an analysis of the fear-experience, then the ontology assumes less significance. What matters now is that we understand the way in which the fear-disposition and the fear-state interact in order to give rise to a fear-experience. Ultimately, James's account of phenomena such as fear involves both the disposition in Chapter 24 and the state in Chapter 25. For some purposes, it might be important to understand what sense of fear should be identified as the fear-emotion. For other purposes, however, what matters is an understanding of the contribution of the different fear-phenomena to the fear-experience. James's account of this experience is best understood by reading the two chapters as offering a single account.

Does it matter that James can be interpreted in these different ways? There are several reasons why we might think that it matters. One reason is simply that we are interested in determining the correct interpretation of a text that is of historical significance. Another reason might be that, through the process of working out what James means, we can clarify the correct way to approach the concept of emotion (indeed, this is Wollheim's motivation). A further reason, however, is that an awareness of the alternatives prompts us to ask which approach to emotion will best facilitate our study of art. Implicit in the separation of the last two reasons is the thought that what turns out to be the proper conceptual analysis of emotion might not end up being the most useful approach to emotion when we are interested in studying the place of emotion in our experience of art. If there is a difference between these two projects, in this chapter we must pursue the account that will be most serviceable in the study of art, rather than the one that might prevail as an analysis of the concept of emotion. Given that James provides us with separate accounts of fear as instinct and fear as emotion, we are presented with two choices. Either we pursue one of the two accounts, as emotion theorists have done in the literature that has developed in response to Chapter 25, or we can try to provide a unified account of experiences such as fear that incorporates James's senses of fear as instinct and fear as emotion. It depends whether we require a theory of the concept of emotion or a theory of emotional experience. In deciding which course to take, we must ask which will most assist our analysis of the emotional experience of art.

Theorizing about emotion and art

In order to develop an account of the emotional experience of art, we must first say something about emotion. We have seen that the experience of an emotion such as fear might involve both a mental state and a mental disposition, and that there are at least three ways in which we might analyse emotion in terms of these. Which analysis we adopt depends upon which we judge to be most useful when we approach the relationship between theory of emotion and theory of art. There are at least two approaches that we might take to the relationship between theorizing about emotion and theorizing about art: the conceptual approach and the experiential approach.

In suggesting that there are two approaches, I am concerned with two approaches to the significance of claims about the ontology and conceptual analysis of emotion for an account of the emotional experience of art. The conceptual approach begins by seeking to resolve the issues about the ontology or conceptual analysis of emotion raised in the previous section, and then recruits the fruits of these investigations for the study of the emotional experience of art. The experiential approach, on the other hand, does not seek to draw ontological conclusions about the nature of emotion before proceeding to analyse the artistic experience. It maintains that we need not resolve the ontological issues in order to investigate the emotional experience of art. By considering these two approaches, we shall establish whether or not it is necessary to have an ontology of emotion before proceeding to analyse the emotional experience of art.

The conceptual approach begins by asking whether the concept of emotion is properly understood in terms of a mental state or a mental disposition. Once this is resolved, emotion is either identified with a certain mental state or with a certain mental disposition. Turning to art, we then need to determine whether the experience of a work of art ever involves the identified mental phenomenon. In this way, the conceptual theorist maintains that an understanding of the connection between art and emotion requires us first to understand what emotion is.

The experiential approach begins by asking what kinds of mental states and mental dispositions our ordinary emotional experiences involve. Once this is resolved, we turn to our experience of art and enquire into whether these experiences ever involve the same mental states and dispositions and, if so, how they are involved. In this way, the experiential theorist maintains, we are able to see the relationship between ordinary emotional experiences and the emotional experience of art.

Which approach is best for delivering a theory of art and emotion? Let us first imagine that we are conceptual theorists. At the outset, we will have to decide whether to identify emotion with a mental state or a mental disposition. Let us say for the sake of argument that we identify it with a certain kind of mental state. We then go to the National Gallery in London and view *Belshazzar's Feast*. As conceptual theorists, we will want to determine whether our experience of the painting involves the mental state that we have identified with the concept of emotion. Either the fear-state is involved in some way or it is not. But what about the fear-disposition? It might or might not be involved in our experience of *Belshazzar's Feast*, but because the disposition has not been identified with the concept of emotion, it does not get a look in. The conceptual theorist is oblivious to the presence of any mental phenomena that attend both the primary experience of fear and the experience of fear upon looking at a painting, if those mental phenomena are not identified with the concept of emotion. In contrast, the experiential theorist is not oblivious in this way. He takes full account of all the phenomena that attend the primary experience and investigates whether all or any of them are involved in the artistic experience in any way. As experiential theorists, we identify both the fear-state and the fear-disposition in a primary experience of fear, and proceed to ask whether either or both are involved in any way in the spectator's experience of *Belshazzar's Feast*.

It should now be clear that the experiential approach is preferable to the conceptual approach for present purposes. The conceptual approach requires us to make a preliminary judgement about the relative significance of mental states and mental dispositions, and in this way restricts our ability to consider the significance that the range of mental phenomena attending experiences such as fear have for the experience of works of art. This is not a criticism of conceptual analysis of emotion. Rather, it is a claim that what interests us when we think about the emotional experience of art is something broader than what might interest us when we engage in conceptual analysis of emotion. The investigation of the emotional experience of art need not be concerned with the ontology of emotion.

It is for this reason that I have used the experience of fear as my standard example in this chapter rather than an experience of "emotion". Depending how one conceives of emotion, fear might involve more than emotion. In

James's terms, it might involve instinct and emotion; in Wollheim's terms, it might involve emotion and feeling. If we want to study the way in which a phenomenon such as fear can be part of an experience such as the spectator's experience of *Belshazzar's Feast*, we are interested in all the salient aspects of our ordinary experience of fear. If the primary experience involves a fear-impulse, and if that impulse is triggered in the ordinary way, or in some other sense, when we see *Belshazzar's Feast*, then that fear-impulse is relevant to our study of the experience of art whether or not the impulse is strictly to be identified with the fear-emotion. The experiential approach can accommodate this in a way that the conceptual approach might not.

Which analysis of emotion does the experiential approach to art and emotion recommend? Of the three options canvassed in the previous section, the second option, that of identifying one of the two phenomena as fundamental, will not help this approach: such a conceptual identification provides the sort of restriction that this approach seeks to avoid. That leaves the first and third options. Of these two, the third is preferable. Although both acknowledge the need to provide an account of the mental state and the mental disposition, the first does so by treating them as discrete concepts, whereas the third treats them as components of a broader phenomenon. When we conceive of an experience of fear as something that involves mental dispositions and mental states, instinct and emotion, emotion and feeling, we conceive of something coherent, albeit something that involves more than one concept. It is this coherent thing that is relevant to our study of art, and it is this that we are best able to account for through the third analysis. So it is this analysis that the experiential approach recommends that we adopt in the current investigations.

Malcolm Budd begins his study of *Music and the Emotions* with a chapter enquiring into the nature of emotion, and he begins that chapter with the claim that although emotion can be understood either episodically or dispositionally, it is as an episode that we are to understand the more basic sense of emotion.[14] He claims that the episode must be more fundamental than the disposition because at least one aspect of the disposition is the tendency to undergo the episode. This does not establish that the disposition can be reduced to the state, but only that one thing we will have to understand in order to understand the disposition is the state. For this reason, it is convenient for Budd to argue that when we are concerned with our emotional experience of music, we should attend to emotion as an occurrent state. What concerns me, however, is that if we begin such a study of music and emotion by asking an ontological question about what kind of mental phenomenon we should be looking for in our experience of music, we assume that we must be looking for *either* the disposition *or* the mental state. If it should turn out that some aspect of the emotional disposition other than the tendency to undergo the episode is relevant to our experience of music, we will be oblivious to this because of the initial decision to restrict our attention to the emotional state.

What is needed is a comparison between the primary experience and the artistic one. This does not require an ontological distinction. Whether we speak of instinct and emotion as James does, or emotion and feeling as Wollheim does, the question is whether either or both of these are aspects of our experience of art. What we require for this purpose is not an account of whether emotion is properly a mental disposition or a mental state, but an account of the interaction between the mental disposition and mental state in our ordinary affective life that we might then compare with the mental phenomena we find in our emotional experience of art.

The emotional economy

What we now require is an account of emotion that allows us to accommodate both the sense in which it is a state that can be a response to the world and the sense in which it is a mental disposition that gives rise to the response as an appropriate response. I shall offer such an account of emotion that incorporates both of these by conceiving of emotional life as an economy or organized system of parts. The basis for this theory of emotional economy may be found in Wollheim's theory of emotion. However, once we have considered his theory, we shall see that certain adjustments must be made so that the mental disposition he regards as the emotion can instead be conceived of as a part of an economy we conceive of as the emotion. Such a system can account for the fear-disposition and the fear-state that attend Belshazzar's experience of fear when he sees the hand writing on the wall. It will also serve as a basis for investigating how certain parts of the system are involved in the spectator's emotional experience of *Belshazzar's Feast*.

Central to Wollheim's theory of emotion is his classification of mental phenomena either as mental states or mental dispositions. Mental states are the transient events that form our stream of consciousness, and include

> perceptions, such as hearing the dawn chorus, or seeing a constellation of stars overhead; sensations, such as pains, and itches, and pangs of hunger or thirst; dreams, and daydreams; moments of despair, boredom, or lust; flashes of inspiration; recollections; images seen in the mind's eye, and tunes heard in the head; and thoughts, both thoughts that we think and those uninvited thoughts which drift into the mind.[15]

Mental dispositions are "those more or less persisting modifications of the mind which underlie this sequence of mental states", such as "beliefs and desires; knowledge; memories; abilities, powers, and skills; habits; inhibitions, obsessions, and phobias; and virtues and vices".[16] Mental states and mental dispositions share the properties of intentionality and grades of consciousness (i.e. they may be conscious, pre-conscious, or unconscious). Only mental states have the property of phenomenology (which property Wollheim refers to as subjectivity).[17] Thus, whereas mental states may be experienced directly, mental dispositions can only be experienced indirectly, through their interaction with mental states.

Mental states and mental dispositions can interact in various ways. A mental state might initiate, terminate or intensify a mental disposition; for example, the mental state that is Belshazzar's perception of the hand writing on the wall initiates his fear-disposition. More importantly, mental dispositions might manifest themselves in mental states; for example, the mental disposition that is Belshazzar's fear of the hand manifests itself in certain thoughts and feelings.

Emotions, for Wollheim, are fundamentally mental dispositions, and he distinguishes different kinds of mental dispositions according to the role they play in our psychological life. He uses the metaphor of a map to explain the different roles of belief, desire and emotion dispositions: the role of our beliefs is to map the world; our desires provide the targets on the map at which we aim; and our emotions tinge certain parts of the map with different emotional colours, making some parts seem desirable and others not so.[18] But what does it mean for emotion to colour experience?[19] For Wollheim, emotion is an attitude to, or way of perceiving, the world. It colours current experience by perceiving it through a lens developed out of past experiences of frustration or satisfaction of desire. To understand how emotion memorializes the past, Wollheim argues that we have to understand the characteristic history through which an emotion usually develops:

(one) we have a desire:
(two) this desire is satisfied or it is frustrated, or it is in prospect of being one or the other: alternatively, we merely believe one of these things of it:
(three) we trace the satisfaction or frustration, real or merely believed-in, actual or prospective, to some thing or some fact, which we regard as having precipitated it:
(four) an attitude develops on our part to this precipitating factor:
(five) this attitude will generally be either positive – that is, tinged with pleasure – or negative – that is, tinged with unpleasure

– though sometimes it may be neutral. And it will generally be positive if it originates in satisfaction, and negative if it originates in frustration, but this is not exceptionless:

(six) the attitude persists:

(seven) the emotion, as it now is, manifests itself in a number of mental states, and it generates a variety of mental dispositions:

(eight) the emotion tends to find expression in behaviour: and

(nine) it is highly likely that the mental dispositions that the emotion generates will include desires, and, if this is so, and if we possess the necessary worldly information, the emotion may generate action, but only indirectly. "Indirectly", for what directly generates action, here as elsewhere, is the motivating conjunction of desire and instrumental belief.[20]

There are no distinctively emotional states for Wollheim. Thoughts and feelings might be initiated by emotional dispositions as outlined in the summary above, but they might also occur independently of such a dispositional framework. And a mental disposition might not manifest itself in a mental state on a given occasion even when presented with the appropriate object:

A man, taken off guard, could be momentarily frightened of a snake without having a dispositional fear of snakes. Or he could have a dispositional fear of snakes, and be frightened of the snake before him, yet his current fright have nothing to do with his underlying fear. For he might have momentarily mastered that fear, and what now frightens him is his knowledge that the snake he confronts is no ordinary snake but has been adjusted by a madman to be the carrier of some synthesized venom.[21]

Mental states that are not the manifestation of emotional mental dispositions are not emotions. Nor are mental dispositions that constitute attitudes to the world genuinely part of our emotional life unless they give rise to responses to the world. They lack phenomenology and so it is only through their interactions with other mental dispositions and mental states (however covert these interactions might be) that they have an impact upon us. The essence of emotion for Wollheim, then, is responses to the world that manifest emotional dispositions and so are responses that arise out of the life I have lived. A response is not emotional unless it has its origin in the life I have lived, and an attitude that colours the world with the lens of my past is not a part of my emotional life unless it manifests itself in mental states that are responses to the world.

This theory can account both for Belshazzar's fear-disposition and his fear-state. We might imagine that he had a desire to maintain his grasp over the Babylonian empire. He perceived this desire to be in prospect of being frustrated and traced this threat to the hand writing on the wall. His attention then shifts from thinking about the sense in which he believes that the hand has precipitated the frustration of his desire to thinking about the hand in light of the frustrated desire, and this is the basis for an attitude to the hand which is "unpleasurable". This attitude – the fear-disposition – persists, and it manifests itself in mental states, generates new mental dispositions and finds expression in his behaviour: his countenance changes, he has frightening thoughts, his joints loosen and his knees smite one against another. The feeling of these changes is the fear feeling state.

It is only as mental dispositions that emotions can perform the role that Wollheim ascribes to them in our psychological life: emotions colour the way we see the world and only a mental disposition can perform this activity. When we use emotion words to describe mental states, we are using them derivatively to describe the states in which the relevant mental dispositions commonly manifest themselves. If Wollheim is emphatic about the importance of identifying emotions with mental dispositions, rather than with mental states, it is because he perceives that theorists since James have failed to do so, and in this way have failed to understand the contribution that emotions make to our psychology as mental dispositions. Even cognitive theorists, who challenge James's somatic account, have provided accounts of emotion in terms of other kinds of mental states such as thoughts or feelings.

I do not propose to enter into a debate about what kind of mental phenomenon emotion should be identified with. That is not required by the experiential approach to art and emotion. If Wollheim's account of emotion can offer anything to the current investigation, it is the thought that our emotional life involves mental dispositions that colour the way we perceive the world, and which manifest themselves in different mental states, initiate other mental dispositions and find expression in behaviour. All of this can be asserted without resolving whether the mental disposition that is the attitude should be identified with the concept of emotion.

For this reason, the major break with Wollheim that I propose is that, while we should retain his conception of a particular kind of mental disposition that colours the world, we should not identify this with emotion. Rather, we should conceive of emotion as an interaction between certain mental dispositions and mental states. Our emotional life is an economy or organized system of parts. The parts of that economy are the mental dispositions and mental states described by Wollheim, and they interact with each other in the ways he suggests. While the idea of an emotional economy might seem like a claim about what an emotion is, it is more fundamentally

a claim that emotion is to be identified with how particular mental dispositions and mental states interact, rather than being identified with either the
mental dispositions or the mental states. It does not need to succeed as an
ontological claim about emotion. It is enough for the study of our emotional
experience of art that it offers us a way of thinking about emotional experiences that takes account of both the mental dispositions and mental states as
constituents of those experiences.

The theory of emotional economy allows us to ask how the parts of the
economy are involved when we perceive a work of art. It can do this without making a claim about which aspect of an ordinary experience of fear is
to be accorded the status of being the emotion. An account of Belshazzar's
fear can then be given in terms of the way that the fear-disposition, which
is one part of the economy, interacts with the fear-state, another part of the
economy, giving rise to his experience of fear. As long as we can identify the
different parts and how they contribute to this experience of fear, we can
then turn to the emotional experience of art and consider whether the same
parts contribute to that experience. We can ask how the emotional economy
is configured when Belshazzar sees the hand appear and we can compare
this with how the emotional economy is configured when we look at *Belshazzar's Feast,* and none of this requires us to be able to identify wherein the
essence of emotion lies. When we turn our attention to the experience of art,
we can examine the sense in which these mental states, mental dispositions
and mental states as manifestations of mental dispositions attend the experience of the work of art.

Psychological reality of emotion

A fundamental feature of the theory of emotional economy, which it inher-
its from Wollheim's account of the emotions, is the repsychologization of
mental phenomena. This is the claim that mental states and mental dispositions both possess psychological reality. In the case of mental states, it might
seem difficult to deny that there are such things as our thoughts, feelings,
pains, sense perceptions and so on. In the case of mental dispositions, however, it has been easier to deny that there is anything more to a mental disposition than ascribing a tendency to undergo a certain mental state (or the
tendency to behave in a particular way). If one adopts such an approach,
then it does not make sense to speak of mental dispositions doing anything,
for there is no sense in which they really exist. There is no fear-disposition
as distinct from episodes of being afraid: the disposition of fear is merely
a way of saying that an individual has a tendency to undergo episodes of
being afraid. Such an approach undermines Wollheim's theory because it is

central to his conception of emotions as mental dispositions that they have a history, that they memorialize this history in the attitude which is at their core and that a mental disposition possesses the ability to manifest itself in a range of different mental states, as well as initiating other mental dispositions and having expression in behaviour. This could not be achieved by a mental phenomenon that lacked psychological reality.

Wollheim describes it as *repsychologization* because, he maintains, our ordinary conception of mental life treats it as comprising psychologically real entities. It is only on reflection that philosophers have challenged the ordinary conception and denied psychological reality. It is in response to this denial that Wollheim argues for a return to the pre-reflective position. Gilbert Ryle's *The Concept of Mind* provides a rigorous attack on the idea that mental phenomena possess psychological reality, and this is Wollheim's departure point in developing his theory.[22] For Ryle, we do not need to suppose that mental dispositions genuinely exist. Rather, we should analyse them as tendencies towards certain behaviour. On such an analysis, the dispositions lack psychological reality. Ryle's own form of analytic behaviourism has spawned a variety of behaviourist positions and, subsequently, functionalist theories of mind in response to perceived inadequacies of behaviourism.[23] For present purposes, we need not enter the debate between these theorists. What matters is that anyone who shares Ryle's conviction that the mind is not a psychologically real entity will reject the conception, developed above, of the emotional economy as the interaction between psychologically real phenomena.[24]

There are two ways in which one might respond to Ryle's approach. First, one might argue, as Wollheim does, that the depsychologized account is ill-equipped to meet the demands that we ordinarily make of a theory of mind.[25] Wollheim observes that we regularly ascribe to mental dispositions explanatory significance that they could not have if they did not exist. We say that Belshazzar summoned the enchanters, Chaldeans and astrologers *because* he was afraid, but if his fear-disposition is not real, it cannot cause him to do anything; thus, for the behaviourist, reference to the disposition only tells us that this is precisely what Belshazzar would do in such circumstances. We also speak of mental dispositions having a certain strength: when the wise men appeared, but failed to interpret the writing on the wall, the king was "greatly affrighted" – he might have been only slightly affrighted, but in fact he was greatly affrighted, and we say that there is a difference in the magnitude with which one might be affrighted. A theory that denies the reality of mental phenomena cannot account for the fact that the same phenomenon can be experienced more or less strongly. And we speak of mental dispositions being in conflict: when Daniel reveals the meaning of the writing, the king's desire to retain power comes into conflict with his belief that his own transgressions have brought about his imminent demise, and the conflict between the desire and the belief results in inner turmoil. Wollheim observes that if a mental disposition is merely an observer's prediction about how a person is likely to behave, then a conflict of mental dispositions is a confusion or uncertainty in the observer's mind about which way the person being observed is likely to behave. This, however, moves the conflict out of the mind of the person whose behaviour is being predicted and places it squarely in the mind of the person making the prediction.

Perhaps arguments about the need to account for explanatory significance, strength and conflict of dispositions can convince us that a depsychologized theory of mind is unacceptable. However, we do not need to resolve this issue for present purposes: it is the nature of art and our experience of art that interests us, not the nature of mind. In order to analyse the emotional experience of art, we require a conception of mental phenomena that allows us to understand the nature of the emotional aspect of that experience. What I want to suggest is important for understanding that experience is not a proper account of the nature of mind, but a proper account of the conception of mental phenomena that Rembrandt or Picasso takes for granted in his work. If they are exploring emotional phenomena in their work, they might misunderstand what they are exploring. If a painting such as *Belshazzar's Feast* or *Guernica* is created in order to offer a particular emotional experience, and succeeds in this ambition, the artist will have refined his technique in a way that allows him to explore emotional life through his medium. If we are to experience the painting as an exploration of emotion, we will have to bring to the experience of the painting a conception of emotion that is at least compatible with the artist's own conception of the emotions he is trying to express. Otherwise, we will not be in a position to have the prescribed experience. To understand this claim, I begin with an analogy.

Let us imagine a tribe of hunter–painters. Their members include skilled rock-artists who paint images of people, animals and spirits on the rock-face of sacred caves. The tribe believe that when they enter the caves and perform certain rituals, the images come alive and the spectators are able to interact with the animated images in various ways.[26] The rock-artist paints the images with this theory in mind, and develops techniques that he intends will enable the spectators of his rock-painting to have an experience in which the painting comes alive. In order to have the experience of the painting prescribed by the artist, the spectator has to share certain of the artist's beliefs. People who do not belong to that tribe may not share those beliefs. They can look at the rock-paintings and they might appreciate them for various reasons, but they will not have the experience of the rock-painting that the artist intended them to have. They could only have that experience if they shared his belief that images come alive under certain conditions. The non-believer can provide an account of the psychology of the artist who painted the images as part of an explanation of what goes on when the initiated spectators perceive the paintings. But in order to have the experience of the painting that this outsider's theory describes, one has to bring the artist's theory to the experience: having the rock-artist's theory is a necessary condition of the proper experience of the rock-painting. Just as the magical experience of the rock-painting is only possible if we bring the rock-painter's magical theory to our experience of the painting, so the emotional experience of *Guernica* will only be possible if we bring to the experience of his painting the conception of emotion that Picasso – however mistakenly – takes for granted in his exploration of emotional life.

If human suffering is a theme that Picasso explores through painting, his success is a matter of his having developed painting techniques through which he can explore the phenomenon that he takes suffering to be. These are techniques that allow the spectator to perceive certain emotional properties in the painting or to respond to the painting with certain emotions. But spectators are only going to appreciate the effectiveness of the techniques through which Picasso explores our emotional life if they bring to the experience of the painting the conception of emotional life that he takes for granted, and which he developed those techniques in order to explore. In other words, they will only be able to appreciate how his technique allows him to explore our emotional life if they share his conception of what our emotional life is. If their conception of emotional life is radically different from his, they may not be able to appreciate how his painterly techniques enable him to explore human emotion as he conceives of it. So a part of the proper experience of Picasso's painting is a purchase on his conception of human emotion.

Given that the proper experience of a work of art requires a purchase on the appropriate theory of mind, it then remains to determine what that theory is. In particular, are we required to determine specifically what theory of mind Rembrandt or Picasso subscribed to? Or is it enough to assume that they both employed the psychological theory of ordinary folk? If it is enough to bring ordinary psychology to the experience of the painting, are we entitled to bring a theoretical version of this psychology, or must it be the ordinary folk psychology?

To say that we will only be able to experience *Belshazzar's Feast* properly if we bring to the painting an appropriate theory of mind does not require us to suppose that Rembrandt had an idiosyncratic theory of mind that we must uncover. It would be too great a burden to expect us to uncover the artist's actual theory of mind. But more than that, it would seem highly unlikely that he developed his own theory of mind. It is perfectly reasonable to assume that, like other folk, he employed a theory of mind that had not been depsychologized: a theory in which mental dispositions possess psychological reality, are felt to have varying degrees of strength or weakness, and have explanatory force. These, it will be recalled, are precisely the aspects of emotion that Wollheim argues the despychologized theory cannot account for, but which a psychologized theory can account for. If ordinary folk are misguided in holding this view, the artist is no less misguided. But it is this ordinary experience of emotion that he is interested in exploring.

Rembrandt and Picasso explore human experience, but not through speculation and theorization. They are interested in exploring what *seem* to be emotional dispositions of unusual strength, *seeming* conflicts of intense emotions and the way in which emotions *seem* to explain our life choices. A painter who succeeds in this pursuit succeeds because he is able to develop appropriate techniques for exploring such aspects as we ordinarily attribute to our emotional life. If we bring to the painting a theory of mind that does not account for the psychological reality of emotional phenomena, we will fail to appreciate the effectiveness of the artist's technique because we fail to appreciate the nature of the subject that the artist intends to explore through the technique. We would fail to have the appropriate emotional experience in something like the way that non-believers fail to experience the rock-painting as coming alive.

To say that we need to bring a theory of mind that is compatible with the artist's to our experience of a work of art might entitle us to bring folk psychology to the experience. However, Wollheim goes a step further than this. He is not content to say that we should bring the folk-psychologized theory of mind to the experience of the painting. Rather, he advocates a particular theoretical repsychologized theory of mind: a psychoanalytically informed theory of mind. This is not the ordinary folk psychology. It supposes mental functioning that ordinary folk would never assume. In Wollheim's opinion, however, it is compatible with folk psychology because it is a theoretical attempt to return theory of mind to the pre-reflective position in which mental phenomena are accorded psychological reality. Indeed, he regards psychoanalysis as providing a depth psychology that is continuous with ordinary psychology.[27] The value of bringing this theoretical psychologized theory of mind to the experience of the picture, rather than the folk-psychologized theory of mind, is that, according to Wollheim, it is capable of revealing more than the folk psychology can. So we have a theoretical account of the mind that is repsychologized, and hence broadly consistent with the folk theory, and hence also, we assume, with the artist's theory of mind. But it is also a repsychologized theory of mind that is more powerful than the folk-psychologized theory, and hence able to access deeper levels of the emotions being explored in the painting. In this way, Wollheim

31

maintains that he can show us how a painting is an exploration of mental phenomena of which the artist might not have been conscious.[28]

Once we accept that Rembrandt had a particular theory of mind when he painted *Belshazzar's Feast*, and that this theory is a constituent of the proper experience of the painting, a theory of mind compatible with the artist's must be employed when we theorize about the proper experience of the painting. Whether or not the behaviourist – or other depsychologized – conception of mind can explain Belshazzar's experience of fear, it will enable us neither to experience Rembrandt's painting properly, nor to analyse this experience. That is only possible if we bring to the experience of the painting a theory of mind that is compatible with the way of thinking about emotional life that the artist takes for granted when exploring emotional life in the painting.[29]

In deciding what theory of emotion the analysis should involve, we have seen that what is of central importance is that we formulate a theory that is consistent with the theory of mind that is an integral part of the experience of the painting. The fact that such a theory might not be the most accurate theory of mind is not to the point. The aim is to analyse the experience of art, not the nature of mind. We will only be able to understand the experience if the theory we use to describe it is also the theory that we employ when having the experience and also consistent with the theory taken for granted by the artist. A theory of emotional economy that makes use of Wollheim's repsychologized mental dispositions and mental states is an appropriate theory for this purpose as it is consistent with the pre-reflective conception of emotion that we take the artist to assume in his explorations of emotional life.[30]

Activity and passivity of emotion

We now have a conception of emotion as an economy that consists of parts, and we are almost ready to begin our investigation of how one or more of those parts might also be a constituent of our experience of a work of art. However, it remains to consider why it would matter whether the experience of art involves one part of the emotional economy rather than another. One reason that it might matter would be if the individual stands in a different relationship to the different parts of his emotional economy.

One way in which we might think about the relation in which an individual stands to his mental phenomena involves asking whether he is active or passive in respect of each of them. R. G. Collingwood suggests that the distinction between active and passive, or acting and being acted upon, is really an instance of a more basic distinction between self and other: I am active in respect of that which emanates out of myself, and passive in respect of that which emanates out of what is not myself (the activity of another upon me).[31] We might then ask whether an agent can regard the various mental phenomena that form parts of his emotional economy as emanating in himself. In order for this to be a useful distinction, however, there must be some relevant sense in which a mental phenomenon can be conceived of as emanating from the self as opposed to emanating from outside the self.

There are various ways in which we might conceive of what it means for an individual to regard a mental phenomenon as emanating from himself, and hence for him to be active in relation to it. First, an individual either has it in his power to initiate a mental phenomenon or he does not. So one sense in which he might be active in respect of a mental phenomenon is if he has the ability to choose whether to initiate it. I can choose, for example, to imagine the scene at Belshazzar's feast, and insofar as I can choose whether to start imagining it, and from which perspective I wish to imagine it, and so on, I might be said to be active in respect of the imagining.[32] Second, even if the individual cannot control a mental phenomenon's initiation, he might still be regarded as active in relation to the mental phenomenon if it comes under his control once it has been initiated. If the memory of reading the story of Belshazzar's feast at Sunday school suddenly pops into my mind uninvited, but I can then choose whether I want to continue thinking about it, or how I want to think about it, I might be said to be active in respect of the memory. A third sense would be if the mental phenomenon provided the agent with some motivational power. If, for reasons beyond my control, I find myself desiring to read the story of Belshazzar in the original tongue, this desire might act as the motivation for learning Aramaic, and the desire might be thought to be active on account of its motivational power. A fourth sense in which the individual might be thought to be active in respect of a mental phenomenon is that, even if he does not have the ability to initiate it, or to control it once it has been initiated, it is a mental phenomenon that arises out of the life that he has lived. If, when I hear the story of Belshazzar's feast, I tense up because of the feeling of frustration with which Sunday school classes about the story are associated, I do not initiate, and cannot control the frustration, but I might nevertheless be said to be active in respect of it; it is not an arbitrary response, but one that has its origin deep within my early childhood experience of biblical stories.

Is the individual active in relation to the mental states that form part of his emotional economy? It seems that, whichever conception of emanating we adopt, the individual is not active in respect of the phenomena that constitute his emotional response to the world. Belshazzar feels his countenance change, his joints loosen and his knees smite one against another. He does not choose to feel these things, and he cannot bring them under his control – if he could, he would stop them. Nor do they seem to provide him with any motivational power. The great king is in a state of fear over which he lacks control and in the grip of which he is powerless to do anything. Belshazzar stands in a passive relation to his fear-state. There is no sense in which the state of being in fear is a matter of being active as the mental states are not emanations of the self.

Is the individual active in relation to the mental dispositions that form a part of his emotional economy? According to Wollheim, the emotional disposition is an attitude that develops when the individual perceives, or imagines, an object to have precipitated the satisfaction or frustration of desire. Nothing in the originating process suggests that the individual can voluntarily initiate the process, or that the attitude comes under his control once it has been initiated. So in a certain respect it does not emanate out of him. In another respect, however, it clearly does emanate out of the individual's past. The attitude colours the object with the lens of the past so that it is experienced in light of the satisfaction or frustration it was once regarded as having precipitated. It is in this respect that the disposition emanates from the self and the individual is active in relation to it. In Wollheim's words:

> When we respond to something towards which we have not formed an emotion, our response can readily be wayward. We are hostages to the moment. However, once we have formed an emotion, our response is something that arises out of us, even if, for reasons connected with imperfect self-knowledge, it does not strike us like this. Our response now derives from how we are, and from how we perceive the world, and ultimately from the history that we have led.[33]

So is Belshazzar active in relation to the fear-disposition? Although he is passive in relation to the mental states that constitute his responses to the hand writing on the wall, he is active in relation to the disposition that manifests itself in these responses. That he feels disposed to respond to the hand in the particular way that he does is not a matter that he has any control over. However, the attitude that colours his perception of the hand and makes him afraid of it is an attitude that arises out of his past – out of the life that he has lived. For it is his own desire to retain power, his own perception that this might be frustrated, and all the things about the life he has lived that lead him to perceive the hand as the precipitating factor of the frustration of his desire, which then form the attitude that develops when he attends to the hand writing on the wall. Were he to respond to the situation without forming an emotional disposition, the same responses would be arbitrary ones, and he would be entirely passive. However, because his response is governed by his fear-disposition, and this disposition is a phenomenon that emerges from deep within him, he can properly be regarded as active in relation to his fear.

In contrast to Wollheim's conception of emotion grounding our response to the world deep within the life we have lived, Spinoza famously says of the emotions, "we are driven about in many ways ... and ... like waves on the sea, driven by contrary winds, we toss about, not knowing our outcome and fate".[34] This suggests that emotional phenomena do not emanate from the self, and that we are fundamentally passive in relation to them.[35] So which is the more accurate conception of our emotional life? Are we active in relation to our emotional economy, as Wollheim maintains, or passive, as Spinoza suggests? It seems that there is more than a grain of truth in both accounts. Spinoza's simile accurately describes the fear-state that is Belshazzar's response to the hand, while Wollheim correctly describes the fear-disposition that initiates and manifests itself in the response. When a mental state is a manifestation of an emotional disposition, it is correct to describe the individual as both active and passive in respect of his emotional experience. He is passive in relation to the mental state and active in relation to the mental disposition. Thus, when these are regarded as components of an emotional economy, the emotional economy involves the individual being both active and passive.

What are we to make of a situation in which it seems we cannot characterize our emotional experience as either wholly active or wholly passive? In an article about perceptual intentionality, Naomi Eilan argues that "getting perceptual intentionality right is a matter of getting right the mixture of activity and passivity distinctive of perceptual experience".[36] She argues that it is a mistake to attempt to characterize perception exclusively in terms of either activity or passivity: perception involves both activity and passivity, as do other kinds of experience, such as remembering. Eilan claims that what marks off one kind of experience from another is the different mixture of activity and passivity that is characteristic of the different kinds of experience.

Peter Goldie has suggested that this analysis might usefully be applied to Wollheim's conception of emotion.[37] Goldie's analysis of Wollheim differs from mine. In particular, he does not use the conception of emotional activity that I maintain is fundamental to Wollheim's theory of emotions as mental dispositions.[38] However, there is still something in his approach that is highly pertinent to the conception of emotion as an economy that I have developed out of Wollheim's conception of emotion. Our experience of the emotional economy involves both our activity and passivity. What is characteristic of our emotional experience is precisely the particular mixture of activity and passivity that it involves. We can distinguish the experience of a mental state that is not a manifestation of a fear-disposition from one that is by pointing out that the first experience involves the agent's passivity whereas the latter experience involves both his activity and passivity. It is when we appreciate the sense in which the agent is active in respect of the mental dispositions and passive in respect of his mental states that we can see the unique mixture of activity and passivity that is characteristic of our experience of the emotional economy.

When we turn to our emotional experiences of art, we shall be interested in investigating whether those experiences involve the characteristic mixture of the emotional economy's activity and passivity, or only a particular aspect of this mixture. Whether the experience of art involves the perceiver's emotional activity, or passivity, or both, will depend upon what part of the emotional economy is engaged in the emotional experience of art. I shall argue that art offers the possibility of engaging both our emotional activity and passivity. To understand why it should matter that we are capable of having such an experience, we shall have to wait until Chapter 5's discussion of what it means to be at home in the world.

Contemporary philosophy of emotion

In this chapter, I have argued that the study of art and emotion needs to begin with a conception of emotion that is expansive rather than constricted, and have suggested that my conception of the emotional economy offers the kind of starting point required for this purpose. The thriving contemporary literature on the definition of emotion has not featured in this account. As previously noted, this contemporary debate can be seen as a response to James's theory of emotion; however, it is a response to an interpretation of James's theory that differs from the interpretation that I have pursued. That debate takes James to identify the concept of emotion with the feeling of changes in bodily states. His critics then argue that this is the wrong mental phenomenon with which to identify emotion. An emotion is variously conceived of by them as a thought, a desire, a feeling or a value judgement.[39] In response to such cognitive conceptions of emotion, the neo-Jamesian positions reassert the claim that emotions are essentially somatic states.[40] So the debate takes the form of arguing about whether emotion is essentially cognitive or somatic; and then if it is cognitive, what kind of cognitive phenomenon it is; and if it is somatic, how James's approach needs to be revised to account for the cognitivists' claims. The debate is further complicated by the claim that emotion is not a natural kind, but an umbrella term that incorporates a range of different phenomena. Theorists pick and choose which they will give account of, depending upon the mental phenomenon in terms of which they choose to analyse emotion.[41]

But the attempt to identify emotion with a particular kind of mental or somatic phenomenon flies in the face of common sense; if there is one thing that is generally accepted about the emotions, it is that they seem to involve a range of different phenomena. Aristotle long ago observed that the emotions are susceptible to analysis in terms of different phenomena: the dialectician will define anger in terms of something like a desire for revenge, whereas the natural philosopher will define it in terms of a boiling of the blood.[42] The philosophical challenge is not a matter of deciding whether to side with the dialectician or the natural philosopher, but to work out how to provide an analysis of anger that accounts for its propensity to be understood both as a desire for revenge and a boiling of the blood.[43] On this point, Aristotle and James are of like mind. We have seen that James is aware of the need to explain both the dispositional and phenomenological aspects of an experience such as fear or anger. The error of the current debate now seems to be that, rather than reading Chapters 24 and 25 of *The Principles of Psychology* together, James's interpreters have attended only to one aspect of his account and then assumed that their task is to assess whether this phenomenon – or some other – is synonymous with emotion. The debate between the contemporary cognitive theorists and neo-Jamesians is as ill-founded as a debate between the dialectician and the natural philosopher on anger, or an interpretation of fear exclusively in terms of James's concept of instinct or his concept of emotion.

Whatever the correct answer to the analytic question is, it is this broader approach that we have seen the current project demands. We are equally interested in investigating whether looking at *Belshazzar's Feast* involves a boiling of the blood, or a desire for revenge on the spectator's part, or both. If the analytic theorists were able to conceptualize emotion in a way that enabled us to combine the various associated phenomena, a definition would not have to reduce emotion to a single mental phenomenon. In this case, the concept of emotion would be sufficiently broad to facilitate the experiential approach to art and emotion. Having surveyed the current literature, Jenefer Robinson argues that rather than choosing between the alternative pretenders to the title of emotion, the solution is to conceive of emotion as a *process* that involves all of these phenomena.[44]

The process involves four components: an affective (i.e. non-cognitive) appraisal that initiates an emotional response to an object; the bodily feelings thus initiated; cognitive monitoring of these responses; and emotional feelings. Robinson argues that once the emotion is identified with the process, we can see why any of the phenomena that comprise the response do not count as emotions if they are not initiated by the appropriate affective appraisals: such phenomena are not part of the process that constitutes the emotion. Likewise, an affective appraisal that has not initiated a response is not an emotion because, regarded as such, it is not yet a component of the process that is the emotion. Robinson's approach explains why each of the theorists has hit on some truth about what emotion involves, without having managed to provide a comprehensive analysis of it.[45]

What are the affective appraisals that initiate the emotional response? Robinson identifies four ways in which they have been characterized in the scientific literature:[46] the preference/aversion approach (e.g. Zajonc),[47] in which the affective appraisal is identified with an innate preference or aversion to certain stimuli; the component approach (e.g. Scherer),[48] which identifies the affective appraisal with a cluster of stimulus evaluations, some of which are present at birth and others of which develop; the goal-orientated approach (e.g. one reading of Lazarus),[49] which identifies affective appraisals with the congruence or incongruence of the object with the promotion of a goal of the agent; and the basic emotion approach (e.g. an alternative reading of Lazarus), which identifies affective appraisals with the basic emotions that can be distinguished physiologically. Each of these meets with certain difficulties, which means that, in Robinson's opinion, no one approach on its own can account for affective appraisals.

It will be apparent that there is some similarity between the relationship between the affective appraisal and the somatic response in Robinson's process and the relationship between the mental disposition and the mental state in Wollheim's theory. The affective appraisal is said to initiate the response and the mental disposition manifests itself in a mental state. So it might be thought that the process theory could serve as a basis for the experiential approach to art and emotion in the same way that my emotional economy theory does. There is, however, an important reason for preferring the emotional economy to emotion as process. Whichever approach (or combination of approaches) to affective appraisals Robinson settles on, in no case will there be a diachronic aspect. The mental disposition that is Wollheim's attitude is said to colour the world with the lens of the past. It can do this because the attitude has its origin in an earlier experience of satisfaction or frustration of desire, which develops into the attitude through the characteristic history. In this way the attitude is a transfigured memorialization of the past. It is because the mental disposition has this diachronic dimension that we can say the individual is active in relation to it. When the mental disposition manifests itself in a mental state, the individual is said to be both active and passive in relation to his mental economy. Because Robinson's affective appraisals lack the diachronic dimension, they lack the sense of activity that comes when a mental phenomenon is anchored deep within the individual's psychological history. Without this sense of activity, the theory cannot account for the sense in which we are both active and passive in our emotional life, which feature we shall find is central to our analysis of the emotional experience of art. For this reason, we should prefer the theory of emotional economy to the process theory.

2

Perception of emotion in the world

There's a certain slant of light,
Winter afternoons,
That oppresses, like the heft
Of cathedral tunes.

Heavenly hurt it gives us.
We can find no scar
But internal difference
Where the meanings are.

(Emily Dickinson)[1]

Crying babies

Emily Dickinson's poem provides us with a vignette of an experience in which the perception of "a certain slant of light" is attended by "heavenly hurt". We are told the "heavenly hurt" is an "internal difference", a modification of our psychological condition, which gives the experience its meaning. In the poem, the perception of the emotional tone of the external object brings about the persona's internal change. If interactions between perceptions of emotion in the world and the perceiver's emotion are a feature of our experience of the world, then we should want to know not just what it feels like to have such experiences, but what it means to have them. The poet captures what it feels like for our perception of the emotional tone of some aspect of the external world to engage with our internal emotional condition. This invites the philosopher to ask what it means to have an experience in which the agent's perception of emotion in the external world interacts with the agent's own emotions. Our investigation of the nature of such interactions begins with three illustrations of experiences in which there seems to be an interaction between a perception of emotion and the perceiver's own emotion. As we shall see, these examples suggest that there is more than one way in which we might conceive of this interaction.

First, a young mother takes advantage of a brief spot of unseasonable sunshine to push her baby around the park in a pram. The baby enjoys the seclusion of the pram with the warmth of its blankets, the crisp fresh air and the view of the clear sky, intermittently interrupted by the image of his mother's face peering over him reassuringly. Other mothers have a similar idea and also take their children to the park to enjoy the sunshine. One child, however, cannot enjoy the simple pleasure of the sun as the others do, and sobs loudly and uncontrollably in distress. When the happy baby in the pram hears this crying, he starts crying too. Now both babies are crying and distressed. The first baby's perception of the other's emotion gives rise to that very emotion in him. Rather as the sound emitted from one violin sets in motion the sympathetic vibrations of a string of a tacit violin, so the one baby's crying seemingly infects the other baby with the same state. This infection is the first sense in which an agent's emotions might attend his experience of emotion in the world: my experience of your being in a particular mental state consists of my being put in the same mental state in virtue of my having perceived your mental state. When an agent is conceived of as having been infected by the emotion he perceives, the problem is then to explain what it means for such infection to occur.

Second, it transpires that the child in the previous example who was heard but not seen cries because he stubbed his big toe, and is now in pain and distressed. His mother saw him stub his toe; she knows that this is why he is crying and that, despite his tears, he is not in danger. Having perceived all of this, we can imagine his mother might have at least two distinct experiences of her son's emotion. Upon becoming aware that her son is distressed, she might be anxious that her child is afraid even though she regards his fear as being unjustified. Alternatively, she might feel exasperated that, yet again, her cry-baby son has become unduly distressed over some trivial accident. In neither case is her emotion identical to the emotion that she perceives the child to have. In one scenario her emotion is distinct, yet sympathetic; in the other it is distinct, but unsympathetic. In both cases, the internal emotion is one that is responsive to the external emotion which is perceived. Such a response has an analogy in an answer to a question. The content of an answer is not generally identical to the content of the question to which it responds, however it must be appropriate to the question.[2] If the perceiving agent's emotion is conceived of as an emotion that is distinct from the perceived emotion to which it is a response, the problem is then to provide an account of what it means for one emotion to be responsive to another.

Third, a man holidaying in New South Wales, Australia, visits the Blue Mountains, where he sees the Three Sisters. As he surveys the famous rock formation, consisting of three lone shafts of sandstone – together and alone – towering over the valley's bush, he suddenly realizes the deep feeling of solidarity that has always bound him, his wife and child together. He has never held his child in his arms, however, having been estranged from the child's mother since she ran off with another woman while pregnant. Looking at the rock formation, he comes to appreciate an emotion which he is aware he has always felt, but which he has not previously comprehended as he now does. This realization attends his experience of the Three Sisters, but it is not a response to the rock formation. The realization is not a matter of his feeling something in response to what he perceives in the landscape. Nor is it the case that he is infected by what he perceives in it. Rather, the perception of the emotion in the landscape is the occasion for his coming to clarify for himself something about what he had already been feeling, but is only now able to comprehend. The man's realization is about himself, not about the Three Sisters, although the experience of seeing the landscape in some way encourages him to comprehend this attitude of familial solidarity that has always been there. If the perception of the external emotion encourages the agent to undertake some reflexive activity with respect to his internal emotion, then we require an account of what it means for a perception to prompt such activity.

These examples illustrate three distinct ways in which the perceiver's emotion and the emotion he perceives in the world might be related. First, the perceiver's emotion might be the same as the perceived emotion: my being aware of your feeling a certain emotion might involve my coming to feel that same emotion (as with the happy baby who starts crying when it hears another crying). Second, the perceiver's emotion might be responsive to the perceived emotion: such is the case when I respond to your emotion with my feeling some other emotion towards you (as with the mother who responds to her child's distress with anxiety or exasperation). Third, the perceiver's emotion might be comprehended on account of having the perception: my perception of something in the world might prompt me to some new comprehension of a pre-existing feeling in me (as with the estranged father who crystallizes his feelings of familial solidarity when he sees the rock formation).

Thus, we have three different interactions between the perceiver's emotion and the perceived emotion: in the experience of infection of emotion they are identical; in the experience of communication the perceiver's emotion is responsive;[3] and in the experience of articulation the perceiver's emotion is comprehended. The distinction is not merely concerned with whether the perceiver's emotion and the perceived emotion are the same or different. What is important about the difference between infection, communication and articulation is a difference in how the emotional condition of the perceived object is related to the emotional condition of the perceiving agent. When my experience of the world involves an emotion infecting me, something about the object of the experience causes me to feel a particular emotion; the perceived emotion dictates the perceiver's emotion. When my experience of the world involves the communication of an emotion, I respond to my perception of the object's emotion with my own emotional response towards the object. In this case the object does not dictate the emotional aspect of my experience: I do not share in the emotion that has been communicated to me, but I have another emotion, one that is directed towards the person who communicated with me, and which seems an appropriate response to the emotion communicated to me. When my experience of the world involves an articulation of emotion, I am doing for myself something that the perception has prompted or encouraged me to do: rather than changing how I feel, perceiving the emotion is the occasion for crystallizing my own emotion. We might observe the way in which the significance of the object changes. In infection, the object did all the work and I did none. In communication, we are partners in my experience: the object poses the question that I must work out how to answer. In articulation, the object prompts me to do something for myself: it puts me in mind of engaging with some aspect of my own emotions, but it does not do this for me.

So we are now presented with three different ways of thinking about the connection between the certain slant of light and Dickinson's heavenly hurt in the poem. The slant of light might be perceived to possess the heavenly hurt, and this infects Dickinson with heavenly hurt. Or the slant of light might possess some other emotional quality, to which Dickinson responds with a feeling of heavenly hurt. Or the emotional quality of the slant of light might encourage Dickinson to comprehend her own feeling as being that of heavenly hurt. We can also say of Dickinson's poem itself that it might have an emotional quality with which it infects the reader, or it might possess one emotional quality and invite the reader to respond with a distinct emotional response, or the poem might encourage the reader to give form to an emotion that he had not previously comprehended. Another possibility, however, is that the poem might have all three of these effects on the reader. The earlier examples were intended to illustrate three experiences in which a single emotional interaction occurred in each experience, but it might also be the case that some experiences involve all three interactions.

Combining emotional experiences

What we now require is an illustration of a single experience that involves all three interactions. This will provide a basis for thinking about the different interactions as aspects of a single experience, rather than as discrete experiences. Aristotle's account of the audience's emotional experience of tragedy can be read as providing an example of an experience that involves all three interactions. To use the account in this way does not commit us to the claim that what follows is the correct interpretation of Aristotle's theory, or that his theory offers the correct analysis of the audience's experience of a Greek tragedy. Nor do I mean to suggest that it is a paradigm for the kind of experience that I shall ultimately argue occurs when the three interactions form aspects of a single experience. Rather, I introduce it merely as a way of demonstrating how we might conceive of a single emotional experience involving different emotional interactions.

The *Poetics* is Aristotle's manual for writing a successful tragedy.[4] A central component of his analysis of tragedy concerns the way in which the audience relates emotionally to the hero. The audience's experience, as it watches the hero submit to his fate, is said to involve fear, pity and κάθαρσις (*katharsis*). These three elements might, I suggest, be understood in terms of infection, communication and articulation: the audience's experience of fear involves its being infected by the hero's fear, while the pity it experiences is a matter of communication. The meaning of Aristotle's concept of κάθαρσις remains the subject of heated debate. One interpretation offered by Martha Nussbaum, however, suggests that κάθαρσις can be understood as a matter of clarifying fear and pity.[5] Working with an interpretation of this kind, κάθαρσις can be seen as something like articulation of emotion. Whether or not this is an accurate account of the experience of tragedy, such an analysis of the audience's experience demonstrates how interactions resembling infection, communication and articulation might form aspects of a single experience rather than being conceived of as discrete experiences.

When watching a tragedy, the audience perceives the protagonist's fear, and this arouses fear in the audience. For Aristotle, fear is an emotion concerned with one's own future. He allows that one might feel fear when someone else's future is in jeopardy, but only if it is a particularly close person, such as a family member, and in this way it is an extension of concern for oneself. This presents a problem for an account of the audience's experience of fear because, on the one hand, the audience has no real reason to fear for themselves while watching the tragedy, but on the other hand they have no reason to feel fear on account of the protagonist's future, as he is not a close relation of theirs. If the audience does experience fear of this kind, it is because they participate in the protagonist's fear rather than because they feel fear for him. There are two ways in which we might conceive of the audience participating in the fear they perceive. First, they might imaginatively identify with the protagonist, and having imagined themselves to be him, then feel the fear that he feels. Second, the audience might perceive that they could very easily be in the protagonist's situation and therefore have reason to think that this might be their future too, a prospect that instils fear in their own hearts. In the latter case, they feel their own fear, which happens to coincide with the protagonist's fear. Jonathan Lear argues that Aristotle cannot be interpreted as having meant imaginative identification, and so the latter must be the correct interpretation.[6] For present purposes, it is not necessary to resolve this issue. What matters is that a constituent element of the audience's experience is feeling the very emotion that they perceive in the object of the experience, and that there is some parallel here with the interaction of infection described above.

In addition to fear, the audience also feels pity, and, in contrast to the experience of fear, the audience's experience of pity involves the audience's emotion responding to the perceived emotion, rather than being the same as it. The audience perceives the protagonist to suffer, and, according to Aristotle, they judge this suffering to be unjust in the circumstances. They then feel pity towards the protagonist in response to his plight, or, more particularly, in response to the injustice of his plight as they have judged it. For Aristotle, there is only one rational way to respond to a situation judged in a particular way. In the case of suffering that is judged to be unjust, the only suitable response is pity. We might take issue with Aristotle's approach, which finds only one response suitable in each situation. We might think that even if one has a particular assessment of a situation, there might still be a number of legitimate ways in which one might respond to the assessment; indeed, Aristotle notes that age, sex, social status and wealth all contribute to emotional responses. However, what remains clear is that whether or not there is choice as to the response to the protagonist's plight, the emotion that constitutes the audience's response to the protagonist is not identical to that which they perceive in him. In a sense, there is nothing remarkable about this. In our ordinary emotional interactions, this is precisely how we behave. We are helped by a kindly bystander and we are grateful; we read about a conceited fool and we feel contemptuous; we are confronted by an impressive hero and we feel humble. You might disagree with some of these responses. You might not find my hero impressive at all. But even if you do find him impressive, you might feel admiration rather than humility. Whether or not we can agree about which emotion is appropriate to feel in the presence of any other emotion, we can agree that it is an appropriate response to feel something other than the emotion that we observe, and to which we are responding. And it is precisely for this reason that the audience's experience of pity is distinct from that of fear. The experience of pity when watching a tragedy is responsive to the protagonist's emotion and in this respect resembles the interaction of communication.

The third aspect of the audience's emotional experience is κάθαρσις. Aristotle does not explain what he means by κάθαρσις, and this has invited much scholarly speculation. Nussbaum interprets Aristotle's approach to κάθαρσις as a response to Plato. Aristotle, she argues, does not employ the word in any technical sense, but rather in what she regards as its primary meaning of "getting clear" or "an improvement in understanding by the removal of some obstacles to understanding". For Plato, emotions such as fear and pity are inherently messy and are the antithesis of cleanliness.[7] Nussbaum suggests that Aristotle's innovation is the claim that fear and pity are the means of achieving a cognitive clearing-up or cleaning-up. Nussbaum understands κάθαρσις as "accomplishing through pity and fear a clearing-up concerning experiences of the pitiable and fearful kind".[8] She argues that for Aristotle the dramatic experience of these emotions has a therapeutic value in that it allows the audience to understand better its own experiences of these emotions in their practical life.[9] On this reading, the audience's experience of fear and pity spurs them on to refine their own emotions of fear and pity. If the κάθαρσις is a cognitive clearing-up, then the audience's experience of fear and pity involves something more than feeling what the protagonist feels or something else in response. It is also an invitation to the audience to engage with their own emotions, and in this respect we can see a parallel with the interaction of articulation.

It is clear that, for Aristotle, the audience only has the appropriate experience if it feels the fear it perceives in the hero, also feels pity in response to the perceived fear and undergoes κάθαρσις. Anything less than being infected by fear, responding with pity and (at least on one interpretation) comprehending one's own emotions through κάθαρσις does not constitute the proper experience. Whether or not this is an accurate account of the audience's experience, it illustrates one sense in which we might conceive of an experience involving different kinds of emotional interactions. When an experience combines these different interactions, we might ask whether the experience has the same emotional intensity as any of the discrete experiences, or whether it involves some increase in intensity. If the intensity is increased, we might understand this as the cumulative effect of the three interactions. However, a further possibility is that the experience that combines all three interactions, as aspects, involves some affect in excess of the combined effects of infection, communication and articulation. To illustrate the sense in which a composite experience might have such a surplus affect, let us imagine that a friend has recently attended a performance of Alan Bennett's *The History Boys*, which he found particularly moving.[10] In

45

a conversation with us, he says that the emotional experience of watching the play totally absorbed him, and he tries to explain what it was about the emotional experience that absorbed him in this way.

Our friend begins by telling us how much he enjoyed the play. In particular, he says that it involved a highly charged emotional experience for him, an experience in which he was totally absorbed. We press him to explain what made the experience so absorbing and he launches into a long tirade about the emotional experience of watching the play. In particular, he talks about the English master, Hector, who is threatened with dismissal for touching his students, and one of the students, Posner, who is particularly impressed by Hector's unorthodox approach to teaching literature. Our friend speaks of the way in which he feels what the characters feel, his reaction to Hector's breakdown in the classroom and Posner's consoling him, his sense that by the end the play has cleared up his own attitude to overcoming awkwardness. To clarify what he has said, we ask whether he would agree that it was an absorbing emotional experience because watching the play allowed him to observe the intense emotions that the characters were feeling. He replies that rather than just identifying the emotions that the characters were feeling, in some sense it was as if he himself felt what they were feeling. After Posner has recited Hardy's "Drummer Hodge", he and Hector talk about the moments when you find in a poem a thought or feeling you've had but never thought anyone else has had, and then a hand comes out of the poem and takes yours. Hector puts out a hand and for a moment it looks like Posner will take it, but then the moment passes. Our friend explains, "As I watched it, I really felt as if I was in the moment, I was feeling what Hector and Posner were feeling at that moment."

On reflection, however, he realizes that this has not fully captured the experience. To explain the intensity of the experience in terms of feeling what is perceived does not capture the sense in which he reacted to what he perceived. At the beginning of the second act, when Hector has a breakdown in front of his students and Posner pats him on the back to console him, our friend's emotional engagement with what he perceived is not that of infection. He explains: "I didn't feel that I was feeling Posner's courage and Hector's sense of his own futility. I felt something different in each case; I felt impressed by Posner's newfound maturity, and I pitied Hector for having to suffer the fate he does." In this case, what he thinks makes it emotional is the sense in which he felt his own emotions in response to those of the characters on the stage as they met with their various fortunes.

And yet this sense of response still does not fully account for the intensity of his experience. Our friend tries to explain that both feeling what the characters were feeling and feeling something else in response were aspects of the experience that contributed to its intensity, but that even then that ignores the more profound sense of the emotional experience: "The sense in which watching the play helped me to comprehend for myself the feelings of holding back and overcoming awkwardness. Before, I had felt what Posner was feeling, but now I can pin down that feeling in a way that I couldn't before." And still it is not the pinning down alone that is fundamental to the intensity of the emotional experience.

"I don't think I could have pinned the feelings down if I hadn't had the emotional reactions and also felt what the characters were feeling. I think when I first said it was a really absorbing emotional experience, I meant it was because of all three. You could explain why it was emotional in terms of any one of them. Each was present and made for an emotional experience in its own right. But I think what I meant about it being totally absorbing really had to do with all three being aspects of the experience."

What makes the emotional experience totally absorbing cannot be iden- tified with any moment at which infection, communication or articulation occurs. It was the performance as a whole in which he felt totally absorbed. It is not simply the fact that our friend is infected by, responds to and articu- lates for himself the emotions he perceives. What is absorbing is something about the way that the experience of the performance is able to draw him in in every respect because it involves his interacting with it in these different ways. This account of watching *The History Boys* suggests that the experi- ence has an intensity that is distinct from the cumulative effect of the dif- ferent interactions between the audience's emotions and the emotions they perceive in the play. To understand such an experience as the cumulative experience of the three separate interactions does not explain why this com- posite experience of emotion might have a surplus intensity in excess of the intensity of the cumulative interactions. To provide an analysis of what is being gestured at in the illustration, we need some way of accounting for the distinctiveness of this experience, and we must wait until Chapter 4 for an account of this in terms of plenary experience of emotion.

In the previous chapter we saw that an emotional economy might be con- ceived of as being composed of parts. The agent is active in respect of some of these parts and passive in respect of others. The suggestion to be devel- oped in Chapter 4 is that, whereas the examples in the previous section illus- trated interactions with one particular part of the emotional economy, in relation to which the agent is either active or passive, the theatrical example illustrates an experience in which we engage with the whole emotional econ- omy, something in respect of which the agent is both active and passive. An engagement with the whole emotional economy involves something more than merely the cumulative intensity of the engagements with the various parts: it offers a plenary experience of emotion.

The theatrical example involved a sequence of events, each of which involved a different emotional interaction. While it is not inconceivable that the various aspects of the experience might all occur simultaneously, it seems unlikely that we could attend to them all at once. So, the kind of experience that we are interested in is likely to be a sequence of events. When our friend tried to explain what made the experience totally absorbing, he found that he could not identify any one of the moments as the totally absorbing one. Rather, it was something about the sequence of events taken as a whole that had the quality of being totally absorbing. We have yet to develop an account of what it means for such a sequence of events to be totally absorbing in this way. However, it is important to note that it is a feature of the experience of the whole sequence of events. It seems that there is a reason to regard this as a single unified experience: the phenomenological report suggests that the quality of being totally absorbing does not inhere in any particular event, but only in the sequence as a whole.[11] So if we can provide an account of what it means for the experience to be totally absorbing (what I shall suggest is plenary experience), we will have said something that only applies to the sequence as a whole and not to any of the constituent events, entitling us to regard the sequence as a whole as the emotional experience requiring analysis.

Analysing emotional experiences

Whether we are interested in developing an account of the experiences of the three discrete interactions or the composite experience in which all three interactions are aspects, the constituents of these experiences are the same. In each case, before attempting to provide an analysis of an experience, we need to enquire into the nature of the two constituents: the object in which the emotion is perceived, and the emotion of the perceiver. We can then study the various interactions between them.

On the one hand, the interaction involves the perceiver's emotions, and any analysis will have to explain what it is about the perceiver's emotions that is relevant to the analysis of the experience. The previous chapter gives us two senses in which the perceiver's own emotion might be part of the experience: the experience involves either a part of the emotional economy or the whole economy. If it involves a part of the economy, then that part is either a mental state or a mental disposition. If the experience involves a mental state, then it involves a mental phenomenon in respect of which the perceiving agent is passive. If it is a mental disposition, then it is something in respect of which he is active. And if it is the whole emotional economy, then it is something in respect of which he is both active and passive. The way in which the perceived emotion interacts with the perceiver's emotion, I shall suggest, depends upon whether the interaction involves an emotional phenomenon in respect of which the agent is active, or passive, or both.

On the other hand, the interaction also involves the object in which an emotional property is perceived. The perceived object might be regarded by the perceiving agent in one of two ways: either as another psychological agent or as a non-psychological object. Perceptual objects regarded as psychological agents are deemed to possess a psychology of their own. (Whether the object actually possesses a psychology is not to the point: what matters is whether the perceiving agent believes or imagines that the perceptual object possesses its own psychology.) People and other animals are the most likely psychological agents in which we will perceive emotional properties. We can also perceive emotional properties in things that we regard as non-psychological objects, that is, objects that are not believed or imagined to possess their own psychology. An emotional property might be perceived in some portion of the landscape, for instance, without any commitment to the landscape's possessing a psychology.

There is a further distinction that we can make with respect to non-psychological objects. We can distinguish between non-psychological objects that are naturally occurring, and non-psychological objects produced by a psychological agent who might have a particular intention in doing so. Just as the nature of the experience is influenced by whether the interaction involves a mental state or a mental disposition, so it is also influenced by whether the perceived object is regarded as another psychological agent, a naturally occurring non-psychological object or a non-psychological object created by a psychological agent. The emotional properties that we perceive, I shall suggest, differ in each case.

It is not just any property of the perceived object that interacts with the perceiver's emotions in the earlier examples. It is a particular kind of property – an emotional property – which the agent perceives in the object. The idea that an agent can perceive emotion in objects of perception raises an immediate problem. An emotion is a psychological phenomenon. Psychological phenomena belong to psychologies. A psychology is not something that we are able to perceive – at any rate, not directly. If we hear distress in a baby's cry, or see pleasure in its smile, we must explain how a psychological property becomes attached to a sound or image that is obviously something that is not itself part of a psychology.[12]

One way in which a perceived sound or image might acquire a psychological property is through its relationship with something that is genuinely psychological. There are two possible psychologies that might be related to the perceived sound or image. Either what we perceive has its genesis in a psychological agent, or it does not. If it does, then what we perceive might acquire its psychological property through its connection with the genetic psychological agent. If the object of perception does not have its genesis in a psychological agent, then we might still perceive some emotional property in the object in virtue of its connection with the perceiver's own psychology. In either case, we will have to explain how a connection with the genetic psychological agent or the perceiving psychological agent can enable us to perceive a psychological property in something that is not itself psychological.

Once we appreciate how our awareness of an object's connection with a psychological agent enables us to perceive a perceptual property in the object, we shall find that we can perceive different kinds of emotional properties in objects of perception, depending upon whether the object we perceive has a connection with a genetic psychological agent, or with the perceiving psychological agent. When there is a connection with a genetic psychological agent, an externalized property might be perceived. We shall see in the following section that such properties are perceived by an agent in the physiognomy of other psychological agents (e.g. the expressiveness of a person's face, the lie of his limbs or the gait of his movements). When the object of perception is a naturally occurring non-psychological object (e.g. a portion of the landscape), the connection can only be with the psychology of the perceiving agent. In this case we might perceive a projective property, an account of which we shall consider below.

Once we have considered both kinds of properties, it will become apparent that it is a distinctive characteristic of works of art that they are capable of possessing both externalized and projective properties and that this fact forms the basis for a special kind of experience: the emotional experience of art.

The experiences we are interested in studying are interactions between the perceiver's emotional economy and the emotional properties of perceptual objects. So an analysis must consider not merely the various forms that both the perceiver's emotion and the perceived emotion might take, but also the various ways in which these affect the nature of the interaction that occurs in each case. In the next chapter, the distinctions we have drawn between the different parts of the perceiver's emotional economy, together with the different kinds of object in which we can perceive emotion, will enable us to analyse the interactions of infection, communication and articulation that were illustrated earlier.

Perceiving externalized properties

Smiles are of many kinds, and we perceive different emotions in different kinds of smiles. One variety is the "innocent and joyous" smile with which Rohinton Mistry delights us in his story "Of White Hairs and Cricket":

> Daddy was still reading the Times at the dining-table. Through
> the gloom of the light bulb I saw the Murphy Baby's innocent and

joyous smile. I wondered what he looked like now. When I was two years old, there was a Murphy Baby Contest, and according to Mummy and Daddy my photograph, which had been entered, should have won. They said that in those days my smile had been just as, if not more, innocent and joyous.[13]

Another variety of smile is the "pleased" smile. Whether a smile is "innocent and joyous" or "pleased", the question is: what does it mean for us to perceive a smile in this way? We can distinguish between an inference that the Murphy Baby is innocent and joyous (rather than pleased), and a perception that his smile is innocent and joyous. Some theorists have gone so far as to conclude that we ordinarily say that a smile expresses pleasure, rather than the person, who smiles in order to express pleasure: the person is pleased, the smile expresses pleasure.[14] Whether or not this accurately captures our ordinary linguistic usage, it captures something about the difference between inferring that a person is pleased and perceiving pleasure in a smile.

When we are concerned with the experience of art, we are interested in what is involved in perceiving emotion in some part of the world, just as we are when we are interested in our perception of emotion in a muscular contortion of the lips or face. A related question concerns whether our perception of the smile enables us to know anything about the mind that produced the smile; for example, does perception of a happy smile permit us to infer that the person is happy? To answer this related question would involve drawing an inference about the happy state of mind from the perception of the happy smile. We could only understand this, however, if we first understood what it means to perceive the smile as being happy. So the preliminary question concerns how we are able to perceive a smile as being happy. It is this question that we must answer in order to provide an account of our perception of externalized properties such as innocence and joy in the Murphy Baby's smile. An account of our ability to perceive externalized properties does not require us to resolve what, if anything, perception of an externalized property might tell us about the inner life of the person who externalized it.[15]

Wollheim considers three analyses of the perception of pleasure in a smile, and concludes that only the third is acceptable.[16] I shall rehearse these analyses and expand the third in order to provide an account of our perception of externalized properties.

The first analysis proposes that there is a natural affinity between an emotion such as pleasure and a muscular contortion such as a smile. On this analysis, we perceive pleasure in a smile because there is something inherently pleasurable about the look of a face pulled in a way that produces the upward curve of the lips.[17] We do not perceive pleasure in a face that is pulled in another way because other facial contortions do not have an affinity with pleasure. A scowl or a frown do not have an affinity with pleasure, and it is for this reason that we do not see pleasure in them, but rather we see anger or disappointment, with which they might be thought to have an affinity. However, while it may be true that we happen to perceive pleasure in a smile, and that this is largely cross-cultural, it is established that there remains some degree of cultural relativism in such perception. If particular facial contortions had an inherent affinity with particular emotions, we should not expect to find any degree of relativity across cultures.[18] This suggests that the perception of emotion in physiognomy is not a matter of perceiving a natural affinity.

The second analysis maintains that although there is no inherent affinity between pleasure and the particular muscular contortion that constitutes the smile, we perceive pleasure in the smile because, in our experience, there is a constant conjunction between the muscular contortion and the mental state of people who contort their face in this way. This explanation holds that although there is nothing inherently pleasurable about the look of a face pulled into a smile, whenever people smile they are always pleased. It is this constant conjunction between a face pulled in a certain way and the frame of mind of the person who pulled it that accounts for the pleasure we perceive in a smile: whenever we see a smile, we know that the person is pleased, and so we come to perceive pleasure in the smile. The problem with this argument, however, is that a smile is not always produced by someone who is pleased. As Wollheim observes, although foolish parents think that their baby smiles with wind, the fact that the baby contorts its face in that particular way does not mean that it is pleased; it is caused by the flatulence rather than a feeling of pleasure. Thus, there is no constant conjunction between a face pulled into a smile and the agent's feeling pleased.

The third analysis differs from the first two in its conception of what constitutes the "smile" in which pleasure is perceived. The two previous arguments were intended to show that we perceive pleasure in a certain muscular contortion. But assuming we do perceive pleasure in a smile, the error might be to equate the "smile" with the facial contortion, and then to ask why we perceive pleasure in a particular configuration of facial muscles. Wollheim suggests that perhaps what we mean by the smile is not the way in which the face is pulled, but an activity intended to give external form to an agent's pleasure by pulling the face in a certain way. If the smile is understood as an intentional activity of this kind, then there will always be a constant conjunction between pleasure and a successful smile (where a successful smile means the realization of an attempt to engage in an activity that externalizes the feeling of pleasure).

This gets us out of the problems encountered by the two previous analyses. If the smile is understood as an intentional activity of this kind, then it

is perfectly possible that the agent might choose to pull his face in a different way in order to give form to his pleasure. Because the concept of a smile
is not now tied to the way in which a face is pulled, but to the realization
of the intention to externalize emotion in a certain way, it is possible that
pleasure might also be perceived in a face pulled in a different way, so long
as it is regarded as having been pulled in that way as part of an activity that
externalizes the agent's pleasure. Furthermore, if a person pulls his face so
as to produce a downward curve of the lips as an activity that externalizes
pleasure, this is now an instance of smiling, rather than being a frown that is
intended to externalize happiness. Also, it is no longer a problem that a face
that is pulled as a smile might also be pulled when the agent is not pleased.
Although the two faces might look the same, the latter has not been pulled
as an activity intended to externalize pleasure. So it does not count as a
smile, since a smile is now the intentional activity, rather than the way the
face is pulled. And a face pulled in the same way without it being intended
to externalize pleasure might resemble that pulled as part of the activity of
smiling, but a face so pulled is not technically a smile.

The look of a face pulled as an activity of externalizing an internal feeling
is a trace of the activity of externalizing that emotion. It is for this reason that
we are able to perceive the externalized property of the emotion in the facial
contortion. The way that the face is pulled when we engage in the activity of
externalizing pleasure through facial expression is a trace of the activity of
smiling. Once we are able to perceive this as a trace of the activity, we can
perceive pleasure in the trace. The fact that a face is pulled in a particular
way does not mean that the person is in fact smiling. There might be some
cause other than the activity of smiling that results in the face being pulled
in that way. However, once we are able to perceive a particular facial contortion as a trace of a smile, we can perceive the externalized property in that
facial contortion even when it is not in fact a trace of the activity of smiling.
So once we have the capacity to perceive the upward curve of the lips as the
trace of a smile, we can perceive pleasure in the upward curve of the lips on
any occasion, even when it is not in fact the trace of a smile.

The perception of the externalized property of pleasure in the curvature
of the lips does not entitle us to infer that the person pulling his face in that
way is pleased. We could only be justified in inferring that if it actually was
a trace of a smile. But we are not currently interested in clarifying when we
can infer things about other minds from the perception of physiognomy.
We can simply note that less is required in order to perceive an externalized
property in another person's physiognomy than is required in order to infer
something about the person's mind from his physiognomy. So Wollheim's
parents are indeed foolish if they infer from the look of their farting baby's
face that it is smiling or that it is pleased. But there is nothing foolish about

their perceiving pleasure in the look of the farting baby's face, or their being infected by this pleasure. Because the look of the face is the same as the trace of smiling, they can perceive the externalized property of pleasure in it even though the baby did not smile.

Smiling is but one activity that leaves a trace in our physiognomy in which we might perceive an externalized property. There is an extensive range of bodily gestures in which we can perceive externalized properties, for example we can perceive anger in a clenched fist. It is also possible for sounds such as shrieks and laughs to be traces of activities intended to externalize emotions such as shock and joy, and once we can perceive these as traces, we can perceive externalized properties in them. However, the trace need not be a gesture that terminates in the body or a noise emitted from it. There could, in principle, be an activity intended to externalize an emotion that involved manual gestures which, rather than involving, say, a clenched fist, involved grasping a calligraphy brush and marking a piece of paper, or grasping a paintbrush and marking a canvas. In this case, the trace of the activity, rather than being a lie of the body, might be an artefact. Once we can perceive an artefact such as a marked canvas as a trace of an externalizing activity, we can perceive an externalized property in it.[19] And we can then perceive a range of different externalized properties in the various ways in which a surface can be marked by an artist as an activity intended to externalize emotion. And once we can perceive particular kinds of marks as traces, we can perceive externalized properties in them even when they are not, in fact, traces of externalizing activities. In this way, we can perceive externalized properties not just in the physiognomy of other psychological agents, but also in non-psychological objects created by psychological agents where these objects are perceived as traces of externalizing activities.

This provides the basis for our perception of externalized properties in works of art. The marks on a page, for example, might be the traces of an externalizing activity. Accordingly, the audience can perceive in the trace the emotion that the artist intended to press out through the activity that terminated in the marks on the page. The audience might, however, lack reason to infer that the artist was, on this particular occasion, engaged in an activity of pressing out an emotion. In this case, the audience will not regard the marks as constituting a trace of an externalizing activity. However, these marks might be indiscernible from the marks in which the audience knows an externalizing activity terminates. Once the audience possesses the capacity to recognize marks as a trace, it can perceive the externalized property in marks that are indiscernible from other marks that it knows to be a trace, without regarding the indiscernible marks as a trace of that activity.

One might accept my analysis of behaviour being perceived as a "pressing out" of emotion, and yet feel that it is very doubtful that this same analysis extends so far as our perceiving externalized properties in works of art. Although my account suggests that there are central cases of this phenomenon, such as smiles, it also suggests that there are more remote cases that can be understood in the same way, despite their remoteness from the central cases. It might be thought that the explanatory power of the account diminishes the further one moves from the central cases: although it is a highly plausible account of our perception of pleasure in a smile, it is a rather improbable account of situations that are remote from physiognomy, such as the expressiveness of the calligrapher's brushstrokes. But to draw such a conclusion is to fail to appreciate that this form of perception is fundamentally imaginative. It is the nature of imagination that it should bound ahead where reason dares not go.

Once we acquire a capacity, such as perceiving externalized properties, the imagination will seek out any opportunity to exercise this capacity. In doing so, it might well venture into contexts far removed from that in which the capacity was developed. When we appreciate the imaginative dimension of perception of externalized properties, we can see how imagination can extend us beyond the central cases in a way that rationality could not. This is why the more remote examples of externalized properties in works of art are dubious examples from which to infer knowledge about the creator's state of mind: they are too far removed from the central cases for rational processes to infer anything, but not too far removed for the imagination to perceive externalized properties. In this way, the central cases of behaviour and physiognomy form the basis upon which imagination can enable us to perceive externalized properties in works of art.

With experience, we become aware of externalizing activities and the traces in which they terminate. Likewise, with experience, our ability to perceive externalized properties in traces, and in the indiscernible counterparts of traces, is refined. There is, however, one further capacity that also develops and refines with experience. Once we are aware of one mark as a trace of one externalizing activity and another mark as the trace of a different externalizing activity, we might also start to imagine that yet further marks are (or might be) the traces of yet further externalizing activities. And so we might come to perceive in these marks the emotions that we imagine have been externalized in activities that terminate in these imaginary traces. We can then perceive externalized properties in marks that are the indiscernible counterparts of these traces, without regarding the marks themselves as traces. So the possibilities for perceiving externalized properties in works of art have rapidly expanded. When looking at a painting, we can perceive externalized properties in marks that are traces of externalizing activities, in marks that are the indiscernible counterparts of traces, in imaginary traces and in the indiscernible counterparts of imaginary traces. The same applies for any other situation in which it is possible to find the trace of an externalizing activity. In this way, a claim about perception of emotion in art need not commit us to claiming that the perceived emotion is a sincere expression of what the artist felt.

This does not provide us with a basis for concluding that we will always be correct in perceiving something to be an activity intended to press out an agent's emotion. We might perceive an externalized property when there was no intention on the part of the agent to press out an emotion, if we are already aware that objects of that kind can be traces of a particular externalizing activity. Furthermore, in cases where we correctly perceive such an intention, we might make a mistake about the particular emotion that it is intended to externalize. For all these reasons, it might not be wise to infer from our perception of innocence and joy in the Murphy Baby's smile that he is innocent and joyous. It is not necessary for present purposes to address these concerns. These considerations diminish the utility of our perception of externalized properties as a means of acquiring knowledge about what the externalizing agent is feeling. But this does not affect the fact that we are capable of perceiving externalized properties. All that we were required to establish is what it would mean to perceive an externalized property in the Murphy Baby's smile. This is sufficient to enable us to investigate the different ways in which a perceived externalized property can interact with the perceiver's emotions.

A final word about the Murphy Baby's smile. At different points I have suggested one might perceive innocence and joy, pleasure or happiness in a smile. It is a cheap trick for a philosopher to assert "a smile expresses ...". There are very many different ways in which we are able to contort the muscles around our lips and face, and our ability to read these fine variations can be exceptionally acute. There is a range of emotions, and shades of emotions, that can be perceived in slight variations of the upturned lips. These emotions might be very fine-grained, and we might lack an emotion-word or label to describe the particular nuance that we perceive in a certain facial contortion. So our perception of emotion in physiognomy is not nearly as simplistic as our ability to read the different colours of traffic lights as signs. Although we can talk about the expressiveness of physiognomy in a rough-and-ready way – and this is sometimes convenient – the emotions that we perceive in physiognomy have more in common with the fine-grained, and perhaps ineffable, emotions that we perceive in some works of art.[20]

Perceiving projective properties

Whereas the externalized property is perceived in an object on account of the object's relation to a genetic agent's psychology, the projective property is perceived on account of the object's relation to the perceiving agent's own psychology. Wollheim provides an account of expressive perception that grounds our ability to perceive emotion in the external world in our ability to perceive correspondences between external objects and our internal psychological condition. Our capacity to perceive such correspondences is again grounded in our capacity for projection, which enables us to project our own psychological condition onto something in the world.[21] I shall not reconstruct Wollheim's argument here, but draw on aspects of it in a way that I believe avoids certain objections raised by Budd.[22]

Our perception of projective properties requires the cultivation of three capacities. The development of each of these capacities follows on from the development of the more primitive capacities, and so they need to be considered in turn. First, the agent must be capable of projection. Second, the agent must become aware that some acts of projection endure. This occurs when the object onto which the emotion is projected bears an affinity for the projected emotion, whereas other acts of projection do not endure because the object onto which the emotion was projected is not appropriate. Third, the agent must be able to perceive a projective property when he appreciates that a certain object has the potential to sustain the projection of a particular emotion if it were projected. Once he perceives this, he can perceive the object as possessing a projective property without having actually engaged in an act of projection.[23]

First, the capacity to project. At the core of Wollheim's account is the psychoanalytic concept of projection.[24] This activity is hypothesized to occur in archaic mental functioning when the mind expels a painful feeling in order to gain relief, or a pleasant feeling in order to preserve it. The benefit is obtained by transferring the feeling to some other part of the world, as if by excreting and smearing it onto that external object, thereby allowing the archaic mind to imagine that the feeling is no longer part of its own psychology. The feeling can be projected either onto another psychological agent, in an act of what Wollheim calls *simple projection,* or onto some part of the environment that does not possess a psychology, in an act of what he calls *complex projection.* In simple projection, the very psychological property that the agent seeks to expel is now thought to be possessed by the other agent, so that whereas the projecting agent once felt afraid, for example, he now believes that someone else feels afraid. Wollheim maintains that the agent cannot conceive of the environment possessing the projected psychological property: the agent is aware both that the portion of the environment in question does not possess a psychology, and that only psychologies can possess psychological properties. Instead, Wollheim hypothesizes that in complex projection, when the archaic mind projects a psychological property, it perceives what he calls a projective property, something similar to – or *of a piece with* – the psychological property, without actually being a psychological property.[25]

Let us imagine that I feel lonely and I seek to remedy this through projection. First, say that I project the loneliness onto my sister. The consequence of this act of projection is that my beliefs about her are changed. I believe that she now feels lonely, and I gain relief from believing that she is lonely, rather than that I am. Second, let us say that I project the loneliness onto a single cloud floating in an otherwise clear sky. The consequence of this act of projection is that I adopt a new attitude to the cloud: I perceive its appearance to be in some sense of a piece with loneliness, and I gain relief from feeling that the environment matches my own emotional condition.[26] There is a difference between these two examples: in one case my beliefs about the object have changed, whereas in the other case my attitude to the object has changed. It is only in that latter case, Wollheim argues, that there is a change in how I perceive the world. Because complex projection affects how I perceive the world, whereas simple projection affects my beliefs about the world, complex projection has the potential to create perceptual properties, which simple projection cannot. Thus, the remainder of our analysis of projective properties is concerned with complex projection, not simple projection.

The second stage in my reworking of Wollheim's account of projective properties involves our observation that some acts of (complex) projection endure whereas others are transient. In our earliest experiences, Wollheim explains, we project emotions onto things in the world indiscriminately. This is initially effective because it is the very act of projecting that provides relief. However, we gradually observe that, in some cases, the projective properties persist, whereas in other cases they do not. Projective properties stick when the emotion is projected onto something that is appropriate to, or in some sense matches, the emotion. In other cases, the object lacks this match and the projection does not stick. What makes some part of the world appropriate to a particular emotion is something that we discover through trial and error as we notice that in some cases the projective property persists, whereas in other cases it is short-lived. So an infant might project either happiness or loneliness onto a cloud, and in either case the act of projection will meet the psychological need. However, the projection of loneliness will persist in a way that the projection of happiness does not. This is because of the affinity between the look of the cloud and loneliness. As the child develops, it might become aware – through experience – that in some cases projective properties persist, while in other cases they do not. This awareness brings new expressive possibilities for complex projection.

What does it mean for a projective property to endure, or persist, in Wollheim's account? The relief that we experience through complex projection is transient. Imagining that some part of the world, such as a cloud, matches my loneliness is sufficient to obtain relief because this eliminates my own feeling of loneliness. But that in itself does not mean that my experience of subsequent similar clouds will be affected by this experience. Once my loneliness has been eliminated, there is no cause to feel the relief on subsequent occasions. However, Wollheim claims that we might find that subsequent experiences of clouds continue to be affected by the earlier projective experience in another way. We continue to perceive something in subsequent sightings of solitary clouds that we did not perceive in them before the projective act: we continue to perceive loneliness in them. In contrast, if we attempted to project loneliness onto a golden daffodil, while we might gain relief on the initial occasion from having eliminated our own feeling of loneliness, we would not find that our experience of golden daffodils on subsequent occasions is affected. The daffodil, unlike the cloud, does not possess an affinity with loneliness, and so it does not sustain the projective property on subsequent occasions.

But to say that we perceive the projective property on subsequent occasions only if there is an affinity prompts the question: what is the nature of the affinity? In particular, does the affinity involve some pre-existing condition that is discovered through the developments of this second stage, or is the affinity something that is created in the act of projection? In Wollheim's system, it seems that the affinity is meant to involve becoming aware of something about ourselves or the world that does not depend on projection. It is precisely for this reason that it is possible to engage in acts of complex projection that do *not* persist: in these cases, the mere act of projection is not enough to generate an affinity. If the affinity were merely a matter of projection, then any act of projection would be capable of persisting. So the affinity must involve something that does not depend upon the act of projection.

For Wollheim, this affinity is a form of matching that occurs in the relation of *correspondence*. This relation is illustrated neatly by Wordsworth's iconic account of his expressive perception of daffodils:

> When all at once I saw a crowd,
> A host, of golden daffodils;
> …
> A poet could not but be gay,
> In such a jocund company.[27]

Wordsworth might be read as suggesting that he perceived the daffodils to be jocund, and that this perception matched, and accordingly gave rise to, a feeling of gaiety within him. On such a reading, he provides an account of an instance of correspondence. Correspondence, as conceived by Wollheim, is a relation between two terms, one of which corresponds to the other. The jocund daffodils are the corresponding term and the poet's gaiety is the term to which it corresponds. Having perceived the projective property of jocundity in the daffodils, the poet's perception corresponds to, or matches, an emotion of his in a way that gives rise to that emotion in him. In this section, I am interested in understanding what it means for the corresponding term to have an affinity with the term to which it corresponds. In the following chapter, I shall consider what is involved in the perception giving rise to the emotion in the perceiver.

Wollheim explains the affinity in terms of our capacity to perceive a special relation of matching between different kinds of mental phenomena.[28] It is helpful to approach this notion of affinity as matching via an instance of another notion of affinity as a causal relation. Synaesthesia is a recognized neurological condition in which one type of stimulation evokes a sensation of another kind in a subject.[29] So, for instance, the sound of a particular tone or chord might evoke the sensation of a particular hue.[30] An explanation of this phenomenon need not make reference to "matching"; the phenomenon simply involves a causal relation in which a sense perception of one kind constantly gives rise to a sense perception of another kind. However, if a sensation of one kind can evoke a sensation of another kind, it might further be claimed that there is not merely a causal relation, but a relation that involves the two sensations matching one another in some sense that holds despite their being different kinds of sensations. It is this idea that Baudelaire has in mind when he famously writes:

> Il est des parfums frais comme des chairs d'enfants,
> Doux comme les hautbois, verts comme les prairies.[31]

What we have here is the suggestion that there is a way of experiencing the smell of children's flesh such that it resembles the sound of oboes and the colour of meadows. This is not a claim that a smell evokes the sensation of a sound or a colour, but that they match or resemble one another. In this sense, the affinity involves a match that might possibly explain why one sensation might give rise to the other. Whether or not the matching accounts for the causal relation, we can distinguish between a purely causal relation and one that refers to our sensation being *appropriate* to another, rather than causing it.

If we are able to grasp the sense of affinity as a match between different sense modalities, exploited by the French symbolists, it is only a small step from Baudelaire's experience of different sense perceptions matching one another in *correspondance* to Wollheim's experience of correspondence, in which a sense perception can match not only another sense perception, but an emotion. Just as the smell of flesh can match the sound of oboes or the colour of meadows, so the appearance of an estuary is said to match the feeling of melancholy.[32] This progression in thought is intended to go some way towards dispelling the mysteriousness that might otherwise seem to shroud the claim that we can perceive a match between two different kinds of mental phenomena.[33] However, even if it gives us reason to entertain the possibility of the kind of relation that Wollheim proposes, it does not explain the nature of the relation that is said to account for the affinity.

Wollheim ascribes four properties to the relation that holds between the perception of jocundity in the daffodils and the feeling of gaiety to which it gives rise in the poet.[34] First, the relation is non-symmetrical: the relation has direction and so the fact that the first term corresponds to the second does not mean that the second corresponds to the first. Thus, the fact that the perception of the daffodils' jocundity corresponds to the poet's gaiety does not entail that his being gay will correspond to perceiving jocundity in the daffodils. It might or might not do so as the relation is non-symmetrical but not asymmetrical. Second, the relation is non-transitive. If the smell of children's flesh corresponds to the sound of oboes, and the sound of oboes corresponds to the colour of meadows, it does not follow that the smell of the flesh will necessarily correspond to the colour of meadows. Again, it may or may not do so, as the relation is non-transitive but not intransitive. Third, the relation is sensory, and we are aware of its holding through our sense perceptions. It is sensory, but only weakly sensory. Both terms might be perceptual or only one; and if both are, they may involve different sense-modalities. So, while correspondence might be a matter of the smell of flesh corresponding to a sound or colour, both terms need not be sensory, as the correspondence of the perception of daffodils to the emotion of gaiety demonstrates.[35] Finally, it is grounded in trains of association. Some trains of association are anchored deeper in the psyche than others, and those that correspondence makes use of tend to be located at a particularly deep level. For these four reasons, Wollheim characterizes correspondence as a subjective phenomenon and contrasts it to the objective relation of fit that holds between the world and a belief when it is true, and between the world and a desire when it is satisfied.[36]

It is the trains of association that are crucial for an understanding of affinity. There is a range of associations that the appearance of an object might have. These might include psychosexual, cultural and biological associations.[37] The appearance of an object might have an association for an individual on account of a connection with some event in his individual psychosexual development, in which case the association will be a private one. (Of course, one might think that individuals share common experiences in their psychosexual development, in which case the associations might not be quite so private.) The appearance of an object might also have an association for all the individuals that are members of a particular species on account of some biological significance, or perhaps on account of the natural selection of individuals with that association, in which case the association will be shared by all members of the species. And the appearance of an object might also have an association for a subset of individuals within a species, on account of some cultural attachment to the object, in which case some, but not all, individuals will share the association. I raise these three possibilities not because they are exhaustive, but because they show that associations might be private, universal or somewhere in-between.

The private, shared and universal associations that the appearance of an object has for an individual are not necessarily associations with a particular emotion. They constitute a network of associations with beliefs, desires, feelings, memories, sensations, perceptions and so on: they are associations with the whole range of mental phenomena. But the network of associations that the appearance of an object has affects its affinity with a particular emotion. If the appearance of the object has one set of associations, it can sustain the projection of a certain emotion, whereas if it has another set of associations, it can sustain a different projection. So the appearance of a single cloud in a clear sky might have one set of associations for Wordsworth, and the host of golden daffodils another set of associations. It is not that the cloud has an association with loneliness and the daffodils an association with jocundity. Rather, the associations (which might be vague or even conflicting) lend the cloud and the daffodils an affinity with certain emotions. Perhaps Wordsworth's mother liked to have a bowl of daffodils in her room, or they reminded him of the onset of spring and its rejuvenation, or they featured prominently at a local fair at which he once bought a book of poems that fascinated him. Perhaps they have all these associations for him. In this case, it is the daffodils' associations with his mother, spring, rejuvenation and the fair that give them an affinity with jocundity. This affinity means that when he projects jocundity onto the daffodils, they sustain the projection.[38]

Note that the perception of emotion occurs only when the appearance of the object is both the object of a train of association and the object of projection. If the affinity lay in the projection of emotion, then the object would sustain the emotion irrespective of the object's associations. In this case, there would be no transient instances of projection: projection would always be sustained. If the affinity with the associations alone enabled us to perceive the emotion, then there would be no need for projection. But we cannot perceive emotion in an object simply because it has associations with a web of non-emotional mental phenomena. Such a web of associations has the potential to sustain an emotion if one is somehow introduced, but it must be introduced by projection or some other means.[39] So the perception of emotion lies in the fact of the coincidence of the appearance as the object of a (possibly arbitrary) train of association and as the object of a (possibly arbitrary) projection. Red, for instance, has very deep associations with blood and the danger of the spilling of bodily fluids. Thus, the appearance of red things has associations that mean that if we were to project fear onto a red object, it is likely to sustain that projection. But we should not expect to be able to find any direct association between red and fear. On the other hand, savannahs perhaps acquired a set of associations with hospitable living conditions, pasture for grazing, food and shelter for our nomadic forebears. If we have inherited our evolutionary forebears' associations, it would not be surprising to find that, were we to project a certain positive emotion, such as tenderness, onto a savannah, the emotion would be sustained by the environment. The projection would be sustained on account of the coincidence of the look of the landscape as an object of association and as the object of projection. So perception of an emotion in an object is no more a function of the object's associations than it is a function of the subject's projective activity: it is a function of something being both the object of associations and the object of a projective act.

A given object might have different private, shared and universal associations for a particular individual. So, while some of the associations that a particular object has for you will be apparent to me, I might only appreciate others if I belong to a group that shares the associations, and your private associations might be inaccessible to me, or at least accessible only with considerable effort. It is also hardly surprising to find that there are fine variations in the emotions with which two individuals perceive the same object to have an affinity. There is still likely to be some degree of convergence, however, if they share similar cultural associations. Indeed, there will be some even looser concurrence with the affinity that the object holds for individuals who have different cultural associations, but are members of a species that shares a common evolutionary psychology. In each case for which there is an affinity, this will involve a combination of these different factors, so that a given object will have a stronger or weaker affinity for different agents. It is this complex web of associations, however, that will make a certain object appropriate to sustain a projection of one emotion but not another. This is a highly complicated situation, which cannot be conveniently presented schematically. But it is a strength of the account that it does not shy away from acknowledging the indefinite and imprecise nature of this affinity.

An objection might be raised that, even if I have established that an object might be perceived to possess the capacity to sustain a projective property, nothing I have said establishes how we get from a conditional awareness of a projective property to actual perception of it. This concern is natural and appropriate when we are concerned with practical reasoning. (To judge that this estuary would be an ideal place to catch a glimpse of a saltwater crocodile does not enable me actually to perceive a croc in the estuary.) But this concern is misplaced when we are considering a fundamentally imaginative activity, such as perceiving melancholy in an estuary. In *De l'amour*, Stendhal speaks of *"une certaine fièvre d'imagination"* ("a certain fever of the imagination") that is central to the lover's falling in love with his beloved.[40] The lover invests his beloved with the properties that would make him love her. He then comes to believe that she actually loves him, and he believes this not because he desires her to love him, but because the fact of her actually loving him would account for his loving her, for his regarding her as an appropriate object of his love. There is nothing rational about this – it is a fever of the imagination. He imagines that she loves him because he regards her as being appropriate to love. My account of perception of projective properties is also concerned with a certain fever of the imagination: conditional awareness of the capacity to sustain enables imagination – but not reason – to perceive the emotion that could be sustained. Perception of projective properties is not a rational activity but an imaginative one. It is for this reason that imagination is able to move us from conditional awareness of suitability for projection to actual perception of a projective property.

Once we are able to project emotions and are aware that some acts of projection endure, we are ready for the third stage, in which we perceive projective properties in things that have not been the object of earlier projections. It is, I suggest, sometimes possible to perceive a projective property in something without that thing having been involved in a prior act of projection. This occurs in cases where we are aware that the object in question has the potential to sustain a certain projective property, were it to be projected onto it. But how do we find out that there is potential for projection unless it means perceiving an affinity between the external object and the internal psychological condition?

Let us say that, through trial and error, I have become aware that certain kinds of things sustain different "coarse" projective properties: an overcast skyscape sustains the projective property of foreboding; slow-moving water sustains the projective property of sluggishness; the rustle of the wind in the leaves sustains the projective property of loneliness; the smell of rotting vegetation sustains the projective property of moribundity. Once experience has given me the ability to recognize that things of these kinds sustain different coarse projective properties, what happens when I am presented with a particular estuary? The estuarine scene is overcast; the water moves slowly; the wind rustles in the leaves; there is a smell of rot in the air. So experience suggests that different parts of the scene would sustain foreboding, sluggishness, loneliness and moribundity. But there is a very "fine-grained" feeling that is not quite any of these, and yet touches on each of them.[41] This fine-grained feeling defies descriptive language, but let us call it "melancholy". Although I have never projected the fine-grained melancholy onto the estuary, my experience of the kind of things that sustain the coarse projective properties, when combined with my awareness that these things are features of the estuary, enables me to perceive the estuary's potential to sustain the fine-grained projective property of melancholy, were I to project it onto the scene. The awareness that the estuary could sustain the projection of melancholy can then serve to affect my subsequent perceptions of the estuary in the same way as the discovery, through experience, that the estuary in fact sustains an earlier projection of emotion can affect subsequent experiences. This awareness enables me to perceive the projective property without having previously projected it.[42]

It is not only kinds of natural phenomena that are observed to sustain coarse projective properties. Obvious candidates for early acts of projection are colours: through experience, I find that red sustains the coarse projective property of terror, whereas blue sustains the coarse projective property of calmness. Similarly, I find that round shapes sustain different projective properties to shapes with acute angles. Once experience has given us the awareness that certain colours and certain shapes sustain different coarse emotions, we can see the potential that different coloured shapes have to sustain certain fine-grained emotions, were we to project them onto the objects. In this way, we can perceive different fine-grained emotions in red triangles, red circles and blue circles. This is not simply a matter of seeing the projective properties sustained by red and roundness in the red circle. Rather, as in the case of the estuary, it is a matter of seeing that a red circle has the potential to sustain the projection of a fine-grained emotion that resonates with both of the coarse emotions. Thus, we can perceive a wide range of fine-grained emotional properties in images of different colour and shape. Indeed, further possibilities will be created by combining different images in a single composition. It is our ability to perceive these projective properties of coloured shapes that accounts for what Kandinsky calls the "spiritual value" of different coloured shapes, and which he believed could account for the expressiveness of abstract painting.[43]

If we can perceive projective properties in paintings, we can also perceive them in music. Major tonalities sustain different coarse projective properties to minor tonalities. Similarly, nasal sounds, such as that of the oboe, sustain different coarse projective properties to shrill sounds, such as that of the trumpet. With experience of the sustainability of projecting coarse emotions onto such sounds, we are able to perceive the potential for a musical phrase in a minor key played on a trumpet to sustain a certain fine-grained projective property. This differs from that which will be sustained by a transposition of the theme into the relative major played on the same instrument, or the projective potential of the theme in the original key when played on the oboe.

In this way, I suggest that our capacity to project emotions, coupled with our experience that certain kinds of things sustain the projection of different coarse projective properties, enables us to perceive fine-grained projective properties in things that have the potential to sustain them. This can occur without our actually having projected the fine-grained emotion immediately prior to perceiving it, or even at some time in the remoter past. Wollheim's attempt to explain a similar position involves his introducing the "intimation thesis", or the claim that our experiences of projective properties intimate, or reveal, their origin in projection.[44] Budd, however, has convincingly discredited this thesis, and, accordingly, an account of perceptual properties should not rely on such a thesis in order to ground such perception in projection.[45] The present theory avoids the need for such a thesis. That fine-grained projective properties can be perceived in the absence of genetic projection is possible because our experience of having projected coarse projective properties enables us to see the potential that a complex object has for sustaining a fine-grained projective property. It is the use that we can make of our experience of successful projections that enables us to perceive new projective properties without having actually projected those particular properties. All of this, it must be remembered, is a claim about possibility, not necessity. But it is a possibility that is important for human flourishing, as we shall see.

Perceiving externalized and projective properties in art

These accounts of perceptual properties, and the objects in which we perceive them, prepare us for understanding the unique possibility that works of art hold for us. I shall make two suggestions that enable us to understand this special possibility, which I shall develop below. First, we can perceive externalized properties, but not projective properties, in other psychological agents. Second, we can perceive projective properties, but not externalized properties, in natural non-psychological objects. In the case of non-psychological objects produced by psychological agents, we can perceive these objects as objects that are suitable to project a projective property onto, and we can also perceive them as traces of behaviour that presses out another agent's inner psychological condition. This means that it is possible for a non-psychological object created by a psychological agent to possess both kinds of perceptual properties: as a non-psychological object, it is suitable for a perceiving agent to project a projective property onto; and as the product of a psychological agent, it is suitable for the perceiving agent to perceive as the externalization of its creator's internal condition.

Unlike human physiognomy or the landscape, a work of art is a non-psychological object created by a psychological agent, the artist. The suggestion that will be developed in later chapters is that in creating a work of art, an artist might exploit his audience's capacities to perceive both externalized and projective properties in it. We shall see that the kind of perceptual property that we perceive bears on the kind of affective consequences that the perceiver experiences. Certain consequences are possible when an externalized property is perceived, and others when a projective property is perceived. If we can perceive both externalized and projective properties in a work of art, then we will have the affective consequences of both the externalized property and the projective property. We shall see in Chapter 4 that it is the nature of a work of art as a perceptual hybrid that gives rise to the possibility of the unique kind of composite emotional experience illustrated earlier in this chapter.[46]

We have considered an account of our capacity for perceiving projective properties in naturally occurring non-psychological objects, such as portions of the landscape. We cannot perceive externalized properties in the landscape unless we regard it as possessing its own psychology. What is interesting about Wordsworth's experience of the daffodils is that although he perceives jocundity in them, he nevertheless perceives them *as* nature: he does not believe or imagine that they possess their own psychologies. In this respect, we can contrast his experience with that of Alice's when she enters the Garden of Live Flowers in *Through the Looking Glass*.[47] Alice regards the Tiger Lily as nasty in the sense that boys might be nasty to her. In doing so, she has ceased engaging with the flowers as non-psychological objects in a way that Wordsworth's poet does not. Thus, she is able to perceive externalized properties in the flowers, but only at the cost of ceasing to engage with them as non-psychological objects.[48]

We might also perceive externalized properties in the landscape if we regard the natural world as the product of a creator or creators who created it as an expression of their own emotions. This requires an appropriate theology.[49] Were one to embrace such a theology, the experience of nature would, I suggest, be the experience of nature *as art*. Such a theist would be precluded from having the kind of emotional experience of nature *as nature* that is open to the atheist (and, indeed, to theists who do not regard nature as the trace of a divine act of externalization). While there might be a number of interesting ways in which we can relate to the landscape, I am only interested in the emotional experience of the landscape *as nature*.[50] When we experience the landscape *as nature* rather than *as art*, as certain theists might, or *as anthropomorphized*, as Alice does, we are able to perceive projective properties but not externalized properties in it.

We have also considered an account of our capacity for perceiving externalized properties in other psychological agents. We do not, however, perceive in other psychological agents the kind of projective properties that

Wollheim describes. To understand why this is so, we have to understand the diachronic nature of Wollheim's account of projection. Projection has its origin in archaic mental activities in which the infant gains relief through phantasizing the expulsion of a painful emotion. Initially, this is a matter of imagining that the actual emotion is excreted and smeared onto something else. This is the basis for Wollheim's *simple projection*. Simple projection is only effective when there is another psychology onto which the actual emotion can be projected. When the archaic mind realizes that simple projection is ineffective for projecting onto non-psychological objects, it develops a further capacity to deal with this contingency: *complex projection*. It is the capacity for complex projection that provides the basis for perceiving projective properties.

It is important to appreciate that, in Wollheim's account, complex projection develops after simple projection, and it develops in order to enable the archaic mind to project emotions when simple projection is not possible. Because the first impulse is to expel an emotion through simple projection, the archaic mind does not have recourse to complex projection unless expulsion through simple projection is not an option. Why would the archaic mind engage in an activity that enabled it to perceive a projective property – something that is *of a piece with* an emotion – if it could engage in an activity that enabled it to perceive the actual emotion? The consequence of this is that, in Wollheim's system, when we want to project onto other agents, we engage in simple projection rather than complex projection. Because our developmental history sees us engage in simple projection rather than complex projection, in relation to other psychological agents, we do not perceive projective properties in their physiognomy.

This position is derived from my interpretation of Wollheim's speculative psychology, a speculative psychology that draws heavily on his own development of Melanie Klein's development of Freudian psychoanalysis. In order for this highly speculative – and, indeed, not particularly intuitive – position to be accepted, even tentatively, it needs to accommodate two intuitions about projection and physiognomic expression. First, it will have to accommodate the intuition that projection does seem to play a significant role in our experience of other people, notwithstanding my claim that we do not perceive projective properties in other people. Second, in precluding the possibility of perceiving projective properties in another agent's physiognomy, it will have to account for the intuition that a perceiver's own mental activity does, on occasion, result in him perceiving a particular emotion in another person's physiognomy, even though the other person did not intend, either consciously or unconsciously, to express it.

To say that we do not perceive projective properties in other people is not to say that projection plays no part in our experience of others. Projection, broadly speaking, might be identified with Hume's observation that "the mind has a great propensity to spread itself on external objects".[51] There are many senses in which the mind might be thought to spread itself on the world through projection.[52] In Wollheim's system, projection can affect our beliefs about, and evaluations of, the world, as well as our perceptions of the world.[53] To say that we do not perceive projective properties in other people is to say that projection does not affect our *perceptions* of other people. It is not to say that projection does not affect our *beliefs* or *evaluations* about them. I suggest that our intuitions about projection in ordinary life are concerned with the way in which, through phantasy, the contents of our own mind spread themselves over other people so as to change our beliefs about them. When we project onto other people, we allow our inner life to affect our beliefs about what other people are thinking and feeling. This, in itself, does not mean that projection directly affects how we perceive them: we do not perceive projective properties in them. However, such phantasies might indirectly affect how we perceive externalized properties in other people.

The second intuition that I suggest we have to accommodate is the thought that, whether or not we perceive projective properties in other people, when we perceive emotion in a person's physiognomy, it is often the case that something about our own inner life affects the emotions that we perceive in others: we often perceive in other people emotions that are not actually the product of an externalizing activity on the other person's part. The account of externalized properties can accommodate this intuition. It will be recalled that we can perceive emotion in a gesture or utterance that is habitually a trace of an externalizing activity even in instances in which it is not, in fact, the product of that activity. Once the foolish parents in Wollheim's example have the capacity to perceive upturned lips as the trace of an activity that externalizes pleasure (i.e. a smile), they can perceive pleasure in their farting baby's upturned lips, even though this is, in fact, a reaction to the flatulence, rather than an attempt at externalization. In such cases, the perceiver perceives in the other person emotion which that person did not actually externalize. But this is not because the perceiver projects something onto the perceived person (at least, not in the sense of simple or complex projection). Rather, it is perceived because the perceiver has acquired a capacity to perceive such gestures or utterances as traces of externalizing activity, even though he might be mistaken in doing so. It is mistake rather than projection that accounts for our perceiving in another person's physiognomy an emotion that that person does not feel. So we need not have recourse to projection in order to explain this phenomenon.

Given that Wollheim provides a diachronic explanation that, I suggest, precludes the possibility of perceiving projective properties in other people, and given that his explanation can accommodate intuitions that might be interpreted as suggesting that we do perceive projective properties in other people, I believe that it is justifiable to claim that we do not perceive projective properties in other people.

The following chapters develop the claim that there is a variety of emotional experience that is unique to art. This claim is premised on the idea that it is only in works of art that we can perceive both externalized and projective properties. However, one might not accept that this only occurs in our experience of art. In particular, one might not accept my basis for maintaining that we do not perceive projective properties in other psychological agents. If one thought that it is possible to perceive projective properties – as well as externalized properties – in other agents, then the emotional experience that I discuss in Chapters 4 and 5 would not be unique to art: it might also occur in our personal relationships. In that case, the following discussion of the emotional experience of art would still serve to exemplify a valuable kind of experience, albeit an experience that can also occur outside of our experience of works of art. In the following chapters, I shall proceed on the basis that I am entitled to claim that it is only in art that we perceive both kinds of emotional properties. In the concluding chapter, however, I shall revisit these assumptions and consider how my argument fares if one believes that there are non-artistic contexts in which we can perceive both kinds of emotional properties.

Perceptual properties and aesthetic properties

O. K. Bouwsma begins his essay on the expression theory of art by seeking to clarify what it means for an agent to perceive some object as being expressive of an emotion.[54] He takes the theorist's primary task to be one of clarifying what it means for an agent to find a piece of music sad, a person sad, a person's face sad or a dog sad. His aim is to show that although "the music is sad", "the girl is sad", "the girl's face is sad" and "the dog's face is sad" all share a common predicate ("is sad"), the predicate means something different in each case, and the different usages present different problems. Now, there might be something significant to be said about the logic of these different statements, but that is very different from clarifying something about the phenomenology of the experiences that prompt one to make these different statements. It is those differences that matter for present purposes. One might think that the only noteworthy feature of the experiences is that they give rise to different statements, which require clarification. But if one thinks that there are substantive differences between the experiences themselves, then it is these experiences that must be studied. We are interested in asking whether the way in which the perceiver's emotion and the perceived emotion interact in the experience of the music, the dog, and the girl are similar or different, rather than how the usage of the same predicate to describe them is similar or different.

Having observed repeatedly that we are interested in the different ways in which the perceived emotion and the perceiver's emotion interact, it is now a commonplace to say that the experiences that interest us are those in which we both perceive emotion in the world and have some affective experience at the same time. So it will not be helpful to investigate experiences in which we only perceive emotion in the world, or those in which we feel an affect without also perceiving emotion in the world. And because we are interested in experiences in which both occur, it will not be helpful to ask whether the emotional aspect of the experience pertains to the fact that we perceive emotion in a work of art, or whether it pertains to the fact that the perception of the formal properties of the work of art gives rise to an emotion within us.

This dispute finds form in the contemporary debate about the relationship between music and emotion, in which some aestheticians argue that we hear sad music as sounding sad — that is, the sadness is to be explained as a perceptual property of the music — while other aestheticians argue that sad music is music that causes us to feel sad or imagine feeling sad when we hear it.[55] There may be some experiences that can be explained satisfactorily in one of these two ways, but they are not the experiences that interest us. What we require is an account that allows us to distinguish experiences on the basis of the different ways in which the perceiver's emotion and the perceived emotion interact rather than an account that forces us to choose between explaining the experience in terms of the perceived emotion or the perceiver's emotion alone.[56] Such an account is offered in the following chapter.

In addition to these highly specialized debates, the earlier discussion of the perception of emotion in the world might also seem to lead us towards more general metaphysical questions concerning the nature of aesthetic properties. If the externalized properties and projective properties with which I have been concerned are aesthetic properties of works of art, this might suggest that I have waded into the current debate about aesthetic properties, which has its origin in Frank Sibley's influential paper on the topic,[57] and the critical literature that emerged in response to his argument for the reality of aesthetic properties.[58] The debate persists in Jerrold Levinson's defence of the realist position,[59] and the challenges that continue to be mounted against his arguments.[60] These theorists share certain of my interests in the perceptual properties of works of art. To establish the amount of common ground that we traverse, it is convenient to identify a number of questions that might be asked about our perception of works of art and the properties that we might be thought to perceive in them:

1. (a) Is it conceivable that there is a higher-order way of appearing that involves perceiving emotion in an appearance?
   (b) Is it conceivable that an emotional response is triggered by an ordinary (or higher-order) way of appearing?
2. (a) Do we actually perceive higher-order ways of appearing?
   (b) Do we actually respond emotionally to appearances?
3. (a) Are higher-order ways of appearing dependent on the subject or the object of perception?
   (b) Are emotional responses to perceptions dependent on the subject or the object of perception?
4. (a) Are aesthetic properties to be identified with higher-order ways of appearing?
   (b) Are aesthetic properties to be identified with emotional responses?
5. Can aesthetic judgements be grounded in aesthetic properties? If so, are they grounded in something that is object-dependent or subject-dependent?
6. How can we conceive of an encounter between our perceiving higher-order ways of appearing and our responding emotionally to appearances?

In this chapter, I have suggested two ways in which we might answer question 1(a) in the affirmative (perception of externalized properties and projective properties). In the next chapter, I shall suggest two ways in which we might answer question 1(b) in the affirmative (what I shall call "primary" and "secondary" experiences of emotion in the perceiver). Having answered these questions in the affirmative, I am then interested in answering question 6. Questions 2(a) and 2(b) are matters for empirical psychology, which the current investigations cannot address.[61] I do not find it necessary to resolve questions 3(a) and (b) in favour of the subject or the object in order to answer questions 1 and 6.[62]

In contrast to my approach, it will be apparent that the established debate about aesthetic properties is primarily concerned with answering question 5. This assumes an answer to questions 4(a) and 4(b), and so also to questions 3(a) and 3(b). Because I am interested in answering question 6 in Chapters 3 and 4, and I do not attempt to answer question 5, I do not address questions 3, 4 or 5, which are not necessary for an answer to question 6.

Both the approach in this book and that in the established debate about aesthetic properties are interested in investigating the significance of the perception of, and response to, works of art for value claims about works of art. The thought progression in the established debate might be represented as follows:

1. The emotions
   What are the emotions?

   2. Higher-order ways of perceiving and responses to perception
      How do emotions figure in our perception of, and response to, art?

      3. Expressive properties
         Does expression involve higher-order ways of perceiving or responding?

         4. Aesthetic properties
            What are aesthetic properties? Do they include expressive properties?

            5. Value claim: aesthetic judgements
               Are value judgements concerned with aesthetic properties?

Whereas the thought progression in this book takes the following form:

1. The emotions
   What are the emotions?

   2. Higher-order ways of perceiving and responses to perception
      How do emotions figure in our perception of, and response to, art?

      3. Encounters between perceptions of emotion and perceiver's emotions
         What can we say about possible interactions between these?

         4. Value claim: contribution that encounters make to our flourishing
            Are these encounters valuable in our "ethical" lives?

This difference in progression means that my approach does not give rise to metaphysical concerns which are central to the debate about aesthetic properties: concerns about whether aesthetic values exist independently of our minds, whether aesthetic properties depend upon the subject or the object and whether aesthetic judgements yield knowledge about the object of judgement.[63] Both approaches have common ground in trying to come to terms with understanding whether it is conceivable that there might be higher-order ways of appearing and responses to perceptions, and whether either of these involves emotion in some way.

Ultimately, any theorizing about art ought to be anchored in the theorist's experience of art. My experience of art leads me down one progression of thought, whereas, I assume, other theorists' experiences of art lead them down another progression. Perhaps the more profound significance of these investigations lies not in the persuasiveness of the particular arguments about higher-order ways of perceiving emotion and emotional responses. Rather, it might lie in demonstrating that an interest in such issues can lead to concerns with value claims that are (at least) a supplement to the established debate's concerns about the significance of aesthetic properties for judgements about aesthetic value.

3

The varieties of emotional experience

Ways of experiencing perceived emotions

Chapter 2 provided an account of our two capacities for perceiving emotion in the world, and some illustrations of experiences involving both a perception of emotion and the perceiver's emotional economy as that was described in Chapter 1. We are now ready to analyse the nature of these experiences. One means of analysing them, an approach that we shall pursue in this chapter, involves studying the different ways in which the perceived emotion can interact with the perceiver's own emotion. Such an approach, we shall see, reveals three distinct kinds of interaction.

It is well to begin with a disclaimer. This chapter is not a catalogue of all the ways in which we can become aware of the presence of emotion in the world. We have investigated two perceptual capacities through which we might become aware of emotion in the world, but this says nothing about other means through which we can infer the presence of emotion without actually perceiving it. Neither is it an account of all the ways in which the world around us can arouse our emotions. We need not perceive emotion in the world in order for the world to affect us emotionally: a judgement about the world might arouse an emotion without involving any perception of emotion in the world. For good measure, we should also note that it is not concerned with the ways in which a perceiver's emotions might affect his perception of the world, or how our perception of the world might affect the formation of our emotions. Those are matters for the theory of affect. Rather, our present concern is with something more focused: the varieties of experience that occur when our perception of emotion in the world interacts with our emotional condition.

There are at least three ways in which this interaction might occur, and we shall analyse each of these possibilities in this chapter. First, when we perceive an emotion in the world, this perception might determine how we feel. This occurs in interactions of "infection", in which we perceive and feel the same emotion.[1] Second, we might distinguish these experiences of infection from the interactions of "communication". In communication, the perceiver's imagination or intellect affects the way in which he interacts with the perceived emotion, so that his perception of a certain emotion is attended by the feeling of some other emotion, which is aroused in response to the one that he perceives. Third, in "articulation", the interaction involves the perceiver relating to his own emotions in a new way through his perception of emotion in the world – a way that makes them comprehensible to him without involving the arousal of any emotion.

This approach to the varieties of emotional interaction enables us to appreciate the richness of our emotional experience. The analysis draws attention to the sense in which emotional experiences can be primary or secondary, voluntary or involuntary, comprehensible or incomprehensible. An appreciation of these different aspects of emotional experience prepares us for understanding the complexity of the emotional experience that art offers and, ultimately, why such an experience might be valuable.

Perceiving externalized properties and feeling perceived emotions

The previous chapter's first illustration of a happy baby that becomes distressed when it hears distress in the cry of another baby is an example of infection. Such instances of infection can be classified a stage further according to which of two subclasses of infection they fall into: resonance and correspondence. So we also need to ask which of the two subclasses the initial illustration exemplifies. This requires an account of the two subclasses of infection, how they differ from one another and why we are justified in regarding both kinds of experience as instances of the same variety of emotional experience, despite their differences. We begin with resonance and then investigate how correspondence differs from resonance.

The earlier example of a person who is infected by the smile of another, like the example of the baby that is infected by another baby's cry, is an illustration of what I shall call resonance. What is common to instances of resonance is that each involves an experience in which an emotion is perceived, and in which the perceiver feels the same emotion as he perceives. In a range of contexts, we find that the mere perception of how those around us feel is enough to stimulate us to feel the same way. Although examples of intimate interactions might initially spring to mind, our capacity to resonate with the feelings of those around us is not limited to such contexts. Spectators at football matches and at rock concerts, like participants at the street carnivals of medieval Europe and the ecstatic rituals connected with Dionysus in antiquity, all share experiences in which people quickly find their own emotional condition resonating with the collective joy or euphoria that they perceive in the crowd around them.[2]

In both the intimate and collective cases, we can identify five moments that distinguish these experiences as instances of resonance:

(i)   Such experiences involve the perception of emotion in the world. They involve perceiving the trace of an activity through which another person presses out an emotion rather than perceiving something to be of a piece with emotion. In other words, they involve perceiving an externalized property rather than a projective property.
(ii) This perception gives rise to the feeling of an emotion in the perceiver.
(iii) The perceiver feels the emotion in the primary sense that we do in our ordinary life.
(iv) The particular emotion that the perceiver feels is determined by the emotion that he perceives.
(v)   The emotion that he feels is identical to the emotion that he perceives.

This analysis can be applied to the experience of the baby that hears distress in the cry of another, becomes distressed, and becomes so distressed on account of its perception of distress. It also applies to the ritual participant who perceives ecstasy in the crowd, becomes ecstatic himself, and feels ecstatic on account of perceiving ecstasy.

Central to Leo Tolstoy's theory of art is the idea that art infects its audience. Although the details are sketchy at times, it seems clear that when Tolstoy speaks of a work of art infecting its audience, it is resonance that he has in mind.[3] Tolstoy's theory of art as the expression of emotion is deeply influenced by Eugene Véron's theory of art as the manifestation of emotion in some external form such as line, colour, sound or verse.[4] For Tolstoy, however, such an account is incomplete: art is an instrument of transmission as well as manifestation. Just as words transmit thoughts from one man to another, so art transmits feelings from one man to another.[5] What makes something a work of art is not merely that it is a manifestation of emotion, but also that the work of art is a conduit through which the feeling is transmitted to the audience, so that all who perceive the work feel the same emotion as each other and as the artist. This last requirement means that it is not enough that the work of art manifests just any emotion. In order for it to be authentic, the emotion that is manifested must be one which the artist sincerely felt. We can see that such an account of art's infectiousness is modelled on the individual's ability to betray an emotion through his physiognomy (i.e. through an externalized property), so that an audience that perceives this will feel the emotion that is perceived. Tolstoy offers a scenario in which a boy encounters a wolf in the forest as an example of infection. The boy is afraid. He returns to the village and tells the villagers a story about the encounter. Upon hearing the story, the villagers become afraid. Their fear resonates with the fear that they perceive in the boy. Tolstoy thinks that the same thing occurs whenever we feel some emotion upon perceiving a work of art: we perceive emotion in the work of art and then we feel the emotion.

There are a number of objections that one might raise to this account.[6] First, one might object that not all art is a matter of expressing emotions and so it is a mistake to define art in terms of such expression. However, even if we concentrate on the theory as an account of infection rather than as a definition of art, there are still problems. Tolstoy provides no account of what it means for an artefact to be an external sign of emotion, or why perceiving such a sign is effective for arousing the same emotion in the perceiver. It is not at all clear that an analogy with words and thought explains this. We require some account of what it means for an artefact to be an external sign of emotion and in what sense exposure to an external sign arouses a feeling in the audience. Furthermore, assuming that perception of the external sign does arouse the feeling in the perceiver, it is not clear why this should require that the artist sincerely felt the emotion that he imbued the work of art with in order for it to be an expression of emotion.

Whereas Tolstoy's theory is open to the objection that it simultaneously asserts too much and explains too little, the account of resonance manages to say a little less and yet also somewhat more. Tolstoy's claim that infection is essential to the experience of a work of art (and indeed to the definition of art) overstates the true position, which is that resonance is merely one possible emotional experience of art, and a possibility that does not even exhaust the infectiousness of art. Furthermore, Tolstoy does not account for how the work of art becomes invested with an emotional property. The foregoing account of resonance, however, makes use of the claim that we can perceive externalized properties in art in order to explain how we perceive emotion in a work of art. Because the claim of resonance is limited to explaining the interaction between what is perceived and what is felt, it is no requirement of this theory that the artist who created the work of art actually experienced the emotion with which the externalized property resonates. It is sufficient that the audience is able to perceive the externalized property as the trace of an activity of externalization of emotion. Thus, while we need not agree with Tolstoy's attempt to define art in terms of its capacity for resonance, or with his assumption that resonance exhausts the possibilities art offers for emotional experience, we can acknowledge that he correctly identifies one possible experience of emotion in art.

It is a fact of life that, even in circumstances in which resonance is possible, it often does not occur. Although the third moment of resonance (feeling an emotion) is a natural concomitant of the first moment (the perception of emotion around us), there are several reasons why the perceiver's experience of perceiving an emotion might not involve his feeling that emotion. First, it is possible that, for reasons which may be more or less apparent to us in different instances, we might suppress the resonance because we do not wish to participate in the emotion that we perceive around us. Second, we might respond to the perceived emotion with a different emotion, in an instance of an interaction which I have called communication. Thus, although we have a natural propensity to resonate with the emotions around us, these two possibilities account for the fact that resonance is not the most common experience of emotion in mature life. It is the most rudimentary emotional experience, but it is easily suppressed in an attempt to avoid emotional engagement, or overpowered by a more sophisticated form of emotional engagement.

Perceiving projective properties and feeling perceived emotions

The second subclass of infection is correspondence. We can develop an account of correspondence by investigating the extent to which each of the five moments of correspondence resemble, or differ from, those of resonance.

Whereas the first moment of resonance begins with the perception of an externalized property, the first moment of correspondence begins with the perception of a projective property. Perceiving a projective property is a matter of perceiving something as matching, or being appropriate to, an emotion, rather than perceiving it to have originated in that emotion, as is the case with an externalized property. Tennyson writes in "In Memoriam A.H.H.":

> Calm is the morn without a sound,
>   Calm as to suit a calmer grief,
>   And only thro' the faded leaf
> The chestnut pattering to the ground.[7]

In this stanza, the poet introduces the sound of a chestnut pattering and the feeling of a particular kind of calm grief. The silent morning is said "to suit a calmer grief". We might interpret this as another way of saying that "the morn without a sound" is *of a piece with* the "calmer grief", in the sense discussed in Chapter 2. In this case, we are able to perceive the projective property of calmer grief in the silent morn. The question, then, is whether it is possible to become infected by a perception that is of a piece with an emotion as opposed to a perception that originated in the emotion.

This brings us to the second moment, in which the perception gives rise to a feeling. There is nothing controversial about the idea that perceiving the sound of the chestnut's pattering might put one in mind of the sound of pattering. Perhaps more controversially, Wollheim wants to argue that perceiving the projective property of calmer grief in the landscape is sufficient to put the perceiver in mind of the calmer grief. In Chapter 2, we considered the sense in which Wollheim thinks a sense perception can match an emotion. It is on account of this matching that we are entitled to maintain that the perception of the projective property is sufficient to put us in mind of the feeling. Assuming that, when the matching relation holds, our perception of "the morn without a sound" can put us in mind of the calmer grief to which the projective property corresponds, the more critical question becomes that of in what sense correspondence puts us in mind of the emotion of calm grief.

The third moment concerns the emotion that the perceiver feels. In the case of resonance, this is an experience of the emotion in the primary sense that we ordinarily feel it. However, there is a range of experiences in which we are affected by the emotion that we perceive in the world, but in which we would not want to say that we have the primary experience of emotion. Reciting Wordsworth's poem about the daffodils might make me feel jocund in some sense, but not in the ordinary sense that I feel jocund when playing backgammon with my friend. Likewise, one might or might not regard sad music as music that makes one feel sad. But even if we maintain that perceiving an emotional property in the music that we hear makes us feel sad in some sense, we might not want to claim that it makes us feel sad in the primary sense of ordinary experiences of sadness, such as experiences that find us on the verge of bursting into tears. The account of resonance that I have given does not account for such experiences. If resonance cannot account for such experiences, it might still be the case that correspondence can account for these more subtle emotional experiences.

In order for the third moment of correspondence to account for such experiences, two extremes must be avoided. First, unlike resonance, it cannot be a matter of having the primary experience of the emotion. Second, the opposite extreme must be avoided. This position argues that the third moment of correspondence does not involve feeling an emotion at all, but rather being put in mind of the emotion in the sense of having a hypothetical thought about it. This might involve judging, for instance, that although I do not actually feel Bacchic fury, as Tovey suggests, when listening to the fourth movement of Beethoven's Seventh Symphony, such fury is just what I might feel; or that if I had composed that music, I would have been feeling furious.[8] Such a conception of the affective component of correspondence is unsatisfactory because it does not explain why correspondence is a genuinely affective experience. We are interested in interactions between perceptions of emotion and the perceiver's own emotion, not interactions between perceptions of emotion and the perceiver's thoughts about emotion. If there is anything remarkable about Wordsworth's experience of the host of golden daffodils, it is that perceiving the daffodils' jocundity actually makes him gay rather than merely making him think about being gay. If Wollheim's theory of correspondence is to avoid these two unacceptable extremes, he will have to provide an explanation of how we can have some sort of secondary experience of emotion.

Does Wollheim provide a suitable account of the kind of experience that the third moment requires? The theory of correspondence will not be plausible if it maintains that the ordinary experience of emotion is involved. Clearly, it is something less than this. So a problem arises in that we cannot claim that the third moment of correspondence is a primary experience of emotion, and yet it cannot simply be a matter of thinking about the emotion. If these two extremes are to be avoided, Wollheim needs to provide an account of an emotional experience that is genuinely affective, but which falls short of the ordinary experience of emotion. Budd observes this problem in Wollheim's theory and argues that what is required is some sort of secondary experience of emotion: "What Wollheim needs is a sense in which an emotion can be present in a person – present in a non-dispositional sense – without the person actually feeling that emotion".[9]

However, he claims that Wollheim fails to provide an account of such a secondary experience of emotion that is neither indefinite nor imprecise. Wollheim concedes to these objections, but suggests that it might not be possible to provide an account in terms that would satisfy Budd: "I wonder whether all philosophical theories of expression and perception are not merely programmatic, and the inadequacies of the concepts used may simply reflect the fact that these are early days".[10]

Can we offer an account of the secondary experience which Budd thinks Wollheim's theory demands? I suggest that the basis for such a secondary experience of emotion is found in Wollheim's earlier thought. Writing on expression in *Art and Its Objects*, Wollheim observes that there are at least two ways in which the mind can entertain emotions other than through the primary experience:

> The first is by the introduction of unconscious feelings. The second is by a more generous conception of the different relations in which a person can stand to the conscious feelings that he has. For it is a fact of human nature, which must be taken into account in any philosophical analysis of the mind, that, even when feelings enter into consciousness, they can be comparatively split off

or dissociated: the dissociation sometimes occurring in accordance with the demands of reality, as in memory or contemplation, or sometimes in more pathological ways.[11]

So what is required is a theory of mind that allows for split-off or dissociated feelings. Such an approach is found in the hypotheses of psychoanalysis, in particular in Freud's analysis of the Rat Man.[12]

In most of his case studies, Freud identifies some difficult emotion that the analysand cannot cope with and which is repressed by being banished to the unconscious. The Rat Man is atypical in this respect. He suffers from incompatible feelings of intense love and intense hatred for his father. Freud might expect to find that one of these is unconscious. However, the Rat Man is conscious of both feelings. He represses the feeling of hatred not by rendering it unconscious, but by dissociating it from the feeling of love.[13] In order for this brief excursus into the Rat Man's case to be of any use to us, the dissociation of the conscious feeling of intense hatred from the conscious feeling of intense love would have to shed some light on primary and secondary ways of experiencing conscious emotions.

When offering his assessment of Wollheim's theory of expressive perception, Budd remarks, "either the affective element ... is an actual feeling of the ... emotion, or it is not".[14] The idea here seems to be that either one actually feels an emotion or else one does not feel it at all. This is compatible with one possible interpretation of the Rat Man's predicament in which he has an "actual feeling of intense love" and an "actual feeling of intense hatred", and the dissociation involves the Rat Man finding a way of simultaneously entertaining the actual feelings by keeping them separate.

After introducing the idea of split-off and dissociated feelings in *Art and Its Objects*, Wollheim remarks, "there are feelings that a man has of which he is not conscious, and there are ways of being in touch with those which he has other than experiencing them in the primary sense".[15] This is compatible with another interpretation of the Rat Man's predicament in which he experiences his feeling of intense love in the primary sense, but has found a way of being in touch with his conscious feeling of intense hatred other than experiencing it in the primary sense. On this analysis, the dissociation of two conflicting feelings for the same object is achieved by simultaneously being in touch with them in different ways.

Why, then, should we prefer an analysis of the Rat Man's predicament that understands the dissociation of the feelings in terms of being in touch with them in different ways, rather than as two actual feelings experienced in the same way, but kept separate from one another? If it were just, as Velleman writes, a matter of the Rat Man's allowing "the two emotions to survive unmixed and hence to continue pulling the patient so violently in opposite directions",[16] we might opt for the latter approach. An analysis in terms of two actual feelings that are kept separate could account for the fact that the love and hatred "were available to his consciousness; he simply disconnected them and reconnected them in such a way as to conceal their true significance".[17] However, as Velleman also notes, what distinguishes this case from Freud's others is the means by which the Rat Man sought to cope: "by repressing his hatred and acknowledging only his love".[18] In this respect, the Rat Man did not merely dissociate the feelings of hatred from the feelings of love but also dissociated the feelings of hatred from himself. As Velleman explains, Freud found that the Rat Man sought "to dissociate himself from his own hatred and hostility".[19] Freud reports that the Rat Man said "that he would like to speak of a criminal act, whose author he did not recognize as himself, though he quite clearly recollected committing it".[20] Velleman's conclusion is that "His hatred was thus something that he had alienated from himself".[21] It seems to me that we have to acknowledge that all of this is a report of a man who, in seeking to dissociate his intense hatred for his father from his intense love for his father, seeks to achieve this end by dissociating the feelings of hatred – but not those of love – from himself. This move is best understood in terms of his having found a way to be in touch with the feelings of hatred that he had other than experiencing them in the primary sense.

The fact that the Rat Man was able to experience two conflicting emotions by dissociating one from the other – and from himself – does not establish that the third moment of correspondence is a secondary experience of emotion. It might, however, suggest that we are capable of being in touch with our conscious feelings in different ways, in which case we might more comfortably entertain the kind of conscious secondary experience of emotion that Budd says Wollheim's account of correspondence requires. If we are willing to entertain the more generous theory of mind that Wollheim gestures at in *Art and its Objects*, and which Freud might be thought to observe in the Rat Man's case, we can then accept the possibility of such a secondary experience of emotion in the context of correspondence.[22]

Whereas our analysis of the first three moments of correspondence draws out the differences between resonance and correspondence, the fourth moment represents one important point of commonality between the two subclasses of infection. In both cases, the perception determines which emotion the perceiver feels. In correspondence, this occurs because the projective property that I perceive provides a reason for experiencing the particular secondary emotional experience that I feel as an appropriate emotion to feel. If I perceive the estuary to possess a certain projective property, say melancholy, this is only good for giving rise to one particular secondary experience of emotion, namely the emotion to which the perceived property corresponds, in this case melancholy.[23] Correspondence cannot account for any other emotion that we might feel in response to the perception of a projective property.[24] What justifies classifying both resonance and correspondence as instances of infection is this common moment – the sense in which the perception determines the affect in both cases. We shall see that what distinguishes experiences of infection from those of communication is that, in both subclasses of infection, the perception determines the affect, whereas in the experience of communication, the emotional response is not determined solely by the perception.

Our discussion of infection began with the observation that such experiences seem to involve feeling the very emotion that is perceived. Indeed, the fifth moment of resonance amounts to just this: not only does the perception determine the emotion that is felt, but it determines that the felt emotion is identical to the perceived emotion. When it comes to the fifth moment of correspondence, the emotion of which we have a secondary experience must be the one with which the projective property is of a piece. So the felt emotion matches the perceived emotion in this experience. But whereas the emotion that I feel in resonance is identical to the emotion I perceive the externalizing agent to have pressed out, in correspondence we cannot go this far. What is perceived in correspondence matches what is felt, but they cannot be identical because a projective property is a different kind of thing to the emotion of which it is a projection.[25] It is something appropriate to the emotion rather than something identical with it. This diminishes the similarity between resonance and correspondence in this moment. Although there is a limited sense in which it is helpful to characterize instances of both resonance and correspondence as experiences in which I feel what I perceive, what really matters is that in both subclasses of infection, there is an experience in which what I feel is determined by what I perceive. Thus it is the common fourth moment (rather than the fifth moment) that is the genuine hallmark of infection.

With the analysis of the five moments of resonance and correspondence complete, we are ready to consider an example of correspondence, and how it relates to resonance. The experience of correspondence occurs in the presence of a landscape or work of art in which we perceive a projective property. When Constable surveyed the scene around Hadleigh Castle, he might have perceived the crumbling ruined fortification, the receding storm clouds and the low tide in the Thames estuary as harrowing. We know that he painted a picture, *Hadleigh Castle, the Mouth of the Thames – Morning After a Stormy Night*,[26] and sensitive scrutiny of the painting reveals that his use of a dark palette and fractured technique to portray this scene imbues the canvas with a harrowing projective property. We also happen to know that Constable was suffering considerably for the harrowing loss of his wife,

Maria, at the time.[27] This might have motivated him to paint the picture in the way that he did.

When we look at the canvas, if we are suitably sensitive, we can perceive a harrowing quality in it, and this perception of harrowing gives rise to a harrowing experience within us.[28] But it is not the ordinary sense of harrowing, that which Constable felt after the loss of his wife, that we experience. If we perceived Constable himself at his wife's funeral, we might become infected by the harrowing grief that we perceive in his physiognomy. This would be an instance of resonance, and we would feel harrowed in the same primary sense that he felt it. But when we perceive a harrowing projective property in the picture he painted (or in the landscape at the mouth of the Thames), we feel harrowed in a different way: it is the dissociated or split-off sense of harrowing that is something more than merely thinking about being harrowed, but something less than the primary experience of being harrowed that Constable has. The experience of the painting is one in which our perception interacts with this secondary feeling, and it is this interaction that is an experience of correspondence. The secondary experience of emotion alone is not what is distinctive about correspondence. What is distinctive about this experience is the interaction between what is perceived and the secondary experience that is felt.

Although I only alluded to the possibility that we might perceive a projective property in Constable's painting, we have established that, in principle, it is also possible to perceive an externalized property in such a work of art. Given that it is possible that we might perceive either kind of property in a painting such as this one, the work of art might either resonate with, or correspond to, an emotion in us. It is possible for both properties to be perceived in a single work of art. Thus the experience of a work of art might involve a primary experience of emotion that resonates with the perception, or a secondary experience of the emotion to which the perception corresponds. It might also involve both a primary and secondary experience of emotion, in which case the one might reinforce the other. This leads us some way towards appreciating the richness of the emotional experience that a work of art can offer.

Responding to perceived emotions

In the previous chapter, we considered two different ways in which the crying baby's distress was experienced: the happy baby perceived the distress, and this resonated with the baby so that it too became distressed, whereas the baby's mother felt something different in response to her perception of the same distress. It is the mother's experience of communication that we now need to analyse. This difference, between how the mother experiences the baby's distress and how the other baby experiences the same distress, can be explained in terms of the difference between the moments of communication and the moments of resonance.

Resonance and communication share the same first and third moments. In each interaction there is a perception of an externalized property (the first moment) and a primary experience of an emotional state (the third moment). It is *how* the perception initiates the primary experience of the emotional state (the second moment) that differs. This difference accounts for the fact that, whereas the perceived emotion determines the felt emotion in resonance (the fourth moment), this perception alone does not determine the felt emotion in the fourth moment of communication. The difference between the second moments in each case also accounts for the difference between the respective fifth moments. Whereas in resonance the perceiver's emotion is identical to the emotion that he perceives, in communication it is different. It is the difference between the fourth moments, and to a lesser extent the second and fifth moments, that provides the basis for distinguishing these as separate varieties of emotional experience. (It will be recalled that it is the similarity between the second and fourth moments – as well as the fifth moment, perhaps – that is the basis for claiming that resonance and correspondence are both subclasses of infection.)

What is it about the second moment that accounts for these differences between the fourth and fifth moments of resonance and communication? I suggest that the second moment of communication introduces some intellectual or imaginative activity that mediates how the perceived emotion is experienced. This answer is not illuminating, however, unless we have an account of the intellectual and imaginative activities that might occur in the second moment of communication.

I turn first to an unsatisfactory account of how we might conceive of an intellectual activity being incorporated into the second moment. This analysis of the intellectual activity is found in Aristotle's account of the tragic audience's experience of fear and pity, which we considered in Chapter 2. When the audience perceives the hero to be afraid, and judges this suffering to be unjust, it feels pity. So it is that when a judgement about the justice or injustice of the hero's fate enters the audience's experience, a response of pity – as opposed to fear – is possible. This provides the first model for understanding the intellectual activity involved in communication: a response occurs, rather than infection, when the perceived emotion is experienced in light of a judgement about the justice or injustice of the perceived suffering. On this model, when the mother responds to the perception of the baby's cry, she forms a judgement about the justice or injustice of the baby's suffering as it does in the particular circumstances, and this enables her to form a response of either anxiety or exasperation. Such an analysis is, however, implausible: we cannot seriously imagine that the mother forms a judgement about whether her child *deserved* to stub his toe. In the case of the tragic hero, it might not seem quite as implausible to ask whether he deserved his fate, but even if this is so, it is not relevant to the emotional response. We can imagine feeling pity for a tragic hero who suffers, whether it is just or unjust that he suffers in this way. Pity is not reserved for those who suffer unjustly: mercy is precisely a matter of having pity even for those who deserve what they get. So it seems that neither in the theatre nor in real life can the emotional response depend upon a judgement of justice.

An alternative account of the audience's emotional response in the theatre is provided by Wollheim in *The Thread of Life*.[29] Wollheim suggests that the audience's response to dramatic characters might be grounded either in an intellectual activity or an imaginative one. His account of the intellectual activity, I suggest, provides a better way of thinking about the intellectual basis for an emotional response than Aristotle's theory does. For Wollheim, the emotional response might involve an intellectual judgement, but whereas Aristotle claims that the response depends upon a judgement about the relationship between the hero and his circumstances, Wollheim claims that what matters is a judgement about the relationship between the hero and the audience. The audience may view the hero with good favour, disfavour or indifference. It may do no more than that: it might make judgements about what it perceives, but not engage emotionally with what is perceived. The formation of this judgement might, however, also enable a voluntary emotional response to the perceived emotion by filtering the way in which the audience experiences the perceived emotion. If the hero's suffering is filtered by a judgement of favour, the audience might feel pity, whereas if it perceives the same suffering in light of a judgement of disfavour, it might feel something more like pleasure. This seems to have ready application in the examples from ordinary life, too. If we perceive someone in light of a judgement of favour, we feel one thing, whereas if we judge him unfavourably, we feel something else. The mother's emotional response to her baby can better be understood in terms of whether she is favourably or unfavourably disposed towards him at that moment than in terms of whether she judges that his suffering is just or unjust. So the judgement of favour is a better candidate for the intellectual motor of voluntary experience than the judgement of justice.

For Wollheim, the response may also involve imaginative rather than intellectual activity. In this case, the audience identifies itself imaginatively with one of the characters in the play and uses its imagination to reproduce within itself how it imagines the chosen protagonist to feel. In this way, the audience experiences the emotion it perceives in that character. But something else happens when it perceives the other characters from the perspective of the character with which it empathizes. Having identified emotionally with one character, the audience imagines how its adopted protagonist would feel about the other characters (and the drama as a whole), and then imagines feeling the same way. In this case, what the audience feels in response to the characters other than the adopted protagonist does not depend upon a judgement of favour, but upon feeling what it imagines the protagonist would feel in response to the perceived emotion. (It should be noted, however, that although the imaginative identification possibility does not involve making a judgement, it assumes the possibility of this. If the character with whom the audience identifies were not deemed capable of making a judgement of favour, that character would not be capable of developing a response with which the audience might identify.) Thus, either imagination or intellect can interpose itself between the perceiver's perception of emotion and the perceiver's own emotions in a way that causes the perceiver to experience the perceived emotion with a different emotion.

Consider an audience watching a performance of *King Lear* at the point when Gloucester's eyes have been put out.[30] The audience might be infected by the anguish it perceives in Gloucester. It might, however, have an experience of communication rather than infection, and there are several conditions that might make this possible. One possibility is that the audience forms a judgement of favour about Gloucester. It might perceive him with good favour, disfavour, or indifference. If it forms a judgment of good favour, it may perceive Gloucester's anguish with pity, whereas if it perceives him with disfavour, it might perceive his anguish with pleasure. The audience might also judge Gloucester's anguish to be just or unjust. But this will not affect the emotional response. An audience that is favourably disposed towards Gloucester may pity him regardless of whether it considers the suffering just or unjust, and an audience that views him with disfavour may take pleasure in the perceived anguish regardless of whether this is deemed to be just or unjust. Another possibility, however, is that the audience might engage its imagination without forming a judgement of favour. The audience might identify with either Edgar or Edmund. If it identifies with Edgar, it will imagine how Edgar would feel pity when he perceived Gloucester's anguish, and the audience then experiences the perceived anguish with pity. If it identifies with Edmund, it will imagine how Edmund would take pleasure in his father's suffering, and it will then experience the perceived anguish with pleasure. These are two different ways in which we might form emotional responses through either the intercession of intellect or imagination in the second moment of communication.

It is when our analysis turns to the fourth moment that we see why communication is fundamentally different from infection. In infection, the perceiver's emotion is determined by the perceived emotion. In communication, the emotional response is not determined solely by the perceived emotion. So one cannot predict, simply on the basis of the identity of the perceived emotion, with which emotion the perceiver will experience the perceived emotion, as one can in the case of infection. We might say that communication is a voluntary interaction, whereas infection is an involuntary interaction.[31] To say this, however, requires us to clarify what is meant by voluntary experience. There are two reasons that lend support to the claim that communication is a voluntary experience.

First, the emotional response in communication is voluntary in the sense that it is not merely a function of how we perceive emotion in the world, but of the way in which we process this perception. The perceiver's intellectual or imaginative activity gives the perceiver a particular perspective on the perceived emotion, and this perspective enables the perceiver to feel an emotion in response to the one he perceives. In this way, the nature of the engagement owes something to the perceiver's own faculties as well as to the impact of the world upon the perceiver. In contrast, an involuntary experience, such as infection, does rely on the agent's faculties in order to be able to perceive the world as he does, but such an experience does not involve him using his faculties to contribute to the way in which he experiences the impact of the world.

Second, the activity does not serve to determine the emotion that is felt, but rather serves to open up a range of possibilities. If the audience perceives anguish in Gloucester after his eyes have been put out, we have already noted that it might do so with good favour, disfavour or indifference, and that how it feels will differ depending upon which judgement it makes. But we can also make a further observation. Say the audience regards him with good favour. It might then experience the anguish with pity. But it might also experience the same anguish with anger or sadness. So the judgement has rendered possible several different ways of interacting with the perception. Furthermore, it also excludes others: it would not be appropriate to perceive the anguish with pleasure, for instance, once one has formed a judgement of good favour. So the judgement generates a repertoire of alternative responses, while excluding other responses as inappropriate. In this way, we can also speak of the interaction as voluntary in the sense that there is no mechanical emotional response once the judgement is formed. If the formation of the judgement meant that there was only one possible response – albeit a different emotion to the perceived one – then the fourth moment of communication would not be significantly different from those of resonance and correspondence.

None of this suggests that the response in communication is voluntary in the sense that we can choose whether we want to have the experience. Rather, it is voluntary in the sense that it is an experience that depends for its character upon how the subject's powers have a hand in shaping the nature of his experience of the perceived emotion. In an involuntary experience such as resonance, there is no place for the subject's intellectual or imaginative powers shaping the way in which he experiences the perceived emotion. Furthermore, although we have seen that there are different activities that enable a voluntary response when interposed in the second moment, these activities are always concerned with the relationship between the perceiver and the perceived object (or perceiver's perspective on the perceived object), not a judgement about the relationship between the perceived object and its circumstances or environment (e.g. a judgement of justice or injustice).

Resonance and communication can also be distinguished in terms of their respective fifth moments. In resonance, the perceived emotion is identical to the perceiver's emotion, whereas in communication the two are different. If the emotional response were a mechanical one, then there would be no significant difference between the fourth moments of the two interactions. In this case, the fifth moment would be the only important difference between them, and what would matter for the distinction between the two varieties of emotional interaction is that in some experiences what we feel is the same as what we perceive, whereas in other cases it is different. Such an analysis, however, would only account for involuntary experiences of emotion, and would fail to do justice to the sense in which some experiences of emotion are voluntary. The effect of the second moment of communication is not simply that the mother feels a different emotion in response to the one which she perceives in her child's cry, but also that this response is a voluntary one, a response drawn from a repertoire of appropriate responses. It is voluntary because it is determined by her intellectual or imaginative processes working on the perceived emotion and there is no formula that can predict what the output of this process will be. So the contrast between the voluntary nature of the one variety of experience and the involuntary nature of the other variety is the significant distinction to be drawn, and this is brought out by contrasting the nature of the fourth moment in each case, rather than that of the fifth.

The problem of responding to projective properties

When we engage with a perceived emotion by responding to it, one possibility is that we form a judgement of favour, and this is why we feel a different emotion in response to the emotion we perceive. But what is it that we form the judgement of favour about? In our interactions with other people, we might form a favourable or unfavourable judgement about a person's external appearance. That, however, is not what is relevant when we say that we view Gloucester's anguish in light of a judgement of good favour or disfavour. It is not the outward appearance of Gloucester in his blood-soaked bandages that we favour or disfavour. Rather, it is Gloucester regarded as another psychological agent about whom we form the relevant judgement.

The point has been made by Scruton, in relation to human beauty, that our interest in such beauty is concerned with "an interest in a person *as embodied*" ("an embodied person is a free being revealed in the flesh"), rather than with the body as "an assemblage of body parts".[32] Although our perception of the flesh is not a perception of the free being, the special and intimate relationship between the two means that we bring our awareness of the latter to bear in our perception of the former. Something similar might be said of the response to a perception of an externalized property: in responding to our perception of anguish in the blood-soaked Gloucester, we are responding to a perception of the outward appearance, but this perception is attended by our awareness of the psychological agent who externalizes his anguish in his appearance.

Likewise, when the mother forms a judgement of good favour or disfavour and responds to her child's distress with anxiety or exasperation, she regards with favour or disfavour the child's psyche, something that cannot necessarily be perceived. But the response is a response to the perceived distress. Because the cry that is perceived is the trace of an externalizing activity of an agent, the mother's judgement of favour about that agent can be applied to the perceived externalized property that originated in the activity of that agent. When the genetic agent and perceived property are related in this way, a judgement about the agent can serve as the basis for a response to the perception of an externalized property deemed to issue from that agent.

Is it possible to form an emotional response to a projective property in the same way that we respond to an externalized property? We have seen that although both externalized and projective properties can infect the perceiver, the difference between the two kinds of property results in two kinds of infection: resonance and correspondence. When we turn to communication, it seems that rather than two distinct forms of communication emerging, this interaction is only possible when an externalized emotion is perceived. The analysis of emotional response in the previous section requires us to be able to form a particular judgement about another agent, and then apply that judgement to a perceptual property that has its origin in that agent. In the case of externalized properties, which have their origin in another agent's externalizing activity, this is not a problem: the judgement is made about the agent and then applied to the perceived trace of that agent's activity. In the case of projective properties, however, the perceived property does not have its origin in another agent, but in the object's capacity to sustain a property projected by the perceiving agent himself. Because we do not suppose the perceived property issues from the activity of another agent, there is no agent to form the judgement about, and hence there is no judgement that can filter the perception of the projective property. Thus, communication is not possible in the case of the projective property.

Our intuitions about emotional response to physiognomy, the landscape and art support this conclusion about the possibility of responding to externalized (but not projective) properties. We might perceive melancholy in each of the physiognomy of the grieving Constable, the landscape around Hadleigh Castle and the picture Constable painted of that scene. Do our intuitions suggest that it is possible to respond emotionally to all or any of these perceptions of melancholy? As regards Constable's physiognomy, it is perfectly natural to think that we might experience this perceived melancholy with pity in response. However, it is not at all intuitive, I suggest, to think that we might respond to the perception of melancholy in the landscape by feeling pity. And whereas I believe we have clear intuitions about the appropriateness of feeling pity in response to Constable's physiognomy and the inappropriateness of feeling pity in response to the landscape, I believe that there is a genuine ambivalence in our intuitions about the appropriateness of feeling pity in response to Constable's painting of the landscape. These intuitions can be supported by the analysis of the circumstances in which a judgement of favour can affect our perception of emotional properties.

We are able to respond to the externalized property we perceive in Constable's physiognomy (rather than resonating with it) because we can form a judgement of good favour, disfavour or indifference about the externalizing agent. Once this judgement is formed, it might then influence the perspective from which we perceive the externalized property. This application of the judgement about the agent to the way we perceive the property is possible because of the special relationship between an externalizing agent and an externalized property that originates in his activity. If we could form a judgement that altered the perspective from which we viewed the projective property that we perceive in the landscape at Hadleigh, emotional response would be possible. The requisite nexus between the judgement and the perception to be filtered would only exist, however, if the perceived property had its origin in some other agent, and the judgement about the agent could then filter the way we perceive the emotion that issued from that agent. The projective property, however, does not originate in the activity of an externalizing agent about whom the perceiver can make such a judgement. Thus, communication is not possible in the case of a projective property that we perceive in the landscape.

To say that we cannot respond emotionally to the emotion that we perceive in the landscape is not to say that we cannot have an emotional response to the emotion with which the landscape infects us. Having had melancholy aroused in me through perceiving the projective property in the landscape, I might feel revulsion or disdain at having allowed myself to feel melancholy. This would be a matter of feeling one emotion in response to another, but it is a matter of responding to the emotion that the perceived emotion causes me to feel, rather than a matter of responding to the perceived emotion itself. It is a meta-response, rather than a direct response to the perceived emotion.[33] That I might have such a reaction to how the landscape makes me feel is interesting, but it tells us nothing about how I engage emotionally with the landscape – only about how I respond to that engagement.

The perceiver's capacity to project his own emotion, rather than the activity of another externalizing agent, serves as the basis for the projective property. So it might be argued that the judgement of favour or disfavour should be formed about the perceiver's own projective experience. However, this is an activity of the perceiving agent. If the perceiving agent were to make a judgement about anything here, he would be judging his own activity with favour or disfavour. It would not be a judgement about the landscape at all. A judgement of favour about myself does not have the requisite nexus with the landscape for filtering my perception of the landscape. I might view with disfavour my being infected by the melancholy I perceive in the landscape. But this is a response to the emotional interaction, not a response to the landscape, which response can form a constituent of the interaction. So it is possible to respond to the emotional experience of the landscape, but not as a moment of that experience. The perceiver might also form some non-emotional response to the perceived emotion; he might have some emotional response to his emotional experience; or he might feel some emotion in response to a belief that he holds about the landscape rather than an emotion that he perceives in it. Such experiences, however, are not engagements between a perception of emotion and the perceiver's own emotion, and thus fall outside of the current investigation.

I suggested that, whereas we have strong intuitions about responses such as pity to physiognomy and the lack of such responses to the landscape, we have reason to feel ambivalent regarding whether we respond emotionally to Constable's painting. The reason for this is that we might perceive either, or both, externalized and projective properties in paintings. The ambivalence depends upon which of the two kinds of properties we are thinking about. When we perceive an externalized property, communication is possible in addition to resonance. When we perceive a projective property in a painting, communication is not possible, although correspondence is. The source of uncertainty about communication with such a work of art is also the source of the richness of the emotional experience of the work of art: if we perceive both externalized and projective properties in the painting, then the perceived melancholy might be experienced with a secondary experience of melancholy and a primary emotional response of pity.

Comprehending perceived emotions

We can distinguish what it means to feel an emotion from what it means to comprehend an emotion. To feel an emotion does not require us to comprehend what we feel: it is possible that we feel something that is incomprehensible to us. Infection and communication are experiences in which we perceive an emotion and feel an emotion. These might occur without comprehension of what is felt or perceived. Comprehending an emotion is a further way of experiencing an emotion, and an account of the third form of emotional interaction – articulation – seeks to explain how perceiving an emotion could effect this shift in the comprehensibility of the perceiver's own emotions.

If articulation is an interaction in which we comprehend our emotions, what is it about our emotions that we comprehend, and how does perceiving emotion in the world enable us to comprehend this? Given the analysis of emotion in Chapter 1, there are three possible candidates that articulation of emotion might involve comprehending: the object of the emotion, the phenomenology of the emotional responses, or the structure of the emotional disposition that gives rise to the various responses as appropriate responses to the object.

I shall suggest that what is comprehended in articulation is the attitude that is the core of the emotional disposition. In Chapter 1, we saw that this attitude develops out of an experience of satisfaction or frustration of desire. Some person, thing or fact is identified as having precipitated this earlier satisfaction or frustration, and then there is a shift in attention from the earlier experience to the precipitating factor, which comes to be perceived in light of the earlier experience. This attitude to the precipitating factor (which we might now regard as the object of the attitude) is a memorialization of the agent's history. The attitude is a matter of perceiving the object through a framework that consists of the life that the agent has lived.

When an emotional disposition determines our response to an object, we are experiencing the object through a framework that is a permutation of our past. This framework has genuine complexity. It is also something that we are not directly aware of, being only directly acquainted with the mental states in which it manifests itself, according to Wollheim. So it is precisely the sort of thing that we might come to comprehend. Becoming aware of the mental disposition's role in our emotional experience might well be thought to offer a way of rendering the experience comprehensible. It is a way of becoming aware of our emotional responses for what they are: responses to the impact of the world that arise out of the life that we have lived, rather than responses that seemingly arise out of the moment.

We can distinguish comprehension from analysis. Given that the mental disposition involves a special transfiguration of an earlier episode in the subject's history, we might want to analyse this disposition by teasing out the different strands of the complex structure. Thus, the analyst might come to understand what actually happened, and how the subject made sense of his frustration or satisfaction of desire in a way that led him to colour his subsequent experience of the world in the way that he did. Such analysis of the disposition is the sort of understanding of a mental disposition that the psychoanalyst hopes to uncover. This is not, however, what we mean by comprehending the mental disposition. Although there is complexity to be unpacked in the mental disposition, we must remember that this is the complexity of a structure of which we are not even ordinarily aware. Before we can address the complexity of the structure, we need to become aware of it. Awareness is therefore a prerequisite for analysis. It is this newfound awareness of the role of the disposition that is the basis for comprehending an emotion through the interaction of articulation. So how might we go about comprehending an emotion?

One reason that an artist might create a work of art is to explore an emotional experience that is otherwise incomprehensible to him. I shall suggest that one way in which an emotion might become comprehensible is by drawing an analogy between the role of the artistic medium and the role of the attitude at the core of emotion. The artistic medium is a framework that interprets and justifies the interpretation of the experience being explored. The attitude at the core of the mental disposition initiates the responses that form that emotional experience, and it justifies them as appropriate responses. Because we lack direct awareness of the attitude, the experience that it initiates and justifies might seem arbitrary, or incomprehensible, to us. However, if we appreciate the role of the artistic medium as a framework, we might, through analogy, come to appreciate the similar role of the emotional disposition. This might enable us to comprehend the emotional experience as a response that arises out of the life we have lived. I shall develop this analysis and demonstrate how it might fruitfully be applied to a reading of J. M. W. Turner's *Staffa, Fingal's Cave*.[34]

Staffa, Fingal's Cave is one of Turner's most famous seascapes. It depicts the sea off Staffa and the setting sun with its "halo" of light (created by rain clouds) about to drop below the horizon. There is a solitary small gull in the foreground, and, beyond that, a tiny steamship, its funnel emitting a billow of black smoke, which dissolves – as if in an act of purification – into the white clouds that dominate the three-quarters of the canvas not taken up by the churning sea. In the background, largely obscured by the clouds, is the island with its cliff face (though the entrance to the island's famous cave is not discernable, and is perhaps on the opposite side of the island). Fingal's Cave was a popular tourist attraction after having been discovered by Sir Joseph Banks in 1772, when it was identified as an appropriate location for the cave that was home to the fictitious Fiuhn Mac Coul – or Fingal, the father of Ossian – and which is mentioned in Walter Scott's *Lord of the Isles*. Turner met Scott in 1831 and then embarked on a tour of Scotland in order to prepare a set of illustrations for an edition of *Lord of the Isles*. It was on this trip that he visited Staffa and entered the famous cave. Upon returning to his studio, he painted *Staffa, Fingal's Cave*.

The title of the painting suggests that it is concerned with the cave. This is supported by the quotation from *Lord of the Isles* that Turner inserted in the catalogue of the Royal Academy exhibition at which it was first exhibited in 1832:

> – nor of a theme less solemn tells
> That mighty surge that ebbs and swells,
> And still, between each awful pause,
> From the high vault an answer draws.[35]

However, the cave is scarcely visible in the background. The painting actually depicts the seascape off the coast, rather than the scene within the cave (although Turner made sketches of this). Yet John Gage observes that if Turner's subject is really the seascape, then he might have chosen to quote a more apposite passage from *Lord of the Isles* which occurs only a few lines earlier:

> Then all unknown its columns rose,
> Where dark and undisturb'd repose
> The cormorant had found.

Given the close interest that Turner had taken in the relationship between poetry and painting in his academic lectures,[36] it seems unlikely that he would simply be casual in selecting the quotation at this point in his career. A better reading of the painting would suggest that what he is interested in exploring in the painting is an experience that is relevant both to the seascape that is depicted and the interior of the cave that is referred to in the title and the quotation. We know, from a letter that Turner wrote to James Lennox many years later, that the trip to Staffa left a memorable impression due to the very poor weather conditions, including "a strong wind and head sea" that delayed arrival.[37] Turner was one of a small number who did scramble over the rocks to enter Fingal's Cave, which, he wrote, was "not very pleasant or safe when the wave rolls right in". After only an hour on the island, he returned to the ship. On the return journey, the poor conditions persisted, and he recalled, "The sun getting towards the horizon, burst through the rain-cloud, angry, and for wind; and so it proved, for we were driven for shelter into Loch Ulver." Perhaps what interested Turner was not the image of the wave rolling into the cave, or the image of the tiny steamship behind the waves, but the very experience of the waves in those inhospitable and dangerous conditions, an emotional experience of the waves that was common both to the experience at sea and in the cave. It is this emotional experience, I suggest, that Turner explores through painting *Staffa*. The sound of the crashing wave that echoes in the cave's high vault is as relevant to this experience as the rising unknown columns of waves surveyed from above by the cormorant.

It was in connection with *Staffa* that Turner made his now infamous remark about indistinctness being either his *forte* or his *fault*.[38] If Turner sought to capture the emotional experience of the waves in these inhospitable climes, we already have an account of the way in which he might use projective properties to achieve the special "indistinct" feeling of this painting. Indistinctness is clearly a feature of this painting. But it is a feature that assists in achieving a distinctive emotional effect: "the very atmosphere in the picture seems to have been manipulated with a sculpturesque precision".[39] It is one thing to acknowledge that Turner succeeds in infecting us with the feeling that he had when he was in this indistinct atmosphere. But that is not to say that he is able to comprehend this emotional experience of waves. There is reason to think that Turner seeks to comprehend these earlier experiences of the waves through the later experience of painting the picture: as Gage writes, "[Turner] surely hoped that his image would stimulate a sort of reverie or speculation, for his aesthetic was pre-eminently an aesthetic of association".[40] I shall suggest one way in which speculating about the indistinct atmosphere in the painting might well enable Turner to comprehend the earlier emotional experiences of the waves in the cave and the sea. This speculation involves drawing an analogy between the artistic medium and the emotional attitude as frameworks for emotional experiences.

The analogy makes use of a conception of an interpretative framework developed by Jonathan Lear in his study of Freudian psychoanalysis.[41] In explaining the development of Freud's theory of catharsis, Lear argues that Freud's practice developed ahead of his theory, in part because he lacked an appropriate conception of emotion. Freud persisted with his quantitative conception of emotion as a kind of charge, despite treating emotion in practice as a kind of cognitive activity, or an attempt at rationality. Lear draws on Aristotle's *Rhetoric* to develop a conception of emotion as a framework through which we experience the world. For Lear, there are two aspects to emotion. First, it is an attempt at making sense of, or interpreting, its object in some way. Second, it is a "claim to rationality": the interpretation carries with it a justification for the interpretation as the correct interpretation of the object. The attitude that we adopt towards an object can offer its own justification, according to Lear, because it is not only the cause for our responding to the object in a particular way, but also serves as a reason for responding to it in this way.[42]

It is the idea that a framework might have a special role in some experiences that concerns us for present purposes. The psychological framework serves to interpret the object for us. Interpreting the object involves responding to it in a particular way. The framework is also thought to offer a justification for its own interpretation: it is not merely that we respond to the object in one way or another, but that we respond to it in the *correct*, or *appropriate*, or *justified* way. The response can be justified because it is not mechanical: the framework is the cause, but it is also the reason for the experience. If we analyse the framework, we will be able to find out why we respond in the way that we do, and why we are justified in doing so. It will, perhaps, already be apparent how the idea of a framework can contribute to understanding the role of the mental disposition in the emotional economy. It is also relevant, however, for explaining the role of the medium in the experience offered by a work of art.

The attitude, as we have seen in Chapter 1, is an attempt at making sense of an object in terms of some earlier experience of satisfaction or frustration of desire that the object is thought to have precipitated. The satisfaction or frustration forms a framework through which the object is experienced, and this framework (i.e. the mental disposition) colours the way in which we experience the object by manifesting itself in a range of mental states, initiating new mental dispositions, finding expression in behaviour, and so on. The responses that it initiates are not arbitrary; they are responses that arise out of the person's past. When the transfigured past manifests itself in certain mental states, it provides a reason for responding to an object in this way rather than another way. It is for this reason that Wollheim regards the person as active in respect of his emotions. And we might also say that this origin offers a justification for the response, whereas a response that is not a manifestation of such a disposition lacks a justification and is arbitrary. So we can regard the attitude as a framework in Lear's sense.[43]

We can also apply the framework analysis to the artistic medium. In the process of painting the picture, Turner experiments with the medium. He manipulates the medium in one way, and then another, and so on until he is satisfied that he has captured the earlier emotional experiences of the waves. Depending upon how he applies the paint to the canvas, the painted canvas might have different sets of associations, and these will give it an affinity with different emotions. When Turner judges that he has captured the earlier experience of the waves, he might settle on how he wants the canvas to look.

When the spectator looks at the painting of the seascape, he might project any number of emotions onto it. But these would not be sustained. The picture will only sustain the projection of an emotion with which it has an affinity. The artist has experimented with the medium until the medium possesses the associations that make it ripe for sustaining the projection of a particular emotion. Similarly, when the spectator looks at the painting, he too engages in experimentation. It might take quite some time for the picture to "reveal" itself to him; he might attempt to project all sorts of emotions onto the canvas. It is only when the spectator grasps that the medium itself has a network of associations through which he is invited to experience the work that he perceives the projective properties that capture the experience of the waves.

The artist experiments with different ways of manipulating the medium in order that it can be both object of appropriate trains of association and projection. The spectator experiments with different ways of engaging with the medium until he grasps the associations and perceives the projective properties sustained by the medium's associations. If we are to have the full experience of the work, we must grasp associations that the medium has and experience the painting in light of them. So we might say that the medium offers a framework of associations through which we can experience the painting. There are other ways in which we might experience the painting. We might project arbitrary emotions onto it. But the painting will not sustain such projections. When we are suitably sensitive to the painting, we become aware of its associations and that the painting commends being experienced in light of the medium's web of associations. So the medium offers a framework of associations through which the work might or might not be experienced, and it commends (or rewards) experiencing the work through the framework as the correct or appropriate way to experience the work.

When Turner seeks to explore his experience of the waves at Staffa through experimentation with the medium of the painted surface of his canvas, two experiences are involved. In each case, there is some kind of emotional experience, and in each case this experience is facilitated by a framework. The particular way in which Turner responds to the waves is determined by an attitude that colours his experience of them: he has the range of responses that he does because he experiences the waves in light of some past experience – although he is not aware of this. So the emotional experience of the waves is caused and justified by a framework that is constructed out of the life he has lived. He then explores this experience through the medium of paint. This involves a second emotional experience. In this case there is also a framework that causes and justifies the experience he has: the medium. It is the medium's framework of associations that gives rise to an affinity for a particular emotional experience and which makes this the appropriate way to experience the painting. Although there are other ways in which one might try to experience the painting, the painting itself does not offer a justification for experiencing it in that way. So both Turner's emotional experience of the waves and the experience of *Staffa* are experiences that are mediated by frameworks.

We are now in a position to draw an analogy between the attitude that initiates and justifies the experience of the waves that Turner seeks to explore in *Staffa*, and the medium through which he explores it. The experience offered by the painting is an emotional experience that is possible on account of the framework offered by the medium and an experience that is appropriate because it is justified by the medium. We can draw an analogy with the sense in which the experience that is being explored by the painter through the painting is itself an experience that is possible and justified on account of a framework – the framework offered by the attitude.

When the artist sets out to explore the emotion, he has (according to Wollheim) no direct awareness of the mental disposition that is the attitude. However, having explored the emotion through the medium, he is directly aware of the artistic medium. So it is natural that he might become aware that the emotional experience offered by the work of art is possible because it is experienced through the framework of the medium. If he does this, he might use this awareness to comprehend the emotional experience that he set out to explore. Given the analogy between the role of the attitude and the role of the medium as frameworks, once the artist appreciates the role of the medium as framework for the emotional experience of the painting, he is in a position to grasp that there must be something similar that serves the role of framework in the experience that he seeks to explore. In this way, through analogy, he can grasp the role played by the attitude in that experience. This might not yet enable him to analyse the attitude, but it will mean that there is a sense in which the initial experience is no longer incomprehensible, for he now appreciates that the emotional response that he is aware of is not an arbitrary one. It is one that arises out of the life that he has lived: it is a response that is justified by his own life, and his awareness of this means that it is no longer incomprehensible to him in the way that it once was.

But the ways in which the life that I have lived can provide a framework through which I comprehend subsequent experiences are many and varied. It is precisely for this reason that Wollheim speaks of the *characteristic* history through which emotions develop. It is not the case that all emotions develop in the same way, and so it is not the case that all emotional dispositions have an identical structure: the framework offered by emotional dispositions is not paradigmatic. And we do well to notice a similarity here with the sense in which the medium serves as a framework for experiencing the work of art. Although a number of artists might explore their emotions through experimenting with the same artistic medium, they do not all experiment with the medium in the same way. Great artists find their own way of experimenting with their medium. In doing so, they develop different frameworks for experiencing their works of art.

If we comprehend an emotion through engaging with a single work of art, we will be aware that there is a mental disposition that serves as the framework for the emotional experience in a way similar to that in which the medium serves the artistic experience. But there is a risk that we might think that we have comprehended something paradigmatic rather than something characteristic. And so it is important that we continue to experience increasing numbers of works of art: our awareness of the many and varied ways in which the medium might serve as a framework prepares us to appreciate the many and varied ways in which the emotional dispositions serve as a framework in emotional experiences.

The audience engages with the medium's projective properties in the same way that the artist does. So if the audience has an emotional experience of art, upon perceiving and corresponding with the projective properties in the medium, it too might grasp the significance of the medium's role as a framework for the emotional experience. Having done so, it might then draw the same analogy that the artist draws between the role of the framework in the experience of the work of art and the role of the attitude in the experience of the emotional economy to which the work of art corresponds. In this way, the audience becomes aware of the role of its attitude in the emotional experience being explored through the painting, even though the audience still lacks any direct awareness of the attitude. The analogy with the role of the medium enables the audience to comprehend the emotional experience as an experience that arises out of himself.[44]

We can analyse this interaction by contrasting it with the five moments of correspondence. It shares a common first moment in that both involve perceiving a projective property. However, the third moment of articulation does not involve the perceiver experiencing a new emotion, but his comprehending an emotion. We can still ask whether the second moment is a matter of the perception giving rise to the comprehension in a way that limits the perceiver's contribution, as in infection, or involves his intellectual or imaginative faculties, as in communication. In articulation, the perception does not itself cause the perceiver to comprehend the emotion. It provides the occasion for comprehending, but the perceiver must take the further step of drawing the analogy. This is something that the perceiver must do for himself. Unlike the fourth moment of infection, it is not determined for the perceiver by what he perceives. There is no fifth moment of articulation: because articulation does not involve feeling an emotion, but comprehending it, we cannot ask whether that which is felt is the same as or different from that which is perceived.

Externalized properties and the problem of comprehending emotion

Articulation involves comprehending that an emotional response is the manifestation of a mental disposition. This involves drawing an analogy between the attitude as a framework and the artistic medium as a framework. The medium might be invested with both externalized and projective properties. Does it matter whether we draw an analogy between the attitude and the medium's externalized properties, or between the attitude and the medium's projective properties?

We have considered the way in which a painting such as Constable's *Hadleigh Castle* might be regarded as possessing both externalized and projective properties. Although both kinds of properties affect our experience of the painting, they do so in different ways. The externalized property is the trace of an activity through which an agent pressed out, or externalized, his emotion. The projective property is a claim about the suitability or appropriateness for projection. The fact that the painted surface is perceived to possess a certain projective property means that it makes a claim about how the medium should be interpreted: it makes a claim that the picture is the kind of thing that one can project a certain emotion onto, and that this is the appropriate way to engage with the painting. Perceiving the externalized property in the painted surface discloses something about the creative process, but that is different to offering a claim about how the audience should engage with the medium. We might say that the externalized melancholy in *Hadleigh Castle* speaks to us by saying something like "this is what I am" or "this is how I feel", whereas the projective melancholy in the picture speaks to us by saying something like "this is how you should make sense of me" or "this is how it is appropriate for you to interpret or experience me". It is only in the latter case, when the medium makes a claim about the appropriate way to experience the object, that there is an analogy with the attitude in emotional experience.

So we can comprehend our emotional experiences only when we draw an analogy between the projective property in the medium as an interpretative framework and the emotional disposition's attitude as an interpretative framework. That is not to say that projective properties are more important than externalized properties. It is only to say that one property provides an analogy that enables articulation of emotion, whereas the other does not. The special experience of art, we shall see, depends upon both kinds of perceptual properties. When we perceive projective properties, correspondence and articulation are possible; when we perceive externalized properties, resonance and communication are possible. It is only when we perceive both externalized and projective properties that infection, communication and articulation are possible.[45]

4

Art and the plenary experience of emotion

Distinctiveness of the emotional experience of art

The argument has now reached a pivot. The two previous chapters provided an account of the varieties of emotional experience and the following chapter will address the value of art. If the previous descriptive material is to form a basis for a claim about the value of art, it will have to be because there is something valuable about the emotional experience of art. In this chapter, we shall ask whether the emotional experience of art is distinctive in a way that justifies us in speaking of a variety of emotional experience that occurs only in our perception of works of art. If we conclude that it is, we can then consider the value of this distinctive experience in the following chapter.

To understand what is distinctive about the emotional experience of a work of art is to understand how it differs from the other varieties of emotional experience. This requires us to place our investigation of the emotional experience of art in the broader context of all our experiences of emotion in the world, and to determine whether there is a sense in which the artistic experience is different from these other varieties of emotional experience. In this way, the previous chapter's discussion of the varieties of emotional experience provides a spectrum of emotional experiences relative to which we can assess what, if anything, is distinctive about the emotional experience of art. It is a weakness of earlier theorists' attempts at analysing our emotional experience of art that they have not sought to analyse it in this broader context. It is only when one situates the emotional experience of art in this context that one sees what is distinctive about the possibility that art offers for emotional experience.

In this chapter we shall develop an account of a distinctive variety of emotional experience, which I shall call the plenary experience of emotion. The value of this experience we shall speculate about in the next chapter. Because the plenary experience of emotion only occurs in our experience of art, I shall want to claim not merely that the plenary experience of emotion is valuable, but that the work of art that offers us the experience is itself also valuable on account of the experience's value. This will require us to explain the sense in which a value claim about the plenary experience of emotion is also a value claim about the work of art that gives rise to it.

It is prudent at this point to remember the limit of my claim about art and the plenary experience of emotion. In maintaining that only works of art give rise to plenary experiences of emotion, I shall not claim that all works of art give rise to such experiences. So a claim about art's capacity to offer plenary experiences does not purport to be a claim about art's essence. Given that the capacity for providing a plenary experience of emotion is not a requirement for something constituting a work of art, it is consistent with the claim that some works of art offer a plenary experience and are valued on account of this, and that other things that count as works of art might not offer such an experience and yet might still be valuable for other reasons. Although we might value the latter works of art for other reasons, we might still value more highly the works of art that offer plenary experiences of emotion than those that do not. An account of our emotional experience of art is not concerned with providing an exhaustive account of art's value, but merely with the possibility that one value that art can have is to be found in the emotional experience that it offers. It is the nature of this distinctive emotional experience that we shall investigate in this chapter.

Expressive perception

To make good the proposal that we should study the emotional experience of art in the context of our other emotional experiences of the world, we need to compare and contrast it with the three varieties of experience analysed in the previous chapter. One means of doing this is to identify some analytic structure that is common to instances of all varieties of emotional experience. We have seen that each of the varieties of experience analysed thus far involves a distinctive interaction between a perception of emotion in the world and an emotion of the perceiver's. When we turn to our experience of art, perhaps the same analytic structure can be used to determine what, if anything, makes the emotional experience of art a distinctive variety of emotional experience.

All of the experiences that we have considered thus far are instances of what we might call expressive perception. By expressive perception I mean a twofold experience in which the perceptual aspect of the experience engages with the affective aspect. Expressive perception, as I conceive of it, does not describe a particular interaction between the two aspects. It is a framework

106

for thinking about different possible relationships between perception of emotion and the perceiver's affective state in experiences of which both are constituents.[1] Experiences that possess both a perceptual and affective aspect can then be classified into different varieties of expressive perception when we identify a distinctive engagement between the two aspects of the experience, an engagement that is present in all and only those experiences classified as instances of a particular variety of expressive perception.

What marks out infection, communication and articulation as different varieties of expressive perception is not only that each experience comprises a perceptual aspect and an affective aspect, but that we can identify a different interaction between the perceptual aspect and the affective aspect of the experience in each case. In infection, the perceived emotion determines the emotion that the perceiver feels. In communication, the emotion that the perceiver feels is determined by a partnership between the perceived emotion and the way in which the perceiver's intellect or imagination works on the perception of emotion. And in articulation, the perception of the emotion provides the occasion for the perceiver to comprehend his emotions for himself. These experiences constitute three different varieties of expressive perception because we can identify three different relationships between the two aspects of the experience. In order for the emotional experience of art to constitute a fourth variety of expressive perception, we need to be satisfied that there is yet another distinctive way in which the perceptual aspect and the affective aspect of an emotional experience can interact. So we need to investigate the interaction between the perceiver's emotion and his perception of emotion when attending to a work of art.

It is desirable to think about our experience of art and emotion in terms of expressive perception for two reasons. First, it encourages us to pay due regard both to our perceptual experience of emotion in art and to our own affective condition as aspects of a distinctive interaction when analysing this phenomenon. If these are not interpreted as aspects of a single experience, the theorist becomes preoccupied with arguing either for the significance of analysing a discrete perceptual experience or for the significance of a discrete affective experience.[2] When we conceive of the problem in terms of a twofold experience, the debate ceases to be a matter of choosing between perception and affect, and becomes a matter of analysing the relationship between them. What matters is correctly analysing the engagement between them.

Second, as has been mentioned, by regarding our experience of art as an instance of expressive perception, we can compare and contrast it with other experiences that we also regard as instances of expressive perception. These instances we can then distinguish into different varieties. We are able to isolate the distinctive character of the expressive perception of art (which will be seen to form the basis for a value of art) by identifying it with the interaction that occurs exclusively in this variety of expressive perception, an experience we can distinguish from the interactions that are the hallmarks of the other forms of expressive perception. This means that when we arrive at an account of the expressive perception of art, we will be able to explain why there is a basis for preferring works of art that permit expressive perception to those works that do not permit it. Furthermore, we will also have a basis for understanding why we might prefer the variety of expressive perception that occurs in some of our experiences of art to the other varieties of expressive perception.[3]

Perceptual aspect of expressive perception

When we analyse the expressive perception of listening to a string quartet or looking at a still life painting, it is natural to begin with the perceptual aspect of the experience: what we hear or what we see. We established in Chapter 2 that there are two kinds of emotional properties that we might perceive in the world – externalized properties and projective properties – and that both kinds of properties may be perceived in a work of art. We are now concerned with understanding whether there is anything distinctive about our perception of emotion in art.

In some works of art we might only perceive an externalized property, while in others we might only perceive a projective property. But these are not the works that interest us for present purposes. There is nothing distinctive about an experience of art in which we perceive merely one or other of these properties. If we perceive only an externalized property, the character of the perceptual aspect is akin to the perceptual aspect of our experience of physiognomy (at least, according to my reconstruction of Wollheim's account of the expressiveness of physiognomy). If we perceive only a projective property, it is akin to the perceptual aspect of our expressive perception of the landscape. Unlike physiognomy or the landscape, we can conceive of a work of art in two distinct ways. On the one hand, we can conceive of a work of art as the trace of an act of pressing out or externalization of its creator's feelings, and in this way we can perceive externalized properties in it. On the other hand, the work of art might also be fashioned in a way that makes it suitable for sustaining the projection of a particular emotion, enabling us to perceive a projective property in it. The perceptual aspect of our experience of art is only distinctive when we perceive both kinds of properties in a single work of art.

An explanation that accounts for the distinctiveness of the expressive perception of art needs to address itself to works of art in which we perceive both externalized and projective properties. (Ultimately, an account of the value of the expressive perception of art will explain why we prefer the distinctive experience offered by works of art in which we perceive both kinds of properties to the experience offered by works of art in which we perceive only an externalized property, or a projective property, or neither.) That the expressive perception of art involves both kinds of properties is identified by Wollheim as the key to a proper understanding of the problem. He misunderstands the nature of his own insight, however, presenting it as a claim about the nature of expressive perception rather than a claim about the special possibility that art holds for expressive perception. The rest of this section is devoted to an analysis and critique of his position.

In *Art and its Objects*, Wollheim argues that any sufficient account of artistic expression will have to include provision for perceiving both externalized properties and projective properties.[4] In adopting such a stance, he advocates a natural rather than a conventional account of artistic expression, and places himself firmly in opposition to the kind of account of expression that E. H. Gombrich gives in *Art and Illusion*.[5] Wollheim argues that despite the force of Gombrich's arguments, our perception of expressiveness is not a matter of being appropriately sensitive to convention (i.e. a certain artist's repertoire and the choice from that repertoire that a particular work of art represents). For Wollheim, it is not merely that Gombrich's arguments are not persuasive, but that they misunderstand the fundamental nature of the experience.[6] Such arguments take no account of our natural capacity to perceive expressive properties in the world outside of a conventional context.

As we are by now well aware, Wollheim identifies two natural capacities that occur in our lives independently of art: the capacities to perceive externalized and projective properties. These are two independent capacities, and Wollheim's claim is that expression is a complex concept that occurs at the intersection of the two discrete notions.[7] Because there are two discrete notions, we might be tempted to try to give an account of expression solely in terms of externalized properties, or solely in terms of projective properties. Indeed, Wollheim argues that an account that is concerned with art as a means of self-expression, such as Tolstoy offers, seeks to explain the effect of our perception of externalized properties in art. On the other hand, a theory that is concerned with accounting for the way in which the work affects its audience, such as I. A. Richards expounds,[8] is, in Wollheim's terms, an account of our perception of projective properties. These theories suggest that we must conceive of the expressiveness of art either in terms of self-expression or in terms of the arousal of the audience, and then offer an analysis in terms of expressive properties or projective properties, whichever the case may be.[9]

Although one can give a discrete account of our perception of externalized properties and another of our perception of projective properties, Wollheim argues that in practice we do not perceive these in isolation from each
other. Accordingly, the best way to understand the phenomenon of expressive perception is to give an account of the practical interaction between the
two perceptual properties. This account of expressive perception maintains
that in practice the two kinds of conceptually distinct perceptual properties
are so closely connected that we cannot understand one in isolation from
the other. It follows from this that to perceive emotion in the world, at least
in practice, should be understood as perceiving both externalized and projective properties. The weakness of earlier theories is that each theory fixes
on one of the two kinds of perceptual properties that we find in art and provides an account of expressive perception in terms of the selected property
rather than providing an account in terms of both kinds of properties.

Wollheim's conception of expression as the intersection between two discrete notions is offered as a way out of an impasse that otherwise seems to
arise in the theory of expression. The conflict between traditional expression theories and arousal theories invites us to choose whether expression
is more fundamentally a matter of attending to how the artist was feeling
when he created the work or how the audience feels when they perceive the
work. Wollheim maintains, however, that artistic expression in fact seems to
involve both of these. He can account for the appeal of the different theories
by explaining that both offer partial accounts of the complex phenomenon:
expression theories seek to provide an account of what happens when we
perceive externalized properties as traces of externalizing activities, whereas
arousal theories seek to provide an account of what happens when we perceive projective properties that match our own emotions. Wollheim thinks
that, as a matter of fact, whenever we perceive externalized properties we
also perceive (or at least make reference to our experience of) projective
properties, and vice versa. So what we really require of a theory of expression is an account of our experience of the practical interaction between
the two kinds of properties. Because the perception of emotion in art will,
in practice, always involve perceiving both kinds of properties, neither of
the influential approaches to the expressiveness of art alone can, in Wollheim's opinion, account for the distinctive experience we have in the expressive perception of art. Rather, these theories demand that we conceive of
our experience of works of art either exclusively in terms of externalized
properties, or exclusively in terms of projective properties. Whatever insight
each offers, the common deficiency of both of these theories is that each
fails to acknowledge that it is the perception of both kinds of properties that
gives the perceptual aspect of the expressive perception of art its distinctive
character.

Clearly, a superior theory would account for our perception of both kinds of properties in art. Wollheim's account of expression as the intersection between externalization and projection achieves this. He accommodates both sets of intuitions by showing that the theories that are motivated by the different intuitions provide only partial accounts of expression.[10] Wollheim is surely correct when he identifies the need to incorporate perception of both externalized and projective properties into an account of the distinctive variety of expressive perception offered by art. To acknowledge this, however, does not commit us to his particular solution. Wollheim's account fails to do justice to the sense in which the perception of both kinds of properties in a work of art is unique to our expressive perception of art. That we perceive both kinds of properties in a work of art has to do with the special possibility that art holds for expressive perception, not with Wollheim's alleged observation that we cannot help but perceive externalized properties when we perceive projective properties, and vice versa.

Wollheim suggests that our perception of physiognomic expression, for example perceiving grief in tears, involves some measure of feedback from judgement. This, he thinks, introduces the sense of "appropriateness" that is at the core of perceiving projective properties and is proof that, in practice, perception of externalized properties involves perception of projective properties. Wollheim may be right that, at some level of consciousness, we modify or revise our physiognomic expression based on our judgements. But this is not to say that we revise it on the basis of its match or appropriateness. We might revise it on the basis of how effective we judge it to be in communicating how we feel to others. Or we might modify it through imitation because we notice other agents seemingly externalizing their emotions in a particular way to good effect. So while the presence of feedback in our externalizing activities would suggest that our judgements can inform our externalization, it does not establish that these are judgements about appropriateness rather than effectiveness or convention.

In the case of our perception of projective properties, Wollheim argues that our perception of the appropriateness of a match between the sensory and the psychological will rarely be independent of our experience of the human body's capacity to externalize an emotional condition in an utterance or gesture of the body that we know to be "constantly conjoined with an inner state":

> When we endow a natural object or artefact with expressive meaning, we tend to see it corporeally: that is, we tend to credit it with a particular look which bears a marked analogy to some look that the human body wears and that is constantly conjoined with an inner state.[11]

111

It is plausible that when we create an artefact that we endow with projective properties, we do regard it as a pressing out of an internal condition. But when we perceive the landscape as possessing a projective property, it is not obviously by analogy with the human body's constant conjunction with an inner state. The glistening of dew drops on spring foliage; the flow of water down rocky rapids or a meandering country stream; the stillness in the air between the heaves of a storm: if these are expressive of emotion, it is hardly because we can see some analogy with the glint of an eye, bodily locomotion or human respiration. I shall not deny that, in some cases, such an analogy might be relevant. But it is not as central as Wollheim suggests. There are any number of other considerations that might influence the perception of such a match. The match between skyscapes and inner states might have more to do with our attitude to bright colours and dark colours than any analogy with the human body. Associations between soft and fluffy things such as cotton wool and the look of clouds may be relevant, but such a consideration, though no doubt drawing on human experience, is not an analogy with externalization. Such an analogy cannot always be relevant, given that we sometimes perceive the presence of power and force in nature that is of a magnitude that cannot be comprehended in terms of any analogy with human activity.[12]

None of this proves that perception of externalized properties never informs perception of projective properties, or vice versa. But it does suggest that Wollheim has no reason for thinking that, in practice, there usually is such a relation between perception of one and the other. When we are able to perceive both externalized and projective properties in something, it is highly likely that our perception of the one strengthens or encourages our perception of the other. Wollheim's claim about the interaction between the two should be limited to this context. This context is art. Wollheim's mistaken conception of the practical interaction between the two kinds of properties prevents him from realizing the genuine insight that he has. While it is not the case that in practice we regularly perceive externalized and projective properties interacting with each other, it is nonetheless true that we do perceive this in (some) works of art. In our perception of physiognomy and the landscape, it is quite possible, however, that we might, in practice, perceive one kind of property and not the other. So Wollheim is wrong to think that it is a fact about expressive perception that it always involves the perception of both properties.

This error does not affect his assessment of the expression and arousal theories. It is true that both of these theories (as he describes them) fail to provide an account of our expressive perception of art, and that they fail because they provide a partial account of what occurs. Wollheim's mistake, however, is to think that they provide a partial account of what it means,

112

even in practice, to perceive expressive properties. In fact, they fail because they provide a partial account of the possibility that art offers for a distinctive experience. To provide an account of our expressive perception of art in terms of one or other of these properties is to fail to acknowledge that we can perceive both kinds of properties in a single work of art, and that this is the distinctive possibility that we need to explain. What Wollheim should have said is not that, in practice, expressive perception involves perceiving both kinds of properties, but that, in practice, we only perceive both kinds of properties in works of art, and this distinguishes the perceptual aspect of our expressive perception of works of art from other instances of expressive perception.

In contrast to Wollheim, we are now well placed to see what is distinctive about the emotional experience of art: art offers the possibility of perceiving both externalized and projective properties. Wollheim shows us that our experience of art involves two kinds of properties and that a false theory tries to explain the experience in terms of one of these rather than both of them. Wollheim's insight is not an insight into the way in which we perceive emotional properties, but an insight into the special possibility that art offers for the exercise of this capacity. This special possibility of art is apparent when one realizes that in other contexts we are only able to perceive one or other kind of perceptual property. To appreciate this requires us to locate our investigation of our emotional experience of art in the wider context of all our emotional experiences, a point that I have repeatedly stressed. We can best appreciate what is distinctive about the perceptual aspect of our expressive perception of works of art when we distinguish it from the other varieties of expressive perception.

When we appreciate what is distinctive about the perceptual aspect of the expressive perception of art, it becomes apparent why this variety of expressive perception requires a different explanation from that which we give of the expressive perception of nature. Aside from Budd's specific criticisms of Wollheim's account of expressive perception in terms of correspondence, on a more basic level he is critical of Wollheim's attempt to provide a "monolithic" account of expressive perception – an account that applies equally to art and the landscape.[13] Budd maintains that our experience of the expressiveness of art is fundamentally different from our experience of the expressiveness of nature.[14] Thus, he thinks Wollheim is fundamentally mistaken in trying to provide a single account of both.[15] However, when we appreciate the difference between the affective aspect of the expressive perception of art and the affective aspect of the expressive perception of nature or physiognomy (i.e. perception of both projective and externalized properties in the former case and perception of either projective or externalized properties in the latter case), we are well positioned to appreciate the need for discrete accounts of the different varieties of expressive perception. Whereas Budd argues that the relevant difference is the standard of correctness that the artistic intention provides in the case of art but not nature, the current theory draws the distinction on a different basis – namely, our capacity to perceive different kinds of perceptual properties in different contexts. By acknowledging that the sense in which the perceptual aspect of our expressive perception of art is different from the perceptual aspect of our expressive perception of nature, we can appreciate the different kinds of emotional interactions that distinguish these varieties of expressive perception.

Affective aspect of expressive perception

Although we have established what is distinctive about the perceptual aspect of our emotional experience of art, what distinguishes the different varieties of expressive perception is not the distinctiveness of either of the aspects of the experience, but the relationship between the two aspects. Our perception of emotion in art is distinctive in that it involves perceiving both externalized and projective properties. We must now consider the affective consequences of perceiving both properties in a work.[16] We can then ask whether there is something distinctive about the way in which the two aspects interact, and whether this interaction justifies regarding these emotional experiences as constituting another variety of expressive perception.

Chapter 3 established that perception of different perceptual properties gives rise to different affects. When we perceive an externalized property, we might resonate with, or respond emotionally to, the perception (Chapter 3, § "Perceiving externalized properties and feeling perceived emotions" and § "Responding to perceived emotions"). When we perceive a projective property, it might correspond to our own emotions, or enable us to comprehend them (Chapter 3, § "Perceiving projective properties and feeling perceived emotions" and § "Comprehending perceived emotions"). So if we ask how our emotions are engaged when we perceive both externalized and projective properties, we can expect that our emotions might engage with the emotions perceived in the work of art through some combination of infection, communication and articulation. Is this enough to establish that our emotional experience of art constitutes a further variety of expressive perception? For such experiences to constitute a new variety, they will have to involve a distinctive engagement between the perceptual and affective aspects. The experiences analysed in the previous chapter might be thought to involve three different forms of expressive perception because they involve three different interactions between the perceived emotion and the perceiver's emotion. The question now is: does an experience in which all of infection, communication and articulation occur involve yet another distinctive engagement?

There are at least three ways in which we might understand the relevance of infection, communication and articulation to the emotional experience of art. First, we might conceive of the artistic experience as one in which three different interactions between the perceptual and affective aspects are *possible*. In this case, what is unique about art is simply that it allows for three possible – but alternative – interactions between the perceptual and affective aspects, whereas in other experiences there is only one possibility for interaction. Second, the artistic experience might be one in which all three discrete interactions actually coincide. In this case, what is unique about art is that it allows for the conjunction of discrete interactions that otherwise only occur independently of one another. Third, we might conceive of it as a single experience that somehow combines all three ways in which the two aspects of the experience can interact.

It is only in this third case that we would have a basis for identifying a distinctive variety of expressive perception in the emotional experience of art. Are we justified in applying the third analysis and regarding the emotional experience of art as a distinctive engagement? We are justified only if we can show that an experience involving infection, communication and articulation constitutes a novel kind of experience rather than simply being a coincidence of the three varieties of experience that we have already investigated.

When we try to characterize what is distinctive about the engagement between the two aspects of our experience of art we face a problem that we do not face when we try to characterize the distinctiveness of the three experiences considered in the previous chapter. What makes each of those varieties of emotional experience distinctive is the unique interaction between the perception of emotion and the perceiver's own emotion in each case. Instances of each variety involve an interaction that instances of other varieties do not. Such an analysis does not reveal anything unique about the experience with which we are now concerned. An experience in which different kinds of interaction coincide does not thereby involve a further kind of interaction between perception and affect that is not found in non-artistic experiences.

If a distinctive engagement requires a unique interaction between the two aspects, then it looks like the emotional experience of a work of art, in which three discrete interactions happen to be conjoined, does not constitute a distinctive variety of expressive perception. Our only hope is to look for some other basis on which we can conceive of an engagement being distinctive without the need for a unique interaction between the two aspects of the experience. If we can show that an emotional experience that involves all three of these interactions involves some novelty in virtue of which we might regard the experience as having a distinctive character, rather than simply having a character that grafts each of these three discrete interactions on to one another, we might yet have the basis for a distinctive engagement between perception and affect, an engagement that could serve as the basis for a distinctive variety of expressive perception.

Plenary experience of emotion

In Chapter 1, we considered an account of our emotional life as an economy of parts. I now want to suggest that we might conceive of an emotional experience either as involving an engagement with a part of that economy or with the whole economy. The three interactions analysed in Chapter 3 are all engagements with a part of the economy, whereas I shall suggest that the emotional experience of art involves an engagement with the whole emotional economy. This, I shall suggest, provides a basis for claiming that there is something distinctive about the emotional engagement that occurs in our experience of art, and which justifies regarding the experience as involving a distinctive variety of expressive perception.

At this point, the analysis of the activity and passivity of emotion that we pursued in Chapter 1 is called into service.[17] It will be recalled that the emotional economy involves some mental phenomena in respect of which the agent is passive and others in respect of which he is active. So the emotional economy, when regarded as a system, involves the agent in both active and passive roles. It is this mixture of activity and passivity that is characteristic of our emotional life. When we turn to the interactions of infection, communication and articulation, we find that each of these interactions involves an engagement with a certain aspect of the characteristic mixture of activity and passivity. Once we have an analysis of these interactions in terms of activity and passivity, we can then return to the emotional experience of art and consider what happens when we analyse that experience in terms of activity and passivity.

Infection is an interaction in which the perception of an emotion determines the emotion that the perceiver experiences when he has the perception. The interaction involves an emotion-state, which need not, in these circumstances, be a manifestation of an emotion-disposition: the baby's cry upon perceiving the distress in another baby's cry does not mean that he is manifesting his own disposition to be distressed.[18] This mental state is a mental phenomenon in respect of which the agent is passive. It is not only, however, that the agent's emotional phenomenon is one in respect of which he is passive. He is also passive in respect of the way in which it is initiated. In both resonance and correspondence, the fourth moment finds the nature of the perceived emotional property determining which mental state is aroused in the perceiver (see Chapter 3). So an experience of infection, whether it involves the crying baby resonating with the distress that it perceives in another's cry or Constable's harrowing feeling when he perceives the harrowing landscape that corresponds to this emotion, is an emotional engagement with the world in which the perceiver is entirely passive in relation to his emotions. He is passive both in terms of how the emotional phenomenon is initiated and in relation to the phenomenon itself once it is initiated.

Whereas correspondence involves an interaction between a perceived property and a mental state of the perceiver, articulation involves an interaction between the same projective property and an emotional disposition that underlies the mental state of the perceiver. This difference in mental phenomena with which the perception can engage accounts for the fact that articulation involves an engagement with emotional activity. The agent is active in respect of his emotional dispositions in the sense that they arise out of the depths of his psychology: they are attempts at making sense of the life he has lived and his experiences of satisfaction and frustration therein (see Chapter 1). We have the capacity to perceive the world as matching or being of a piece with our emotions (see Chapter 2). When such perception occurs, we might grasp this (see Chapter 3). If the perceiver does become aware of the match between his perception and his mental disposition, it is something that he must do for himself. It does not occur as a consequence of perceiving the projective property. So whereas the secondary emotional experience that occurs in correspondence is determined by perception of the projective property, the comprehension that occurs in articulation is not determined by the perception. It requires that the perceiver actively does something more for himself. In this way, the perceiver is active in relation to the mental phenomenon with which the projective property interacts in articulation: he plays an active role in making the interaction happen; he must realize for himself how the perception is related to the disposition and, in doing so, give himself an awareness of the emotional disposition. This is not simply a consequence of perceiving the emotional property.

Like infection, communication involves the perceived emotion interacting with the perceiver's mental state. So, once again this is an interaction with an emotional phenomenon in respect of which the perceiver is passive. However, whereas infection is an involuntary experience in which the emotion that the perceiver feels is determined by the emotion that he perceives, in communication, we have a voluntary experience of emotion ("voluntary", that is, in the sense discussed in Chapter 3). Both judgements of favour and imaginative identification, through which the emotional response might be initiated in communication, involve mental dispositions in respect of which the perceiver is active. However, they do not form part of the emotional economy. They represent instances of activity outside of the emotional economy initiating mental phenomena, which form parts of the perceiver's emotional economy and in respect of which he is passive.

Whereas we can analyse infection in terms of passivity alone, communication involves the agent being active in relation to the process that initiates the mental state (a mental disposition that is not part of the emotional economy), but passive in respect of the mental state that is part of the emotional economy. So, in contrast to the two previous interactions, the perceiver is neither wholly active nor wholly passive in communication: it is a mixed experience that involves both activity and passivity. Having said that, we need to be clear about the sense in which the interaction is *not* a mixed experience. It does not involve parts of the emotional economy in respect of which we are active, as well as other parts in respect of which we are passive. There are two senses of activity and passivity at work here. In the narrower sense (of the characteristic mixture of emotional activity and passivity), the agent is passive (but not active). In the more general sense, he is both passive and (non-emotionally) active: the agent's activity does not form part of his emotional economy and so is not part of the characteristic mixture of emotional activity and passivity.

We now have two alternative analyses of the three discrete interactions. We can analyse the discrete interactions illustrated at the beginning of Chapter 2, not only in terms of the different ways in which the perception of emotion interacts with the perceived emotion, but also in terms of the mixture of activity and passivity that we established is characteristic of our emotional life (Chapter 1). In this way, we find that what distinguishes the varieties of emotional experience is also the sense in which each involves an engagement with a different aspect of the plenitude of emotional activity and passivity: infection is a passive engagement with emotional passivity, communication is an engagement with emotional passivity and non-emotional activity, and articulation is an active engagement with emotional activity. Whereas the Chapter 3 analysis offered an account of the different ways in which a perception can interact with the perceiver's emotions, the new analysis enables us to investigate how these emotional experiences are also engagements with different aspects of emotion's characteristic mixture of activity and passivity.

What advantage has been gained by demonstrating that we possess a second means of distinguishing between the three discrete interactions in terms of emotional activity and passivity? Even if there is no utility in drawing this distinction in yet another way, there may be some further utility if we are able to use the new analysis to demonstrate the distinctiveness of the engagement found in a further variety of experience, which distinctiveness was not apparent on the original analysis. The variety of experience I have in mind here is the emotional experience of art.

The discrete interactions are engagements with the different parts of the emotional economy and, as such, are engagements with particular aspects of the characteristic mixture of emotional activity and passivity. What distinguishes each of the discrete interactions is that each involves a different aspect of the characteristic mixture of emotional activity and passivity. But it follows that what they all have in common is that each involves only a single aspect of the characteristic mixture. We can contrast all of these experiences with an experience that involves all of the aspects of the plenitude of emotional activity and passivity. This latter experience I shall call a plenary experience of emotion, or simply a plenary experience. The emotional experience of art is an experience that involves all three interactions. As such, it involves an engagement with the whole emotional economy and all the aspects of the characteristic mixture of emotional activity and passivity: the emotional experience of art involves a plenary experience of emotion.

The plenary experience of emotion constitutes a distinctive way of engaging with emotion. We saw, in the previous section, that an experience that combines three otherwise discrete interactions between the perceived emotion and the perceiver's emotion does not thereby generate a fourth interaction. However, an experience that combines all three interactions can also be said to be an engagement with the different parts of the emotional economy. As such, it is an engagement with the whole emotional economy. An engagement with the emotional economy is distinctive in a way that involves more than merely the conjunction of interactions with its various parts. It is distinctive in the sense that it is an engagement with the plenitude of the emotional activity and passivity of the perceiver's emotional economy. When we have a plenary experience of emotion, the world engages with us as the kind of emotional creatures that we really are: it is an engagement with our emotion as in one sense something that happens to us, and in another sense something that we do. This distinguishes it from the other ways of engaging with emotion. None of the other experiences involve an engagement between the perception of emotion and the perceiver's emotion as the active and passive phenomenon that it is. If the plenary experience of emotion is a distinctive way in which the perception of emotion in the world can engage with the perceiver's emotion, the plenary experience that occurs in the emotional experience of art affords us a basis for regarding the expressive perception of art as a distinctive variety of expressive perception.

Artists and plenary experience of emotion

There are three distinct perspectives from which we might analyse the plenary experience of emotion: the theorist's perspective, the artist's perspective and the audience's perspective. The theoretical perspective examines the conditions under which the plenary experience of emotion is possible. We approached it from that perspective in the previous section, and have considered why this distinctive experience is only possible in our emotional experience of art. In this section, we approach the plenary experience from the artist's perspective. If an artist not only creates something that offers the audience a plenary experience, but intends the audience to have such an experience, we might enquire into the nature of the artist's intention: did he want to reproduce in the audience an earlier experience of his, or to create something that offers an experience he has not previously undergone? Finally, the audience's perspective is the one from which we contemplate the phenomenology of the plenary experience in the next section. The difference in perspective of artist and audience is a matter of the difference between two roles rather than two persons: one person can assume both roles, and this always occurs when the artist is the initial audience of the work he creates.[19]

Given that the artist creates something that offers its audience a plenary experience, the artist is either indifferent to the possibility that the work of art might offer a plenary experience throughout the creative process or else this possibility assumes some significance in motivating his activity. In cases in which at least part of his motivation is concerned with creating the possibility of a plenary experience, we might ask whether this involves creating something that allows for the repetition of an earlier experience of the artist's, or something that allows the artist to have a new experience, one which he has not previously had. The earlier analysis from the theoretical perspective has suggested that we only encounter the conditions necessary for a plenary experience in a work of art. So it cannot be the case that an artist creates the work of art in order to reproduce an earlier plenary experience. If creating a plenary experience is at all a part of his motivations, it must be that he seeks to create something that will enable him to undergo a new experience, an experience that was not possible before the work of art was brought into existence. The artist might previously have felt an emotion, or he might have perceived an externalized or projective property. The perceived property might even have interacted with the artist's own emotions in a particular way. But all of this falls short of a plenary experience.

Turner might have comprehended his emotion at Fingal's Cave, just as Constable might have experienced correspondence at the mouth of the Thames. They might then have set about painting pictures that offer an experience of articulation or infection. In each case, the emotional experience offered by that picture could reproduce the kind of experience offered by the landscape. This would only require them to invest their respective canvases with the appropriate projective properties. They might also, however, create pictures that offer a plenary experience. In this case, they will invest their canvases with externalized properties as well as projective properties, although they only perceived projective properties in the landscape (according to my analysis rather than Wollheim's). So while they might have had some emotional experience prior to executing the work of art, and while this might have involved infection, communication or articulation, it could not have been a plenary experience of emotion. The plenary experience is only possible when they engage with the works that they create.

A work of art might offer only an experience of infection, communication *or* articulation, and in this case the artist might have created the work of art in order to reproduce in himself and his audience an earlier experience of this kind. A work of art might also offer a plenary experience, however, and in this case it cannot be a matter of reproducing an earlier experience because it is not possible to have the plenary experience prior to perceiving the work of art. The plenary experience may well be central to the artist's intention, but it is central in a different way. If the artist is concerned with the plenary experience, he is concerned with creating something that will enable him to undergo an experience for the first time, rather than with reproducing an earlier experience. Even if a work of art enables an artist to have a plenary experience for the first time, this might be incidental to his primary artistic intention. To say that his primary intention in creating a work of art is undergoing a plenary experience assumes that a plenary experience is sufficiently rewarding to justify all this effort on the artist's part. We shall have to wait until the next chapter to understand why he might so desperately want to have a plenary experience. Assuming that the plenary experience is valuable, however, and that the artist creates a work of art because this is the only way to have a plenary experience, then an evaluation of the work of art in terms of this experience is the correct way of appreciating it as a work of art.

In this respect, the account of the plenary experience is radically different from Tolstoy's transmission theory, but shares a marked similarity with Collingwood's theory. For Tolstoy, the whole point of creating a work of art is so that artist and audience alike can undergo an experience that the artist has already had and which he wishes to reproduce in those who perceive the work of art. There is no place in such a theory for an emotional experience that is only possible through engaging with the work of art. It must be possible to have the emotional experience described by Tolstoy's theory independently of the experience of the work of art, for the artist's aim is to reproduce his earlier experience through the medium of the work of art.

According to Collingwood, however, the artist creates the work of art specifically in order to have an experience through the medium of the work of art, an experience it was not previously possible for him to have. For

Collingwood, the artist is dissatisfied with the nature of his emotional experience prior to creating the work because it is incomprehensible to him. The artist engages in the process of creating the work of art in order to undergo a special experience that renders the emotion comprehensible. Such a theory makes the experience offered by the work of art necessary for the valued experience: there is no way of comprehending the emotion except through the medium of the work of art. The emotional experience of art, when conceived of as a plenary experience, is fundamentally different from Tolstoy's conception of the artistic experience as reproducing an earlier experience. It is closer to, albeit distinct from, Collingwood's theory of the artistic experience as comprehending something previously incomprehensible, in that both theories require the experience of the work of art in order to have the emotional experience that the respective theory describes as valuable.

Audiences and plenary experience of emotion

Turning to the audience's perspective, we ask whether the theory of the plenary experience can account for the phenomenology of the audience's emotional experience of art. I suggest that we can appreciate the audience's perspective by considering the fundamental similarities that surface when we use the plenary experience theory to analyse the audience's experience of emotion in a piece of music, such as Elgar's Cello Concerto, and in a painting, such as Manet's *Woman with a Parrot*.

Music historians often speak of the peculiarly intense emotional qualities of Elgar's music. A typical account is offered by Michael Hall at the beginning of *Leaving Home*, his study of music in the twentieth century, when he wants to describe the musical world that is about to be left behind:

> The expansiveness and nobility of Elgar's music contains within it an insecurity that seems to be public as well as private. The characteristic feature of *The Dream of Gerontius* is the contrast between the assurance that Cardinal Newman conveys in his account of the Soul's journey through judgment to purgatory, and the anxious nature of Elgar's chromaticisms. This dichotomy is also present in Elgar's symphonies, the first movement of the second (1911) in particular. Elgar never took any part in the folksong revival that led composers such as Delius and Vaughan Williams to evoke the English countryside as a "land of lost content", but in the Violin Concerto (1910) and especially the Cello Concerto (1919), he was able to express a sense of loss by recalling earlier material as if it were a memory to be lingered over.[20]

And comparing Mahler and Elgar:

> Mahler belonged to the same generation as Elgar and, like Elgar's, his music can overflow with self-confidence one moment and express a deep sense of loss the next. It is as if both men were conscious that the world they loved would soon crumble away. Elgar's sense of loss is conveyed by recalling earlier material nostalgically – as in the Violin and Cello concertos, for instance – whilst Mahler's comes from the nature of the material itself.[21]

Let us take the first movement of the Cello Concerto as representative of Elgar's music, and investigate the kind of experience we might have when we listen to a fine performance conducted by Daniel Barenboim, with Jacqueline du Pré as the soloist. The piece was written at the conclusion of the Great War and perhaps addresses the tremendous sense of public loss that this catastrophe entailed. As it happens, we also know that the night that Elgar returned home from the hospital where he had undergone an operation for infected tonsils, he wrote down the long, wandering melody that is the theme of the first movement.[22] So we might well have reason to think that the music addresses his personal suffering at that time, as well as the public mood. If we, as audience, do experience loss, nostalgia and anxiety interspersed with moments of self-confidence, expansiveness and nobility when listening to the concerto, can the theory of plenary experience make sense of this?

What would our theory have to do to make sense of such an account? It would need to explain that the experience of nostalgia, loss, anxiety and so on in the concerto involves perceiving externalized and projective properties; that these perceptions interact with the listener's emotional economy through infection, communication and articulation; and that these interactions are aspects of a plenary experience of emotion, which is an engagement with the whole emotional economy.

A preliminary problem might arise, however, if I suggest that anxiety can be perceived in a particular musical figure, whereas you say that you perceive melancholy in it. Does it matter that our reports disagree about which emotion we perceive in the music? There are two possibilities here. The first is that we, in fact, agree about the phenomenology of what we hear, but we prefer to give it different labels. This is not a significant problem. In any case, the emotions that we perceive are far more fine-grained than any of our emotion-terms can do justice to.[23]

The second scenario might seem more difficult. In this case, the disagreement is about the phenomenology. Even when we can agree on the use of words, the music might seem to me to match a different emotion to the one you perceive it to match. If the purpose of the plenary experience were for the composer or the performer to communicate a particular emotion to the audience, then it would be a serious problem that two people perceived different emotions in the same music. At least one of them would have to be wrong. However, if the purpose of plenary experience is not that the audience experiences a particular emotion, but that it experiences an emotion in a particular way (or to be more precise, a particular combination of ways), then it is no impediment that people engage with different emotions as long as they engage with them in the right way, that is, they have a plenary experience of them. So if I have a plenary experience of anxiety and you have a plenary experience of melancholy, this is not a significant problem. What is important is that the artist has created something that enables us to have a plenary experience at all. It is only to be expected that people will perceive slightly different emotions in the same music just as they perceive slightly different emotions in the same facial expression.

Preliminary matters aside, we must first be able to hear externalized emotions in the concerto. In passages such as the unaccompanied solo cello line in Figure 1, we might hear traces of activities in which feelings such as loss and anxiety are pressed out, or externalized, by an agent. To hear this involves hearing such parts of the music as being a pressing out of an inner psychological state. To hear the passage in this way is not to suggest that it resembles the sounds a person makes when he externalizes such emotions vocally. Rather, once we have acquired the ability to perceive sounds and gestures as traces of externalization in the primary context of the human body, we are able to apply it in more sophisticated – albeit more remote – contexts, and we can hear the sound of the solo cello in the concerto as traces of du Pré's externalizing activities.

Budd considers and rejects two senses in which we might hear music as the expression of emotion.[24] First, music might imitate the vocal sounds that we make to express emotion. Second, we might make-believe that we are hearing the vocal expression of emotion in music, and we might make-believe this even though the resemblance between our experience of the music and an actual human voice is tenuous at best.[25] It will be apparent from the discussion in Chapter 2 that I do not regard the perception of emotion in the concerto as either a matter of the musical passage above actually resembling vocal expression, or make-believing that it is vocal expression. Rather, I suggest that we can perceive some musical sounds as the trace of an externalizing activity. Once we have the capacity to perceive traces in activities that terminate in facial physiognomy such as smiles, bodily gestures such as clenched fists, vocal utterances such as shrieks, and manual activities that terminate in a marked canvas, it is no huge leap for this capacity to enable us to perceive the sound that results from the activity of drawing a bow across

Figure 1 Elgar, Concerto in E minor Opus 85 for Violoncello and Orchestra, first movement, bars 7–8. *Source:* arrangement by the composer, © Copyright 1919, 2004 Novello & Company Limited.

a string as the trace of an activity intended to externalize emotion. I do not claim that this always occurs in our experience of music, but the concerto form is a dialogue between two voices – solo and tutti – and so of particular relevance in this regard. Virtuosic cadenza passages, such as in Figure 1, are prime candidates for being perceived as the trace of an externalizing activity on the part of the soloist. This is not to suppose that we imagine some indefinite backgrounded persona such as Levinson suggests.[26] Perhaps we might imagine such a persona in some music. But at least in the case of the sound of the solo cello in a performance of Elgar's Cello Concerto, it is natural for a listener who is sensitive to the concerto form to hear this as the trace of an externalizing activity on the part of the soloist.

Second, we have to be able to perceive projective properties in the music. We might perceive the setting of the first subject in this movement as sounding appropriate to sustain the projective property of nostalgic yearning for a lost world. After the initial eight bar cadenza, the violas and cellos provide the first statement of the wandering melody without any accompaniment (Figure 2).

This melody is then repeated five times without development. The second *pianissimo* statement of the melody by the solo cello is accompanied by intermittent horn and clarinet chords (Figure 3). The strings then offer a harmonized rendition of the melody, which the solo cello joins with a counterpoint melody before it again states the same melody. The soloist's second statement of the melody is *fortissimo* rather than *pianissimo*, and is now articulated in two-note phrases, rather than six-note phrases, with block chords in the lower strings and woodwind accompaniment (Figure 4). This culminates in the fifth statement of the melody by the whole orchestra – including the brass – playing *fortissimo* (Figure 5), but dying away at the end of the phrase to give way to the final *mezzo forte* statement by the solo cello, using the original six-note phrasing, and accompanied by occasional chords.

The middle section of this ternary movement is a lighter melody in E major. At its conclusion, we hear four more renditions of the wandering melody. It begins with the solo cello playing the melody *mezzo forte* in the original six-note phrasing with very thin accompaniment including the occasional ascending scale. The orchestra then plays the melody twice: first, *pianissimo* with the soloist in counterpoint; and for the last time *fortissimo*. The movement ends with the soloist providing the final statement of the melody, this time in four-note and two-note phrases and a very sparse accompaniment, which dies away to almost nothing.

Figure 2 Elgar, Concerto in E minor Opus 85 for Violoncello and Orchestra, first movement, bars 9–14. *Source:* arrangement by the composer, © Copyright 1919, 2004 Novello & Company Limited.

Figure 3 Elgar, Concerto in E minor Opus 85 for Violoncello and Orchestra, first movement, bars 15–20. *Source:* arrangement by the composer, © Copyright 1919, 2004 Novello & Company Limited.

Figure 4 Elgar, Concerto in E minor Opus 85 for Violoncello and Orchestra, first movement, bars 27–31. *Source:* arrangement by the composer, © Copyright 1919, 2004 Novello & Company Limited.

Figure 5 Elgar, Concerto in E minor Opus 85 for Violoncello and Orchestra, first movement, bars 33–38. *Source:* arrangement by the composer, © Copyright 1919, 2004 Novello & Company Limited.

There is something about the way in which the same musical idea is repeated ten times without any development that seems to make this appropriate to sustain a nostalgic projective property: the simple melody, which hardly seems deserving of any attention, is pored over by soloist and tutti, being lovingly amplified by forces that it did not originally possess. The soloist tends so carefully to what has been lost: was it a six-note phrase, a two-note phrase, or a four-and-two-note phrase? Then after a break it returns. But its spirit is broken: although the idea lingers on, the last four statements have decidedly less strength than the earlier ones. One cannot say that any of this resembles the mind or behaviour of a nostalgic person, but it seems nevertheless to match it. Its trains of association make it precisely the sort of sound that would sustain a projection of nostalgia, were we to project it. Thus we can perceive a projective property of nostalgia in the movement. This is different from hearing a melody as a pressing out of emotion. As a pressing out, we hear it as something produced by another agent with a certain intention. As a projective property, we hear it as the kind of thing onto which it is appropriate for our own agency to project a psychological condition.[27]

Once we are satisfied that we can perceive both externalized and projective properties in the movement, the question is then how we experience these properties. The listener might be infected by the externalized nostalgia that he perceives. In this case the externalized property will resonate with his own emotional condition and he will experience the perceived nostalgia with his own primary experience of nostalgia. However, the listener might also communicate with the externalized property that he perceives in the music. In this case, he might hear the nostalgia with disfavour and respond to the perceived nostalgia with a primary experience of exasperation at the nostalgic setting of the melody.

Even if the listener responds to the externalized property, he might still be infected by his perception of projective nostalgia. This projective property might correspond to his own condition and be experienced with a secondary experience of nostalgia. So the listener might have a primary experience of exasperation and a secondary experience of nostalgia when he hears nostalgia in the music. In both of these cases, what is aroused in him is a mental phenomenon in respect of which he is passive. But the perceived nostalgia might also engage with an emotional phenomenon in respect of which he is active: the listener might engage with the music through articulation. He perceives a projective property of nostalgia in the way in which the theme is constantly restated without being developed. He is able to draw an analogy between the way that the music serves as a framework for his secondary experience of nostalgia and the role of the attitude as a framework for his primary experience of nostalgia. In this way, he becomes aware of, and is able to comprehend for himself, the role of the mental disposition that gives rise to episodes in which he yearns for the past. This emotion was previously incomprehensible to him, but is now comprehensible because he becomes aware, through analogy, that it is a response that is initiated and justified by a framework that interprets his experience in terms of the life he has lived.

When the listener's emotional condition corresponds to, is responsive to and is comprehended through hearing the emotional properties in the music, the listener has an experience in which all the parts of his emotional economy are engaged with the emotion he hears in the music. In this way, listening to a performance of the first movement of Elgar's Cello Concerto involves having a plenary experience of emotion. Can the same analysis be applied to the experience of looking at a painting, an experience that might in many other ways seem dissimilar to listening to music?

In Manet's single-figure paintings, such as *Woman with a Parrot*,[28] we encounter a remarkable sense of momentary reverie.[29] This experience of reverie in the painting can be analysed in the same way as the experience of nostalgia in the piece of music when we make use of a unique reading offered by Wollheim, in which this experience of reverie is explained using the device of the spectator in the picture.[30] Wollheim writes of these single-figure paintings:

> What is common to the works ... is a shared psychological subject-matter: they present us with figures characterizable in the same mental terms. They are figures who, at the moment at which we see them, are turned in upon themselves by some powerful troubling thought: they are figures who are temporarily preoccupied, figures who have retained and cherish, who cosset, a secret, to which their thoughts have now reverted. A moment later and the mood may dissipate, but until it does, they are absent from the world.[31]

To appreciate what Manet achieves in these pictures, Wollheim suggests that we must look at them in relation to his multi-figure pictures. In pictures such as *Le Balcon*,[32] Manet presents a small group of people who are in close physical proximity and yet emotionally distanced from each other. They are together, yet they are alone. Wollheim observes that in this respect there is a superficial resemblance with Degas's small-group paintings such as *Duc et Duchesse de Morbilli* or *Au Café*, in which there is psychological distance between the people that Degas paints. The difference, however, is that the loneliness in Degas's pictures arises out of the people in the picture; they are chronically unhappy, and we see this aspect of their personality depicted. In Manet's paintings, however, we see something quite different.

The people are not fundamentally sad and detached from one another. Rather, Manet has caught a brief moment in which each happens to be lost in his own thoughts. We are given a brief moment in which each person fails to make eye-contact with any of the others as they are caught up in their own moment of reverie.

When it comes to capturing the same emotions in paintings of single figures, Degas is free to paint them in the way that he paints his groups, as his effect is achieved by capturing the persistent condition of each subject, and this is no more difficult whether there is one or many subjects. For Manet, however, there is a special difficulty. His subjects are not fundamentally sad and detached. Rather, he captures a special moment in which this occurs. He captures the moment not by bringing out the persistent condition, but by painting the way in which they fail to engage with each other in that moment. When he paints a single figure, this technique is not possible. So how does he capture the moment of reverie? Wollheim suggests that he makes use of the device of an internal spectator. The internal spectator is located in the painted space, but outside of the view of the space captured within the picture frame.[33] Manet invites us to imagine this spectator, identify with the spectator in the picture, and look at the single figure in the way that that spectator does. Thus, we see the single figure in a moment of isolation as one of the figures in the group painting would see the other figures in that painting. Can the theory of plenary experience account for the experience of reverie in such a painting? In order to determine this, we must consider whether we perceive the relevant properties in the painting, and whether they then interact with our emotional economy.

We can perceive externalized properties in the painted surface when we see marks as having been made as an externalization of the painter's psychological condition, and we can perceive projective properties in the painted surface when we see it as being suitable for projecting one of our emotions onto. When we engage with certain paintings, it is immediately apparent how the marked surface bears the trace of a pressing out of emotion by the painter: the agitated impasto brushwork of van Gogh or de Kooning, for instance, being obvious examples of this. In other paintings, such as Manet's *Woman with a Parrot*, the externalized properties of the trace of the artist's activity are more subtle. Our experience of the acute examples might facilitate our awareness of the more subtle instances. But there is also another way in which our ability to perceive the subtle cases is enhanced. Our perception of the painted surface as the trace of an activity through which the painter externalizes an emotion might be reinforced by the content that he chooses to paint.

Whereas the concerto is a non-representational art form, painting is often a representational art form. In this case, Manet has depicted a woman standing next to a parrot. So it is possible for the artist to depict in the woman's physiognomy – the vacant look in the eyes gazing out to the corner of the picture, the pursed lips and the lie of the hands – a feeling of one lost in her own thoughts. We might perceive an externalized property in this representation of the trace of an externalizing activity.[34] To say that we perceive the woman's physiognomy as a pressing out of how she feels is not to say that we perceive in this a pressing out of how Manet feels. However, I see no reason why our experience of the painting might not involve both the perception of externalized properties that we imagine the represented woman has pressed out, and externalized properties that we see in the painted surface as the trace of a painting activity through which the artist pressed out his emotions.[35] And our perception of each of these might reinforce our perception of the other. Whereas it might be easier to perceive the trace of the artist's externalizing activity in the agitated impasto brushwork of a van Gogh still life, our perception of externalized properties in the figure that Manet depicts serves to reinforce our sensitivity to the more subtle sense in which the painted surface is the trace of an activity through which Manet presses out his own emotion.[36]

We must also be able to perceive a projective property in the picture. Does Manet present us with an image that it seems would sustain a projection by the spectator of his sense of reverie? It is not a matter of projecting the spectator's emotion onto the woman, but onto the whole picture: the monochrome background; the intimately situated live parrot on a stand; the half-peeled fruit discarded on the floor; not to mention the texture of the brushstrokes with which Manet depicts these, and the composition, in which the woman takes up the full length of the picture. All of this combines to produce something that is appropriate to sustain the projection of a particular emotion.

Having perceived these two properties, the perception might then interact with the spectator's own emotion. The feeling of momentary emptiness perceived by the spectator corresponds to his own feelings, putting him in mind of the feeling of such reverie. Because we perceive an externalized property, communication is possible. It is here that Wollheim's claims about the internal spectator become significant. For we are encouraged, Wollheim suggests, to imagine another figure, just out of view, who seeks – but fails – to gain the woman's attention. If we can identify with this figure, then we can respond to her from the figure's point of view.[37] In response to her feelings of momentary loss, we now feel perhaps tedium, frustration or rejection.[38] At the same time, when we draw an analogy between the two interpretative frameworks (the painted surface of the picture and the mental disposition within us that manifests itself in moments of reverie), we are able to comprehend something about the life we have led, which gives rise to occasional empty moments: something about ourselves that was previously incomprehensible to us. Because looking at the painting offers the possibility of these interactions with both our emotional activity and passivity, we have the possibility of a plenary experience of emotion. In this way, despite all the ontological differences between a painting and a musical performance,[39] and all the differences between aural and visual perception, the theory of plenary experience facilitates a similar analysis in each case. This demonstrates that there is something interestingly similar about the phenomenology of the emotional experience of the painting and the phenomenology of the emotional experience of the performance.

5

The value of art and
the practice of life

Value of the plenary experience of emotion

Two central questions that a theory of art must address, if it is to be useful to us, are "Why do we value works of art at all?" and "Why do we value some works of art more than other works of art?" These are questions to which the earlier chapters have not provided answers. We have an account of a distinctive experience that is possible only when we perceive a work of art, but we have not yet established any reason to value that experience, let alone the work of art that gives rise to it. It should be clear that if the preceding argument has prepared us to assert anything about the value that works of art have, it will be a value derived from having a plenary experience of emotion. What we now require is an account of why the plenary experience of emotion is valuable, and why the possibility of this valuable experience in our expressive perception of art makes art valuable for us. If we can provide such an account, the distinctive nature of the experience of art will be shown to account for a value that is unique to the category of art, and one that some individual works of art might be judged to possess to a greater or lesser degree than other works of art.

There are at least two ways in which we can think about an experience such as the plenary experience of emotion being valuable. An experience might be one that we value simply because it is pleasurable and we enjoy having it. It might also be valuable, however, because there is some pre-existing need that the experience meets. The plenary experience might be pleasurable. Indeed, our experience of art might be pleasurable whether or not it involves a plenary experience of emotion. In claiming that the value of art is derived from the value of the plenary experience, however, it is not the pleasurable nature of the experience that concerns us, but the need that the experience meets. It is in meeting this need that we shall find that the experience makes a unique contribution to the good life.

This approach requires us to identify the particular need that the plenary experience meets. We shall see that when a creature possesses both its own emotional condition and the ability to perceive emotion in the world around it, the need for an engagement between the perception of emotion and the perceiver's own emotional condition arises. Without emotional engagement, how we feel about the world cannot take account of the emotion that we perceive in the world, leaving us in an intolerable state in which we are not at home in the world. One value of the plenary experience of emotion, I shall suggest, lies in its ability to meet the need for engagement between the perception of emotion and the perceiver's emotional condition.

In arguing that one value of works of art is their ability to provide us with experiences that negate emotional isolation, I need not argue that this is the only value of art.[1] I do not propose to provide a comprehensive statement of all the values that art has for us.[2] Nor do I propose to argue for a value that every work of art possesses. What I do propose to demonstrate, however, is that because some works of art offer a special kind of experience – the plenary experience of emotion – they make a valuable contribution to the good life.

Such a claim about art's contribution to the good life leads us into debates about the relationship between aesthetic and ethical value. The development of axiology in analytic philosophy during the twentieth century saw a shift from a commitment to a fundamental similarity between the aesthetic and ethical domains (be they one and the same thing[3] or both similarly wanting in their pretentions to constitute unique types of knowledge[4]), to an interest in studying the interactions between two domains that theorists have come to treat as fundamentally disanalogous.[5] The study of the interaction between these two independent domains has progressed largely through the investigation of the impact of moral commitments on the evaluation of art, notably in the writing of Berys Gaut.[6]

Gaut identifies five distinct issues that tend to become entwined in discussions about art and morality.[7] First, there is a causal issue, concerning the effect of a particular work of art on an actual audience, a problem that requires empirical research. Second, there are questions of public policy, both regarding the appropriateness of state censorship of art that is deemed to have undesirable effects on its audience and state sponsorship of art deemed to have beneficial effects on its audience. Third, there is the conceptual issue of the analytical connection, if any, between the aesthetic and the ethical. Fourth, there is the issue of whether there is an intrinsic relation between art and morality. And, fifth, there is the issue of whether the aesthetic and ethical domains have a symmetrical structure, such that a philosophical account of one will also apply to the other. Gaut is primarily concerned with addressing the intrinsic issue and, to the extent that it is relevant to this issue, the analytical issue.

In investigating the relevance of morality for the appreciation of art, Gaut leads the analytic philosophical establishment down a well-trodden path. There is a long tradition that maintains that a work of art's aesthetic value is entirely dependent upon its ethical value.[8] Unsurprisingly, there is an antithetical tradition that maintains that aesthetic value is entirely independent of ethical value,[9] and another tradition that argues that aesthetic value can be directly enhanced by the lack of ethical value.[10] A middle road acknowledges that aesthetic value, although not dependent upon ethical value, can nevertheless be affected by ethical considerations.[11] Gaut belongs to this tradition. He argues that a work of art is always aesthetically flawed to the extent that it contains an ethical flaw that is aesthetically relevant (which, because Gaut equates aesthetic value with artistic value, means a flaw that is relevant to our appreciation of the work as the artist intends us to appreciate it). My concern is not with how he argues for this position so much as with some of the assumptions that underpin the investigation.

Of the fourth of his five issues, Gaut writes, "The intrinsic question ... is not about the effects of art, but about an internal relation of the aesthetic to the moral domains: does the moral value of works condition their aesthetic value?"[12] There are two insights here. First, that we can study the internal relations between the aesthetic and ethical domains independently of our study of the causal effects of art on particular audiences. Second, that the important question about the internal relations of the aesthetic and the ethical concerns whether ethical value conditions aesthetic value. Gaut's presentation of these two insights might suggest, however, that the significance of ethical value for aesthetic evaluation of art exhausts the study of the internal relations between the aesthetic and the ethical domains, or at least that it is the most fundamental enquiry to be made into the internal relations between those two domains.

It is not my intention to cast aspersion on Gaut's project, nor on his achievement in it, though others have questioned the extent of the latter.[13] However, one would do well to challenge the tacit assumption that the internal relations between the two domains are primarily (if not only) to be understood in terms of the significance of ethical commitments for the estimation of aesthetic value. Just as the intrinsic relations involve the implications of the ethical domain for evaluations in the aesthetic domain, so too might there be intrinsic relations moving in the opposite direction.

The current argument is concerned with one way in which the aesthetic domain might be thought to make some intrinsic contribution to the ethical domain. That contribution involves a particular way of experiencing art that facilitates the flourishing of ethical life. It is not concerned with the causal issue, namely, whether a particular work of art has a certain effect on any actual audience. Rather, it is concerned with demonstrating why the intrinsic nature of the emotional economy gives rise to a need that must be fulfilled in ethical life if we are to flourish, and why works of art are intrinsically suited to offering experiences that meet this need. As such, I conceive of it as a supplement to the existing literature's investigations into some of the intrinsic relations between the two domains.

Elizabeth Schellekens observes that the five issues identified by Gaut raise three main kinds of concerns: experiential or phenomenological concerns "about how we engage with and are affected by artworks, and whether that should be conceived as part and parcel of any function artworks ought to serve";[14] epistemological issues, in particular how "we pick out features salient to aesthetic and moral assessment, and the possibility of developing or educating these dispositions";[15] and metaphysical issues concerning the application of metaphysical theories to the two fields of experience and the way in which they interact with each other. Schellekens notes that Gaut's approach to the intrinsic issue "takes us back to the epistemological and metaphysical concerns".[16] What will be apparent is that my interest in the intrinsic issue involves attending to the experiential or phenomenological concerns. This does not mean that the phenomenological concerns are more important than the epistemological or metaphysical concerns, but rather that the intrinsic issue is not exhausted by attending to the epistemological and metaphysical concerns, as the literature might seem to suggest.

Need for emotional engagement

In our ordinary life, we have a commerce – or exchange – with the world around us. We engage with the world: the world impacts upon us in one way or another, and respond to this impact in various ways. It might seem trite to say that when we respond to the world, we respond to it as we perceive it to impact upon us. But it is a crucial feature of how we live our lives that we are able to engage with the world on the same terms that it impacts upon us. The very possibility of human flourishing, or a good life, requires that a person stands in this relation to the world, a relation that I shall call "being at home in the world".[17] To say that a person is at home in the world is not to say that he is happy. But it is to say that he stands in the kind of relationship to his world in which it is possible for him to be happy. So long as I am capable of engaging with the world on the terms in which it is felt to impact upon me, it is at least possible that I might be happy; my relationship with the world is such that it is at least possible for me to try to find a way of engaging with the world in which I can flourish. If I cannot engage with the world in this way, I am liable to find the world a hostile place: a place in which I cannot even begin to be at home. One basic requirement for being at home in the world is that our engagement with, or involvement in, our world has a certain "fit" between our awareness of the world and our response[18] to the world. Unless we have at least some experiences in which we respond to the world in the same terms that it impacts upon us, we are likely to feel isolated from the world that we inhabit, and we will not be at home in the world.

The thought that art and the aesthetic are intrinsically connected to an experience of being at home in the world is not a peculiarity of my approach to emotional experience. The connection is also apparent from the central place that the idea occupies in Roger Scruton's treatment of beauty.[19] In discussing natural beauty, he suggests that "The experience of natural beauty is not a sense of 'how nice!' or 'how pleasant!' It contains a reassurance that this world is a right and fitting place to be – a home in which our human powers and prospects find confirmation."[20] Beauty, Scruton maintains, allows us to feel that we belong in the world on account of how we perceive it: "In the experience of beauty the world *comes home* to us, and we to the world. But it comes home in a special way – through its presentation, rather than its use."[21] We feel that we belong in art no less than in nature. In *The Waste Land*, T. S. Eliot presents us with images of and allusions to the soulless desert that is the modern city. However, his presentation allows us to affirm, through our experience of the poem, precisely that which our experience of the city denies us: "If we can grasp the emptiness of modern life, this is because art points to *another way of being*, and Eliot's poem makes this other way available."[22] By offering us a special way of being in the world, Scruton thinks that Eliot addresses a deep human need that can only be addressed through art:

> Our need for beauty is not something that we could lack and still be fulfilled as people. It is a need arising from our metaphysical condition, as free individuals, seeking our place in a shared and public world. We can wander through this world, alienated, resentful, full of suspicion and distrust. Or we can find our home here, coming to rest in harmony with others and with ourselves. The experience of beauty guides us along this second path: it tells us that we *are* at home in the world, that the world is already ordered in our perceptions as a place fit for the lives of beings like us. But – and this is again one of the messages of the early modernists – beings like us become at home in the world only by acknowledging our "fallen" condition, as Eliot acknowledged it in *The Waste Land*.[23]

For present purposes, we need not commit ourselves to Scruton's analysis of beauty. I introduce his discussion only in order to demonstrate that, whatever one's particular thoughts about the beauty or emotional experience of art, there is good reason to think that their relevance to the value of art lies in how they anchor art's value in its ability to address our need to be at home in the world.

As we have seen, our emotional life involves an engagement with the world. So how we engage with the world emotionally will have a bearing on whether we feel at home in the world. One way in which we might avoid the emotional isolation that leaves us feeling alienated from the world would be through an emotional engagement with the world: an engagement in which our response to the world is a response to the world as the world impacts upon us. The earlier analysis suggested that an important part of how the world impacts upon us involves our perception of emotion in the world. Given that part of the impact of the world involves the perception of emotion in the world, feeling at home in that world will involve engaging with the emotion that we perceive in that world. A creature that perceives the emotion, but can only respond to the world in a way that does not involve responding to the perceived emotion, would feel alienated from the world that it inhabited. It would not be possible for such a creature to flourish because it is not at home in the world it inhabits. This problem of not being at home in the world will only arise for a certain sort of creature. We can see this when we consider three different kinds of hypothetical creatures.

The first hypothetical creature is capable of having an emotional response to the world, but is incapable of perceiving emotion in the world. Often our emotional responses to the world involve responses to emotions we perceive in the world (such as the mother's emotional response to her perception of distress in her child's cry in Chapter 2), but in principle this need not be the case. It is conceivable that a creature might not perceive emotion in the world, but might nevertheless respond emotionally to the impact of the emotionless world upon it. The sight and sound of my grandmother's teapot smashing on the floor elicits a feeling of sadness in me. In this case, I respond simply to the sight and sound of the event and the associations that the teapot holds for me. The experience does not involve a perception of emotion. The experience of seeing the expression on my mother's face when she drops her mother's teapot, however, might also elicit an emotional response. In this case, the perception of emotion in my mother's face is part of the experience. Thus, while our emotional condition can be affected by the perception of emotion, changes in our emotional condition need not involve the perception of emotion in the world. In principle, we could imagine a creature that had a flourishing emotional life despite never perceiving emotion in the world. The creature would perceive and respond to the smashing of a teapot, but would neither perceive nor respond to the physiognomy of its mother when she dropped the teapot.

Second, there is a creature with which we are more familiar. This creature perceives emotion in the world. Like the first creature, this creature engages emotionally with the world, but, unlike the first creature, this includes engaging with the emotion that it perceives in the world (but which the first creature does not perceive). This more closely resembles the kind of creature that we considered in the earlier chapters: the human creature. When it witnesses the smashing of the teapot, it perceives the emotion in its mother's physiognomy and this perception forms part of the world that it responds to when there is a change in its own emotional condition in response to the perceived situation. It is the varieties of this interaction that we were concerned with in the earlier chapters.

Finally, there is a third creature that is more emotionally advanced than the first, but less so than the second. It can perceive emotion in the world, and it can engage emotionally with the world. But it cannot engage emotionally with the emotion that it perceives in the world. Although it perceives emotion in its mother's physiognomy in the way that the second creature does, its emotional experience (when it perceives the teapot smash) is the same as the first creature's: although it is capable of perceiving emotion in its mother's physiognomy, it is incapable of responding to this perception. It responds to the sound, sight and associations, but not the perceived emotion. There is a change in this creature's emotional condition when it hears the crash of the teapot on the floor, and it does perceive an externalized property in its mother's face when she drops the teapot, but there is no connection between the change in the creature's emotional condition and its perception of emotion in its mother's face. This is a creature that can only engage emotionally with certain aspects of the way in which the world impacts upon it.

As far as the first of these creatures is concerned, its emotional engagement does not raise a problem for its sense of being at home in the world: because it does not perceive emotion in the world, the question of its not being able to respond properly to what it perceives does not arise. There is a potential problem for the second and third creatures, however. They perceive emotion in the world, and so, if they engage with the emotion that they perceive in the world, they will be at home in the world; if they are incapable of engaging with the emotion that they perceive, they will not be at home in the world. The second creature, although vulnerable to this risk, has the capacity to avert it: it can engage with the emotion that it perceives. The plight of the third creature is that, unlike the second creature, although it perceives emotion in the world, it lacks the capacity to engage with the emotion that it perceives. So it lacks the possibility of engaging with the world as the world is perceived, and consequently lacks the possibility of being at home in its world.

Ovid tells us that when Diana caught Actaeon watching her bathe, she turned him into a stag, so that "it was only his feelings that stayed unchanged".[24]

Obviously, Actaeon suffered great misery as his dogs tore him apart. But what was the nature of that misery? Any stag would suffer great pain when being attacked and killed in this way. But Actaeon does not merely suffer in the way that a stag does, as, say, Galanthis might suffer as an ordinary weasel does, or Arachne as an ordinary spider. For him, the misery is not just the physical suffering, but the plight of one who retains the feelings of a hunter, but can only behave like a stag. The misery would not be so great if the world impacted upon him as it does upon the hunted, or if he were able to respond as the hunter can. It is the misery of having the hunter's awareness of the world, but only the hunted's ability to respond to the world. This illustrates one sense in which we can conceive of a creature being unable to engage with the world in a way that is commensurate with its awareness of the world.[25] It prepares us for understanding the sense of inability to engage with the world that I have suggested occurs when we are not at home in the world.

In Rohinton Mistry's story "Of White Hairs and Cricket", we are provided with a vignette of the life of a fourteen-year-old Parsi boy, Kersi, an inhabitant of a Bombay apartment block called Firozsha Baag.[26] Every Sunday night, he is required to pluck the white hairs out of his father's scalp with tweezers, so that the chronically unemployed man will appear youthful in the unlikely event that he has a job interview during the following week. On one occasion, he tells his son that somehow they will find the money to send the boy to America. Then, Kersi recounts:

> His face filled with love. I felt suddenly like hugging him, but we never did except on birthdays, and to get rid of the feeling I looked away and pretended to myself that he was saying it just to humour me, because he wanted me to finish pulling his white hairs.[27]

In this vignette, Kersi perceives love in his father's face; however, he is overwhelmed by what he perceives and is afraid of responding to it. So he contrives a way of dealing with the situation without having to respond to the perceived love: he engages in simple projection; this changes his belief about why his father is behaving in the way that he is; he then responds to what he phantasizes his father to be thinking, rather than responding to the perceived externalized property. The strategy is ultimately an unsuccessful one, and leaves him feeling miserable: the last paragraph has his face buried in a pillow, wishing that he could bring himself to weep for his failure to respond to what he perceived (not to mention a litany of similar regrets).

In the story, Kersi is miserable because he chooses not to engage with the emotion that he perceives in his father's face. But what if, rather than making this poor choice, he in fact had no choice? What if, just as the world impacts upon Actaeon as a hunter, but he can only engage with the world as the hunted does, Kersi were able to perceive emotion in the world that he inhabits, but were unable to engage with the emotion that he perceived in the world? That is, rather than choosing not to engage with what he perceives, he is incapable of engaging with it. In this scenario, his misery would not merely be the result of the outcome of his choice, but the misery of not even being able to engage with the world as it impacts upon him: he would be miserable because he is not at home in the world.

If he could not engage with the world as he perceives it, he is in the position of the third hypothetical creature, whereas, if it is possible for him to do so (but he chooses not to), he is in the position of the second creature. The second creature has the capacity to be at home in the world because it has the capacity to engage with the world in the way that the world impacts upon it. This is a precondition for flourishing. Given that we are the kind of creatures that do perceive emotion in the world, experiences that enable us to engage with that perceived emotion will be valuable to us because they enable us to be at home in the world.[28] They will give us the advantage that the second creature has over the third.

There is no assurance that a world in which there is emotional engagement will be agreeable. When the individual's emotional condition engages with his perception of emotion in the world, this might give rise to a range of painful emotions in him, emotions that he would not otherwise experience. Although this might be unpleasant, it puts him at an advantage: he is now capable of interacting with the world as he perceives it. He can seek out pleasant interactions and find ways of coping with distressing ones if he so chooses. The value of emotional engagement is the possibility that it creates, not that it ensures an agreeable interaction with the world.

Engagement with the emotional economy

Given that being at home in the world requires an emotional engagement with the emotion that we perceive in the world, attention then turns to the kind of engagement that is necessary in order to be at home in the world. The previous chapters analysed four ways in which perceived emotion can engage with a perceiver's own emotions: infection, communication, articulation, and plenary experience of emotion. So the question is now whether these varieties of emotional engagement are all equally good for the purpose of being at home in the world, or whether one of them more effectively enables us to be at home in the world.

Chapter 1 suggested that we can conceive of emotion in terms of an economy or an organized system of parts operating as an organic whole. The parts of that system are constituted by mental states and mental dispositions that interact in different ways, most notably through the manifestation of mental dispositions in mental states. We have considered the different ways in which one or other of these parts of the economy can engage with emotion and, in Chapter 4, the way in which the whole emotional economy is said to engage with the perceived emotion in the plenary experience of emotion. So the question about whether it matters what kind of engagement we have becomes a question about whether being at home in the world requires an engagement with any part of the emotional economy, a particular part of the emotional economy or the whole economy.

Chapter 1 discussed the sense in which an agent is active in relation to some of his mental phenomena and passive in relation to other mental phenomena. His emotional economy involves the interaction between both kinds of mental phenomena, and so he participates in his emotional life both in active and passive capacities: he both acts and is acted upon. When we ask what kind of emotional engagement is necessary for the agent to feel at home in the world, we now find that we are asking whether this requires the perceived emotion to engage with something in respect of which the perceiver is emotionally active, passive or both active and passive. Just as being at home in the world requires us to be able to engage emotionally with all the aspects of our perception of the world, being fully engaged also requires that all the aspects of our emotional condition be engaged. That is, the perception must engage the plenitude of our emotional activity and passivity: to be at home in the world is as much about the world's impacting on all the aspects of our emotional condition as it is about our emotional condition being able to respond to all the aspects of the world's impact. Thus, being at home in the world requires us to have experiences in which the emotion we perceive in the world engages with our whole emotional economy. Although other engagements are possible, they will not be as effective in making one at home in the world.

It is one thing to say that we need to have experiences that engage our emotional activity and experiences that engage our emotional passivity in order to be at home in the world. It is another to say that we require the same experience to engage our emotional activity and passivity. If it were only the former that is required, one might argue that surely it is enough that we can have experiences of infection, communication and articulation. As long as I am aware that I am capable of having all these experiences, and consequently that I am capable of having each part of the emotional economy engaged in one experience or another, why do I need something more than that to feel at home in the world? Why do I need to have a special experience in which both emotional activity and passivity are engaged?

My analysis of the emotional economy has suggested that our emotional life involves an organised system of parts. It is this system that is central to the kind of creatures that we are. In saying that we have a need for experiences in which we are emotionally engaged, such engagement must be an engagement with the system. Plenary experience engages the peculiar mixture of emotional activity and passivity that is the hallmark of the system that constitutes our emotional life. Knowing that it is possible to have experiences that engage different aspects of this mixture of activity and passivity is no substitute for having plenary experiences that engage the plenitude of emotional activity and passivity. A creature that has an emotional economy of this kind is only at home in a world in which the plenitude of emotional activity and passivity of its economy can be engaged. This occurs when it has experiences that engage all aspects of its emotional plenitude, not when it merely has a range of experiences, each of which engages some different aspect of that plenitude. A creature that had an emotional economy of the kind that I have described, but could only have experiences that engaged one aspect or another of its emotional economy, would not be able to engage with the world as the kind of creature that it is. By way of contrast, however, such an engagement would be sufficient for a creature that possessed said mental states and mental dispositions, but in which these were not organized into a system.

So, given the kind of creatures that we are, in order to be at home in the world we need to have experiences in which the whole emotional economy engages with the emotion we perceive in the world. Do we have such experiences? It has been anticipated that we can have such experiences in the emotional experience of art. If we do have such experiences when we engage with works of art, one reason for valuing these experiences is because they enable us to be at home in the world. In order to establish this, it will not be enough to argue that in artistic experience there is an engagement between a part of the emotional economy and the perceived emotion. While such an engagement might have some benefits, it will not give us what we are looking for. The kind of artistic experience that will make a profound contribution to our lives is one that enables us to be at home in the world.

Art and emotional engagement

If our experience of art makes such a contribution to human flourishing, we require an account of how our experience of art provides an engagement with the whole emotional economy. When we consider the existing literature on art and emotion, however, we are unable to find any account that suggests that art provides such an engagement. Because the literature does not distinguish between engagement with a part of the emotional economy and engagement with the whole economy, the need for an engagement with the whole economy is not discussed. Instead, the debate is focused on which part of the economy should be engaged with the perceived emotion. When we turn to the accounts of the expressiveness of art offered by Tolstoy and Collingwood, we find that each offers an account of an engagement with a different aspect of emotional activity or passivity. The disagreement concerns which is the significant aspect. Thus the proper objection in both cases is to the aim of the project, rather than the argument offered in favour of engaging with a particular part of the emotional economy.

For Tolstoy, what is valuable about our experience of art is that it infects us with the very emotion that we perceive in the work of art.[29] In the context of his broader theory, this is significant because it gives rise to the possibility of creating a community in which the same emotion is shared by all. What is significant, for present purposes, is that the valuable interaction can be identified with the first of the three interactions we distinguished in Chapter 3. This involves the perceiver experiencing a mental state that is the same emotion as he perceives. What we can now see is that Tolstoy's account is concerned only with an engagement between the perceived emotion and a part of the emotional economy in respect of which the perceiver is passive.

One way to criticise this approach is to argue that it attaches significance to the wrong kind of interaction. We can interpret Collingwood's implicit criticism of Tolstoy in this way. Collingwood acknowledges the possibility of infection, but does not attach significance to it. For him, what matters is the experience in which emotion is articulated.[30] The significance of this interaction in his broader theory is that the artist encourages the audience to comprehend for itself an emotion that is otherwise incomprehensible, rather than causing it to feel a new, yet incomprehensible emotion. On this analysis, the problem is neither that Tolstoy errs in positing his interaction nor that he gives the wrong account of it. Rather, the problem is that this is not the valuable interaction. So the debate takes the form of Collingwood demonstrating that, in addition to the interaction identified by Tolstoy, there is another interaction, which turns out to be the significant one. Collingwood seeks to establish that it is the experience of comprehending – rather than feeling – emotion that is valuable. The question, however, is whether the significance of articulation negates any value that infection might have.

We established in Chapter 3 that Collingwood's articulation of emotion is, on my exposition of the emotional economy, the comprehension of the mental disposition rather than the mental state. Hence it is an interaction with a part of the emotional economy in respect of which the individual is active. Tolstoy, however, provides an account of an engagement with a mental state. What appeared to be a debate about the most important way of engaging with an emotion is now seen to be the juxtaposition of an account of an engagement with a part of the emotional economy in respect of which we are passive (infection) and an account of an engagement with a part in respect of which we are active (articulation). Now, the debate appears to be a matter of determining whether we are interested in how our perception of emotion engages with our emotional activity or our emotional passivity. However, we have already established that what is required is an engagement with the plenitude of emotional activity and passivity.

The established debate is not going to resolve this problem because it pits an account of an engagement with one part of the emotional economy against an account of an engagement with another part of the economy, rather than comparing alternative accounts of our engagement with the whole economy. Once we see that the project is to explain the relationship between the whole emotional economy and the perceived emotion, Collingwood's is no more the last word than Tolstoy's. The problem is not whether articulation or infection is more valuable, but to demonstrate how both can be seen as aspects of a single valuable experience in which each of the active and passive parts of the emotional economy engages with the perceived emotion. Each theory provides only a partial answer: a clue to what an engagement with the whole economy would involve.

Plenary experience as engagement with the emotional economy

What is required is a theory of art that explains how our emotional engagement with works of art might involve the whole emotional economy. Chapter 4 advanced the claim that our emotional engagement with a work of art might involve a plenary experience of emotion. In doing so, it made the stronger claim that it is only in our experience of art that we have a plenary experience of emotion. This chapter has argued that the plenary experience is valuable because it enables us to be at home in the world. So we are now able to appreciate why the emotional experience offered by works of art is not only unique, but also valuable.

To say that the plenary experience of emotion only occurs in our experience of art is not to say that all works of art offer that experience. If some works of art offer us this valuable plenary experience, then it is in our experience of those works of art that we will feel most at home in the world. Might this explain why we prefer these works to others? Does a claim about the value of the plenary experience of emotion tell us anything about the value of the works of art that offer it? It requires a further step to establish that, because a plenary experience of emotion is valuable, a work of art that offers a plenary experience of emotion is also valuable.

In developing her "new romantic theory of expression", Jenefer Robinson seeks to affirm the significance of articulation of emotion for a theory of artistic expression.[31] Her approach can accommodate claims that expression involves comprehension (what she calls articulation and individuation), as well as pressing out of emotion, recognition of emotion, and perhaps feeling emotion. Robinson takes herself to be addressing two questions that Levinson has been at pains to tease apart: "What is expression?" and "How do works of art achieve expression?"[32] Having answered the first question with her new romantic theory, she proceeds to show the different ways in which the second question is answered with respect to the different art forms. It is over a hundred pages later, in the epilogue, that she reveals her interest in a further question. She writes:

> Part of my subtext has been to show why it's so important to continue to engage with the great novels and poems and pieces of music ... It's not just that these works engage our emotions ... – most importantly – they actively encourage us to reflect about our emotional responses and learn from them.[33]

What this "subtext" reveals is a concern with a third question: why is artistic expression one of the values of art? In answering this question, she squarely identifies the value of expression with the way in which we learn about our emotional life through reflecting upon it in our engagement with works of art that are expressions of emotion.

Our investigations have not been concerned with "artistic expression", but with the idea of "emotional experience of art". The approach that we have taken elevates Robinson's third question from the subtext: understanding the value of the emotional experience of art is no less prominent a concern than understanding the nature of the emotional experience of art. This approach has the merit not only of affirming the significance of a question that might otherwise be subordinated, but of inviting us to attend to one of the values of art that might otherwise be neglected. Whereas Robinson seeks to establish the significance of artistic expression for our understanding of our emotional life, our approach invites us to appreciate the significance of the emotional experience of art for our feeling at home in the world. These two values of art need not be inconsistent.

Intrinsic and instrumental values of art

A central concern of the philosophy of art is to understand what it means for one work of art to be a finer work of art than another. We now have an account of the value of the emotional engagement that might attend our experience of art. The question, then, is whether the value of emotional engagement can account for the value of the work of art that offers it. If it does, our emotional engagement with some works of art will account for why we regard them as finer works than others. Our answer requires us to proceed in two stages. First, we must establish what kind of value claim would justify regarding one work of art as a finer work of art than another. Then, we can ask whether a claim about emotional engagement constitutes the requisite kind of value claim.

There are many senses in which we might find a work of art valuable. Some ways of valuing a work of art need not have regard for it as a work of art. Grinling Gibbons's carved font cover in All Hallows by the Tower, in the City of London, might have some practical value as a font cover. It might also have religious value as an icon of devotion, status value as an expression of the donor's wealth or the commissioner's power, or cultural value as an indication of social developments and achievements of the society in which it was created. It may be particularly valuable in any of these regards, without being particularly valuable as a work of art. We might regard another carving as a finer work of art, whilst still valuing this carving more in terms of its practical, religious, status, historical, or cultural value. Likewise, a simpler, more functional font cover might have greater practical value than this one, and yet we would still prefer the Grinling Gibbons as a work of art. What we want to know is whether there is a basis for preferring the Grinling Gibbons carving as a work of art to a carving executed by an incompetent member of the master's studio. The apprentice's carving might be competent enough to have the same practical or religious value, and yet we still prefer the master's as a finer work of art. What accounts for this kind of preference? Once we know what it means to prefer one thing to another as a work of art, we can then ask whether the capacity to offer emotional engagement is a suitable basis for valuing a work of art in this way.

There are at least two ways in which we might try to explain the basis for judging one thing to be a finer work of art than another: we might make a judgement in terms of the essence of art, or the experience of art. Given an account of the essence of what it is to be a work of art, we might prefer works of art that are better able to meet the criterion of art to works that are less well-equipped to meet that criterion. In this case, preferring one work to another would be a matter of reckoning which work possesses a higher degree of the essential property. If, for instance, one thought that the essential property of being a work of art is the capacity for emotional engagement, then a particular work of art might be more or less valuable as a work of art depending on its capacity for emotional engagement. However, whether or not there is some essential property of art, it has been no claim of mine that the capacity to offer emotional engagement is a necessary or sufficient condition for being a work of art. Rather, I have argued that it is in some works of art, and only in works of art, that we are able to perceive the two kinds of perceptual properties required for a plenary experience. So this approach to artistic value will not help us as far as the plenary experience of emotion is concerned, because emotional engagement is not offered as a definition of art.

The second suggestion, developed by Budd, is that the basis for preferring one work of art to another has to do with our finding the experience offered by the one work of art more rewarding than the experience offered by the other.[34] The experience that the work of art offers is the experience one has when one interacts with the work "in whatever way it demands if it is to be understood".[35] This experience will vary from art form to art form, and, within an art form, from work to work. So one experiences a Sibelius symphony as a work of art when one listens to it and ignores the sound of passing traffic outside the concert room, and one experiences a Jackson Pollock painting when one stands in front of the surface that is marked and looks at it from the appropriate distance, whereas one experiences a Henry Moore sculpture as a work of art when one looks at it while walking around it, and one experiences a novel as a work of art when one comprehends the language in which it is written and reads its chapters in the appropriate order. These experiences might or might not be rewarding, and we shall have to consider why one might be more rewarding than another. But in each case they involve an experience of the properties of the work of art. If we find these experiences rewarding, it is because the properties of the work of art reward our attending to them in a particular way. This is a claim about the work of art that possesses the properties, not merely a claim about the experience. If the experience of the properties is rewarding, then it is the work itself that is rewarding, and it is for this reason that a judgement about which work offers a better experience might serve as a judgement about which is the finer work of art.

Budd acknowledges both that an aspect of an experience of art and a consequence of an experience of art might be valuable. But these constitute different kinds of values of the work of art. An aspect of an experience of a work of art might be intrinsically valuable, in which case it constitutes an intrinsic value of the work of art. A consequence of an experience of a work of art might also be intrinsically valuable, but as the experience of the work of art is simply one means to this intrinsically valuable consequence, the work of art has instrumental value as a means to the intrinsically valuable end. Given that works of art can be valuable for various reasons, Budd is happy to accept that they can have both intrinsic and instrumental values. However, he argues that only intrinsic values can serve as the basis for a claim about which is a finer painting or a more rewarding piece of music to listen to as a work of art. A judgement about the relative instrumental value of two works of art will not result in a judgement about which is the finer work of art, but rather a judgement about which set of consequences is preferable. This is not a claim about the experience of the properties of the work of art. It is a claim about a discrete state of affairs that might be realized through acquaintance with a work of art, or by some other means.

In *Through the Looking Glass*, Alice makes the following remark after reading "Jabberwocky":

> "It seems very pretty," she said when she had finished it, "but it's *rather* hard to understand!" (You see she didn't like to confess, even to herself, that she couldn't make it out at all.) "Somehow it seems to fill my head with ideas – only I don't exactly know what they are!"[36]

There is something about the way in which the experience of reading the poem fills Alice's head with ideas that she finds rewarding. She regards the poem itself as "very pretty" on account of the way in which her experience of it seems rewarding.

In *Maurice*, E. M. Forster describes what happened when, late in life, Maurice's grandfather took to reading:

> He took to "reading", and though the direct effects were grotesque, a softening was generated that transformed his character. The opinions of others – once to be contradicted or ignored – appeared worthy of note, and their desires worth humouring.[37]

In this case we are told something about the beneficial effect that Forster believes reading had on Maurice's grandfather's character. But we are not told whether Maurice's grandfather actually found the experience of reading itself rewarding. If Maurice's grandfather and Alice read the same work, they would both have benefited from reading it – but in different ways. Alice found a particular aspect of the experience rewarding (the way it filled her head with ideas as she read it), whereas Forster regards a particular consequence of reading the poem as beneficial for Maurice's grandfather (the way in which it softened his character).[38] While Alice is able to describe the poem as "pretty" on account of her experience, Maurice's grandfather, assuming that he agrees with Forster's judgement, could not make such a claim about it. Alice can say that that is a better poem than another because reading it filled her head with ideas in a way that another experience did not. She can do this because what she values is an aspect of the experience of the properties of the poem. Maurice's grandfather could not say that this was a better poem than another one. He could only say that it had a better effect on him than another poem did. The effect is not an experience of the properties of the poem: it is a separable consequence that might have been obtained in another way. His character might have been softened through the natural process of ageing, or through psychoanalysis, or some other process, and the same beneficial effects obtained. But Alice's experience is only possible when she reads the poem. What she values is a property of the poem.

Alice's experience of an aspect of the poem reveals the intrinsic value of a poem. Maurice's grandfather's experience of a consequence of reading reveals the instrumental value of what he read. Softening of character might itself be intrinsically valuable, but reading a poem is instrumentally valuable when it has, as a consequence, the intrinsically valuable effect of softening the character. The same work of art might be both intrinsically valuable and instrumentally valuable. But whereas a claim about which of two works of art has the greater intrinsic value tells us something about which is the finer work of art, a claim about the relative instrumental value of each is not a claim about which is the finer work of art. It only tells us which has the finer consequences, rather than telling us which work of art has the finer properties, as only an experience of those properties can disclose.

When a work of art offers a plenary experience of emotion, is this plenary experience an aspect of the experience offered by a work of art, or a consequence of that experience? If it is an aspect, then the intrinsic value of a plenary experience will also be an intrinsic value of the work of art. In this case, the plenary experience offered by some works of art would provide a basis for finding those works more rewarding than others. If it is a consequence, then the intrinsic value of the plenary experience will be an instrumental value of the work of art, and not a basis for judging its value as a work of art.

Plenary experience as an intrinsic value of art

Chapter 4 argued that the conditions required for a plenary experience of emotion only occur in our emotional experience of art, and that the artist creates the work of art in order to have a new plenary experience, rather than to reproduce an earlier experience. However, if the plenary experience is to serve as a basis for judgements about which works of art we regard as finer than others, we require something more than this. We are required to establish that the plenary experience is an aspect of the experience offered by the work of art, rather than a consequence of it. In the absence of this, we might be able to claim that the experience of one work of art is a more efficient means of obtaining emotional engagement than the experience of another work of art (or indeed than something that is not a work of art), but we will not be able to claim that it is a finer work of art than the other.

The theory advanced above might seem to resemble Tolstoy's transmission theory. According to Tolstoy's theory, the valued experience is clearly a consequence of the experience offered by the work of art, rather than an aspect of it. For Tolstoy, the perception of the work of art gives rise to the discrete experience of feeling the emotion. Tolstoy ascribes a special value to the experience of feeling the emotion. This valuable emotional experience is a consequence of perceiving the work of art, not an aspect of that experience. How could perceiving the work of art be part of the valuable emotional experience when the valuable experience is said to be a repetition of an experience that the artist had before he produced the work of art?

Tolstoy's account does not provide a theory of the value of the experience offered by the work of art. This problem with the transmission theory is a consequence of conceiving of the work of art as a conduit for emotional experiences, rather than the object of an emotional experience. As a theory of value, it is a theory of the value of an experience that may be an effect of exposure to a work of art, just as it may be an effect of some non-artistic experience. This is hardly surprising given that what Tolstoy values is the emotion the audience feels upon perceiving the work of art, rather than valuing the way in which the audience's emotion engages with the perception of emotion in the work, which is what I have claimed is distinctive (and which we are yet to see is also valuable). For Tolstoy, the perceptual experience of the work of art is discrete from the emotional experience to which it gives rise. The perceptual experience is of instrumental value in so far as it gives rise to the consequent intrinsically valuable experience of emotion. What we are interested in, however, is an account of what is valuable about the kind of experience we have of a work of art, not what is valuable about one of the consequences of having the experience of the work.

It is by now a commonplace that what is distinctive about the plenary experience is its engagement between the perceived emotion and the perceiver's own emotion, an engagement that involves multiple interactions. The perceived externalized and projective properties are properties that are perceived in the work of art. It is, after all, the appropriateness of the appearance of the work for projection that gives rise to a projective property, and our perception of the work as the trace of an externalizing activity that gives rise to the externalized property. So it is an experience of the work of art's properties that is the foundation of the perceptual aspect of the expressive perception of art. There is also, of course, the affective aspect, in which the perceiver feels (in a primary or secondary sense) the emotion that he perceived, responds to it with another emotion and participates in an act of comprehending the emotion. It is not one or other of the perceptual or affective aspects of the experience of emotional engagement that is valuable, but the engagement between the two aspects of the experience.

Given that this engagement involves a special way of experiencing the actual properties of the work of art, the plenary experience must be an aspect of the experience offered by the properties of the work of art. It cannot be a consequence of the experience offered by the work of art since it involves how we perceive the work of art. Unlike Tolstoy's account, the plenary experience is not a case of a perceptual experience triggering a discrete affective experience. It is a twofold experience in which a perceptual aspect engages with an affective aspect. In this way, we are justified in regarding the plenary experience as intrinsic to the experience of the work of art. Even if we could conceive of having the affective aspect of a particular instance of the expressive perception of art in isolation from the perceptual aspect, we cannot conceive of having the plenary experience as an experience separable from the experience of perceiving the emotional properties, for the plenary experience describes a certain relationship between the perceptual and the affective.

Once the plenary experience is regarded as an aspect of the experience offered by the properties of the work of art, the value of emotional engagement can be regarded as an intrinsic value of the work of art itself. So it can now serve as the basis for judgements about which of two works of art is finer: the work of art that offers emotional engagement is finer than the one that does not. This is a claim about which is a finer work of art, not a claim about which experience has better consequences.

In Chapter 4 we considered two illustrations of the plenary experience of emotion: listening to Elgar's Cello Concerto and looking at Manet's *Woman with a Parrot*. We are now in a position to determine not only what is distinctive about these experiences, but why they are valuable and why one might value the works of art accordingly. Listening to the Cello Concerto involves all the parts of the listener's emotional economy being engaged with the emotion he hears in the music. This emotional engagement enables the listener to feel at home in the world while he is listening to the music. So we find that the contribution that listening to Elgar's Cello Concerto makes to the good life is that, for a few minutes, the listener's emotional participation in the world is complete. When we look at *Woman with a Parrot* with the aid of an internal spectator, as Wollheim suggests, looking at the painting also offers the possibility of interactions with both our emotional activity and passivity, and thus the possibility of a plenary experience of emotion. While we are absorbed in looking at the painting in this way, our emotional activity and passivity are engaged with the emotion we perceive in the world, and again we are at home in the world. As in the case of listening to the Cello Concerto, the emotional engagement we have when looking at the picture contributes to the good life by making us at home in the world.

This much allows us to judge that a work of art that offers a plenary experience is finer than a work of art that does not offer it.[39] But what of two works of art that both offer a plenary experience? Are we able to say that one of these is finer than the other? Perhaps there is some other artistic value that the experience of one has in addition to its plenary experience. But setting that possibility aside, is it possible to prefer one work of art to another on the basis that, although both offer a plenary experience, one offers a better plenary experience of emotion? Either we have a plenary experience of emotion or we do not. An experience that does not quite manage to engage both the perceiver's emotional activity and passivity is not a plenary experience at all. So we cannot say that although two works offer a plenary experience, one is "more plenary" than the other.

However, I might find that although it is possible for me to have a plenary experience when I listen to "La Cathédrale Engloutie" from Debussy's *Préludes*, I prefer the one I have when I listen to the first movement of Elgar's Cello Concerto. So I might prefer the concerto to the prelude as a work of art. A plenary experience involves experiencing both externalized and projective properties in the work of art. There need not be any special relationship between the externalized and projective emotion: a plenary experience is possible even if the externalized and projective emotions seem to be arbitrarily related.

Certain plenary experiences might, however, involve the perception of complementary externalized and projective emotional properties. We might perceive in the work emotions that are subtly different, which reinforce one another in an interesting way that gives rise to a highly focused experience. The appeal of Elgar's concerto over Debussy's prelude might be that, although both offer a plenary experience, the externalized and projective emotions that I experience in the concerto movement not only enable me to be at home in the world, but in doing so give me a highly focused experience of loss and nostalgia. I might also feel at home in the world when I listen to the prelude, but if the externalized and projective emotions seem to be only arbitrarily related, I might prefer the more focused experience of being at home in the world that the concerto offers. Leaving Debussy aside, we might say that the apprentice acquires the ability to imbue his creation with externalized and projective properties without having acquired the ability to control this technique in the way that the master does. The great artist is one who has the insight to select projective properties that complement the externalized ones. This might be what Wollheim has in mind when he speaks of the psychological achievement that is the development of an artist's individual style.[40]

The artist's achievement might be in the convergence of externalized and projective properties, but it might also be in the deliberate divergence. In "Une charogne", Baudelaire provides an account of a lover reminiscing with his mistress about an experience in which they discovered a rotting corpse by a bend in the path.[41] The poem might be deemed to be obscene on account of the way in which it seems to involve both sexual arousal and revulsion. But this is a quality that, it has been noted, might be an aesthetic virtue.[42] If the poem were thought to offer a plenary experience of emotion, one way of analysing the relationship between the conflicting emotions might be to say that we perceive externalized sexual lust and projective revulsion. In this case there is no convergence between the projective and externalized emotions, and yet we might regard this as a highly successful work of art because the divergence is not arbitrary. The poet has deliberately created a work of art that offers a plenary experience involving a creative emotional tension. One reason that we might prefer this emotional tension to an arbitrary divergence of perceived emotion is that there is a sophisticated relationship between the two perceived emotions. Through communication, we might experience the externalized sexual lust with a different emotion, one that complements the conflicting projective emotion. In this way, the tension that occurs in the plenary experience is something to be appreciated, and the work is to be preferred to one that has an arbitrary divergence of emotions in the plenary experience. Again, the artist's genius is to be found in what his individual style enables him to do with plenary experience.

So while I value Debussy's prelude for the plenary experience that it offers, I might prefer Elgar's concerto to Debussy's prelude on account of my finding that the concerto's plenary experience offers a focused experience of yearning for the past, whereas I find the emotions with which I engage in my experience of the prelude to be arbitrary. I might also prefer Schoenberg's *Pierrot lunaire* to Debussy's prelude. In this case it is not because the plenary experience involves converging emotions, but because of the creative tension in the plenary experience. Schoenberg's setting of Giraud's poems results in songs that are full of ambiguities, which juxtapose opposing emotions. One analysis of such a situation is to suggest that a certain externalized emotion is perceived in the music and an opposing projective property. Part of the success of the music might then be the way in which our experience of the opposing externalized and projective properties is harmonized through the emotional response to the externalized property complementing the projective property. In this case I might prefer the plenary experiences offered by both Elgar's concerto and Schoenberg's songs to that offered by Debussy's prelude, even though I prefer them for different reasons.

You might agree that all three pieces of music offer plenary experiences. However, whereas I respond positively to the externalized emotion that I perceive in the concerto, you might respond with a different, negative emotion. In this case, although you have a plenary experience, your emotional experience of the concerto is not as convergent as mine is. So you might prefer the emotional tension of the songs to the experience offered by the concerto. We can agree that all three are valuable in virtue of the plenary experience that we have when we listen to them, but still disagree about which plenary experience we prefer, depending whether the plenary experience seems to involve arbitrary emotions, converging emotions or a creative tension between divergent emotions. In this way, we have two different reasons why we might prefer some plenary experiences to others. This analysis has an advantage over Collingwood's analysis: whereas he can only say why we prefer successful works of art to unsuccessful ones, the theory of plenary experience allows us to say why we might prefer some successful works to other successful works, while still valuing the less successful works for the plenary experience that they offer.[43]

We can contrast these plenary experiences with other valuable experiences that do not offer emotional engagement. In Chapter 3, attending a football match was an example of an experience in which spectators become infected by the collective euphoria that surrounds them. The spectators can perceive the externalized property of euphoria in the crowd, but not a projective property of euphoria: they do not perceive something inanimate that has an appearance appropriate to sustain a projective property. So the spectators' experience cannot involve a plenary experience, and, although it might be valuable for other reasons, it cannot succeed in making us at home in the world. Similarly, a walk through the Lake District might be an enjoyable experience that enriches our lives. The hiker who arrives at Wast Water might perceive an ominous pensiveness in Scafell Pike, with its peak shrouded in mist and its desolate base strewn with scree all the way to the shoreline and beyond, penetrating further down into the unseen depths of the region's deepest lake. Such an experience of a projective property might be valuable for the experience of correspondence of emotion that it offers. But, again, whatever value it has, it is not the value of emotional engagement, because the hiker is not able to communicate with the emotion he perceives. These are examples of valuable experiences that are pleasurable in part because of the emotional experience they offer, albeit one that does not enable the subject to feel at home in the world. There are other pleasurable experiences, such as eating a good meal, which are also potentially pleasurable, although they do not involve perceiving emotion in any sense. Experiences in which it is not possible to perceive emotional properties, or only possible to perceive one kind of emotional property, have the potential to be pleasurable, but not the potential to make us at home in the world. Hence they are valuable, but not in the way that art is.

We can contrast these experiences with the experience of listening to muzak in an elevator on the way up to a doctor's surgery, or looking at a framed photograph of a Bakelite radio in the doctor's waiting room. The muzak and the photograph both have the potential to bear externalized and

155

projective properties, and yet their blandness means that we do not perceive either kind of property in them. In a sense, these experiences are similar to those of the spectator, hiker and gourmand. All fail to offer a plenary experience. But the difference is that whereas the match, the mountain and the meal do not have the potential to offer plenary experiences, the muzak and the medic's photograph do. They fail to realize their potential and, as such, their value as art is diminished.

We can say that Elgar's concerto is finer music than the muzak, and Manet's painting a finer picture than that in the waiting room. Like the other things, the muzak and the photograph might be valuable in their own way. But unlike the others, they might also be valuable as works of art. Their failure to offer emotional engagement can be seen as a basis for claiming they are inferior works of art. Emotional engagement is a value that we can say some fine works of art realize and inferior works of art fail to realize, although they have the potential to do so, but which other sources of pleasure do not have the potential to realize. Not only is the value of plenary experience unique to art, but the discussion of Elgar's Cello Concerto and Manet's paintings demonstrates that the theory of plenary experience applies across the art forms. This confirms our earlier claim that the plenary experience is a possibility of all art and so offers a basis for evaluating works of art as art.

This analysis has prepared us to make three kinds of evaluations. First, we have a reason for valuing art over non-art: art offers the valuable possibility of plenary experience, which non-art cannot offer. Second, we have a reason for preferring expressive works of art to non-expressive works of art: expressive art realizes the valuable possibility of being at home in the world, a possibility that is unique to art, whereas non-expressive works of art do not. Third, we have a reason for regarding some expressive works of art as finer works of art than other expressive works of art: some works are arbitrary, whereas others have a creative focus or creative tension.

In Chapter 2, Aristotle's theory of tragedy was discussed as a way of introducing the idea of a composite experience in which the interactions of infection, communication and articulation might constitute aspects of a single experience. We have now seen that the value of these experiences is the emotional engagement that they offer. It will be recalled, however, that Nussbaum takes the value of the audience's comprehension of its own emotions to be a matter of self-improvement, and this gives the experience of κάθαρσις a moral value. Unlike Nussbaum's conception of κάθαρσις, the account of articulation that we have been considering does not suggest that the experience improves the psychological life of the audience by changing it so much as it allows the audience to stand in a new relation to the existing condition. The plenary experience of emotion (which involves articulation) does not make me a better person. Rather, watching the tragedy, like listening to Elgar's concerto, or looking at Manet's painting, allows me to be at home in the world I perceive. The value of this experience is not presented as a therapeutic one. Unlike Nussbaum's theory of the value of κάθαρσις, the value is not now that it improves the way we behave, but that it alleviates a sense of isolation. At least for the duration of the performance, we are offered an experience that allows our whole emotional economy to be connected with the emotion we perceive in the world and thus enables us to be at home in the world. By meeting a need within us as we are, rather than by improving, changing, or refining us into something better, the emotional experience of tragedy can be seen to make a contribution to the good life.

To say that the possibility of emotional engagement is an intrinsic value of art is not to say anything of the other reasons for which we might value works of art that do not offer emotional engagement. Nor does the value of a work of art as a realization of the possibility for emotional engagement deny that there might be additional reasons for valuing such a work of art. Works of art might, for instance, also be valuable on account of what they tell us about the culture in which they were produced, or their place in the history of art, or in virtue of their formal properties.[44] Such values are compatible with the value of emotional engagement. Indeed, we need not commit ourselves to the claim that emotional engagement is the only value a work of art has in virtue of being a work of art. We need only agree that emotional engagement is a valuable possibility exclusive to art, and that this offers a basis for preferring works of art that realize this possibility to those that do not. If we prefer this value to any other values of art, it is because this value is not only unique to art, but is one that makes a supreme contribution to the good life.

It follows from the compatibility of the value of the plenary experience with other possible values of art that pleasure is also a possible value of art. In the tradition of Tolstoy and Collingwood, however, I have been at pains to demonstrate that, however pleasurable the experience of art may be, such pleasure is not the ultimate contribution that it makes to the good life. I have not argued this because I believe that the pleasures of art lack value. Rather, I have endeavoured to show that there is a deep need that must be met if we are to flourish, and that this can only be met by the emotional engagement that occurs in the expressive perception of art.

Conclusion

Broader contexts

Over five chapters we have developed the thesis that art is valuable because it can offer a plenary experience of emotion, an experience in which we are able to escape emotional isolation. As such, we can conceive of the thesis as a claim about overcoming emotional isolation, as a claim about how one might experience art, and as a particular way of thinking about emotion and perception. In each case, we can locate the claim in a broader context. How does the claim about overcoming emotional isolation sit with our intuitions about other ways in which we might overcome emotional isolation, perhaps through personal relationships? (A claim concerning practical philosophy or ethics, broadly conceived.) How does the claim that our experience of art is valuable, because it involves a plenary experience of emotion, sit with theories that value the experience of art on account of its disinterested nature or hedonistic tone? (A claim to be considered in the context of historical approaches to artistic value.) How seriously is the thesis threatened if one rejects certain aspects of the psychoanalytically informed theory of an emotional economy involving psychologically real mental states and mental dispositions, their activity and passivity, and our capacities to perceive things as being suitable to project such emotions onto? (A claim about theory of mind and psychology.) It remains to investigate the implications for the thesis that we have developed when we locate it within these broader debates in practical philosophy, aesthetics and theory of mind.

Emotion, perception and complex projection

In developing my claims about the nature of our experience of art, what is distinctive about it and why this is valuable, I have proposed that we should think about our own emotions and our awareness of emotion in the world in a manner that might seem to some readers to be idiosyncratic, if not unacceptable. There are at least three points at which one might be concerned about my approach to issues in the theory of mind.

First, the theory of emotional economy might be thought to offer an inadequate ontology of emotion. Although not intended to provide an ontology of emotion, this account of emotion as an economy of parts, however unsatisfactory it might seem in some quarters, can be seen as a way of responding to the kind of concerns that Jesse Prinz suggests, in his recent *Gut Reactions*, that a theory of emotion must address.[1] He argues that the state of contemporary philosophy of emotion requires a theory of emotion to propose solutions to what he calls the "problem of parts" and the "problem of plenty". The problem of parts arises when, like Aristotle in the *Rhetoric*, one realizes that there are a number of components of emotional experiences, each of which might, for different reasons, be identified as the essential feature of emotion. The problem of plenty then arises when, rather than trying to choose between these different parts, one endeavours to provide an account that incorporates them all. Prinz provides his own solution to these two problems and would, no doubt, reject mine. Even so, one can see that the emotional economy speaks to the problems he identifies in the contemporary philosophical study of emotion.

The emotional economy is a solution to the problems of parts and plenty that draws heavily on folk psychology, or what Wollheim describes as the repsychologization of mental phenomena. Contemporary philosophers of mind may well argue that this is not the best way to provide an account of the mind. Yet they will concede that it is the way that we do conceive of the mind in our ordinary life. I have argued that if we want to understand the emotional properties that artists invest in their works of art, we need to work with the artists' own conception of emotion. That conception is nothing more remarkable than the folk psychology that we all embrace in ordinary life. This approach might not be appropriate if our aim were to provide a theory of mind. But it is an appropriate response to the problem of parts and the problem of plenty when we seek to provide a theory of artistic experience. When investigating an experience that employs a false theory, an account of that experience might quite properly make use of the false theory that is part of the experience under investigation when providing an analysis of that experience.

Second, there is a tendency to think that the philosophical problem of expression needs to be resolved either in terms of perception or affect: the problem is fundamentally a matter of determining whether we require a discrete account of our awareness of the presence of emotion in some part of the world, or a discrete account of the emotions that we experience when we attend to that part of the world. Such an intuition makes my approach seem misguided. My approach emphasizes that what matters is analysing the special engagement between awareness of emotion and experience of emotion. At this point, I do not propose to challenge the alternative intuition. I wish only to point out that there are other intuitions that encourage one to employ a theory resembling mine, when thinking about the emotional experience of art.

That perception and emotion are more closely entwined than we are in the habit of thinking is very much apparent to Collingwood, who emphasizes the intimate relation between sensation and emotion:

> When an infant is terrified at the sight of a scarlet curtain blazing in the sunlight, there are not two distinct experiences in its mind, one a sensation of red and the other an emotion of fear: there is only one experience, a terrifying red. We can certainly analyse that experience into two elements, one sensuous and the other emotional; but this is not to divide it into two experiences, each independent of the other, like seeing red and hearing the note of a bell.[2]

Collingwood attributes our failure to appreciate this intimacy to a habit of "sterilizing" our perceptions "by ignoring their emotional charge", a habit "not equally prevalent among all sorts and conditions of men":

> It seems to be especially characteristic of adult and "educated" people in what is called modern European civilization; among them, it is more developed in men than in women, and less in artists than in others. To study the so-called colour-symbolism of the Middle Ages is to see into a world where, even among adult and educated Europeans, the sterilizing of colour-sensa has not taken place; where any one who is conscious of seeing a colour is simultaneously conscious of feeling a corresponding emotion, as is still the case among ourselves with children and artists. In persons who are likely to read this book, the habit of sterilizing sensa has probably become so ingrained that a reader who tries to go beyond it will find it very hard to overcome the resistance which hampers him at every move in his inquiry.[3]

More recently, Jerrold Levinson has made a similar observation, when he laments that "recognizing emotion in music and experiencing emotion from music may not be as separable in principle as one might have liked".[4] The fact that he does not like to acknowledge that perception and experience of emotion are not separable might facetiously be attributable to his having to write from the unfortunate perspective of a modern European non-artistic adult male who has been conditioned into sterilizing his perceptions of their emotional charge.[5] Such observations encourage us to take seriously an approach that combines awareness and experience of emotion.

Finally, there is the most controversial aspect of my approach: the use I make of Wollheim's concept of complex projection. Wollheim, a Kleinian, develops the idea that the archaic mind's primitive capacity to project its emotions into the world can be used to explain much more sophisticated capacities, such as the ability to perceive projective properties in paintings. This claim requires us not only to be prepared to entertain some general notion of projection, but a very specific notion, one that relies on a rather technical distinction, in order to distinguish between how we project emotions onto other people and inanimate parts of the world. Wollheim's distinction is employed in my theory to explain why we cannot perceive projective properties in an artist's physiognomy, but why we can perceive it in his work of art. This is crucial to the claim that the plenary experience is only possible in the emotional experience of art.

It is particularly difficult to justify these claims to a philosopher who objects to the use of the hypotheses of psychoanalysis. However, the details of my account of projective properties may well seem unacceptable even to philosophers who are not, in principle, hostile to psychoanalysis. The diachronic account of the relationship between simple projection and complex projection is intended to explain why we do not perceive projective properties in other people. However, one might be willing to entertain the idea of projective properties without accepting that, as a contingent matter, we do not attempt complex projection when simple projection is possible. In this case, I should prefer to concede the lesser point and retain a qualified version of the theory. It would be broadly consistent with my ideas to hold that both simple and complex projection are possible ways of projecting onto other agents. In this case, we would be able to perceive projective properties in other agents as well as in non-psychological objects. This is not the position that I have wished to defend, but it is one that I am prepared to accommodate.

Personal relationships and emotional engagement

Whether or not art provides a good means of overcoming emotional isolation, human intimacy might seem like a more obvious way to achieve this. So it is strange that I have emphasized that emotional engagement is achieved through art alone. In arguing that it is only in our emotional engagement with art that we are able to be at home in the world, it might seem that

I have neglected an obvious intuition: that personal relationships can be a source of such emotional engagement and that they are valued for this very reason. It is, of course, a consequence of my theory that personal relationships cannot be a source of emotional engagement. But if our intuitions suggest that personal relationships are a source of emotional engagement, then we should ask whether the theory is incorrect insofar as it neglects this fact.

It should be remembered that I have employed a technical conception of "emotional engagement" as an engagement between the perception of emotion and the perceiver's own emotions. I have endeavoured to demonstrate that the possibility for such an engagement is necessary if one is to be at home in the world. However, it has been no claim of mine that the possibility of such emotional engagement is sufficient for human flourishing: emotional engagement might be one of a host of factors that are necessary for human flourishing. So, while there is a special form of emotional engagement that is only possible in art, there may yet be some other aspect of our emotional life that also makes another contribution to human flourishing and which is only possible through personal relationships.

This is not the context for considering the contribution that personal relationships make to the good life. However, I would gesture at two ways in which they might supplement, rather than duplicate, the contribution made by art. First, there is the more general observation that personal relationships offer the possibility of reciprocity: however I engage with another person, that person can engage with me in the same way, and I can experience her as responding to me. This experience of reciprocal engagement is something that cannot be achieved in our experience of art. Like the emotional engagement analysed above, this might also be necessary, although not sufficient, for human flourishing.

Second, although I have been interested in how we experience the emotions that we perceive in the world, there are other ways in which we might be aware of emotion in the world: we might also form beliefs about the presence of emotion in some part of the world. In the initial discussion of externalized properties in Chapter 2, I suggested that our interest in the expressiveness of physiognomy might lead us in two directions. Our ability to perceive something as the trace of an activity that presses out an agent's inner psychological condition might be of interest to us because it enables us to perceive emotion – a component of a psychological system – in gestures and utterances that occur in the physical world that we perceive. An alternative source of interest, however, lies in the possibility that it might enable us to draw inferences about the inner life of other agents, a life to which we otherwise have only restricted access. The former project, we pursued; the latter, we did not: my interest was in explaining why our ability to regard the activity of pulling a face as a smile enables us to perceive pleasure in the upward-curved lips. We might also be interested in establishing whether our perception of the face pulled in this way enables us to form the true belief that the agent who pulls his face in this way is pleased. Whereas the literature on expressiveness has tended to regard the epistemological issue as more fundamental than the phenomenological issue, I have presented an approach that adopts the opposite emphasis. I have been interested in the experiences that we have when we have perceptions of pleasure rather than the experiences we have when we form beliefs about pleasure.

The difference between perception of emotion and belief about emotion is central to Wollheim's theory of projection. For Wollheim, because simple projection involves a change in our belief about another person's state of mind rather than a change in our perception of that person, it cannot serve as the engine for generating a perceptual property. This is not to say that our beliefs about other people's emotions are not very important to the way we live our lives. They are. But their importance is different from the importance of our perception of emotion in those same people, and in other parts of the world. As creatures that form beliefs about other people's emotions, we might well have needs that can only be met in personal relationships. Such a creature might need to ensure that its own emotional condition stands in a certain relation to the beliefs it has about other creatures' emotional conditions. A proper account of this would require us to explore the significance of a creature's beliefs about the emotional state of other minds for its own emotional condition. This is beyond the scope of the present investigations. It suggests, however, that being at home in the world might involve being able to respond appropriately to beliefs about other people's emotions as well as being able to engage with the emotions that we perceive in the world.

My analysis precludes the possibility of emotional engagement through personal relationships because emotional engagement occurs in the plenary experience of emotion. The plenary experience involves the perception of projective properties. These properties require complex projection, which I have argued does not occur in our experience of other people. However, in the previous section, I conceded that some readers might reject the reasoning that supports this claim. They might hold that, since complex projection enables us to perceive projective properties, it enables us to perceive them equally in the inanimate world and in other agents. If this qualified position is embraced, the foregoing argument does not preclude the possibility of my narrow sense of emotional engagement in the case of personal relationships. In this case, aside from whatever other value personal relationships might have, they are also valuable in virtue of their ability to make us at home in the world, as I have argued that only art does. On this analysis, the plenary experience of emotion is exemplified by art, as I have suggested, but it is not unique to art.[6]

Value of art and personal relationships

As his epigraph to *Howards End*, E. M. Forster takes the words "only connect ...". Throughout the novel, he explores the different ways in which we can connect with people and places. He has Margaret explain to her future husband about her protégé, Mr Bast:

> "We want to show him how he may get upsides with life. As I said, either friends or the country, some" – she hesitated – "either some very dear person or some very dear place seems necessary to relieve life's daily grey, and to show that it is grey. If possible, one should have both."[7]

We find here the idea that one can connect with the world either through another person or through a place. Forster might be claiming that it is important for human flourishing that one has a particular kind of connection, and that one can make that connection equally well with a person or a place. He might also be saying, however, that there is one kind of important connection that we make with a person, and another kind of important connection that we make with a place, both of which make a positive contribution to human flourishing. But for Forster, ideally, we should have connections both with people and places. This suggests to me that he regards both connections as desirable because they represent different ways of connecting – or engaging – with the world: two ways of engaging that meet different emotional needs.

Even if Forster is concerned with two kinds of connection, there is nothing to suggest that he is distinguishing between aesthetic experience and practical experience. It is more likely that he is interested in two kinds of practical experience. However, we have been investigating the contribution that our connection with a work of art can make to how we live our lives. So whereas he is interested in engagement with a place, I am concerned with an engagement with a work of art (which might include a place), and I ask the same question about our connection with a person or a work of art that I have asked about Forster's connection with a person or a place.[8] As in the novel, I think that human flourishing requires us to connect with both people and art because we connect with them in different ways, and these make different contributions to human flourishing.

My inkling is that we are able to form different kinds of connections with people and works of art. I have endeavoured to provide an account of an engagement that is possible with a work of art, and have only gestured at the kind of relationship that might be unique to our experience of other people. Given that there is a difference between the two kinds of relationship, it is also conceivable, as I have suggested, that they are valuable to us for different reasons. In this way, the intuition that human flourishing involves connecting with art and people in different ways is compatible with the claim that complex projection is possible in one case but not the other. So a general theory of the good life would have to take account not only of the special contribution that the emotional experience of art makes to our lives, but also the complementary contribution that personal relationships make to life, although the latter has been beyond the scope of the present investigations. Furthermore, given the importance of art and personal relationships for human flourishing, we would ultimately want a political theory to explain how society can be structured in a way that promotes opportunities for its members to overcome emotional isolation through art and personal relationships and thereby flourish.

An alternative intuition, however, would suggest that there is only one way in which we form emotional connections with both people and works of art. In this case, we would not have a reason for arguing that the experiences make different contributions to human flourishing, and the value of the emotional experience of art might also be the value of the emotional experience of humanity. This intuition is compatible with the claim that complex projection is possible in both contexts, and, consequently, that we can perceive both projective and externalized properties in physiognomy and art indiscriminately. In this case, perhaps art offers the possibility of an education in the kind of meaningful engagement that we can have with the world: a preparation, perhaps, for more significant engagements with other people.

Now we have drawn together the alternative positions on complex projection and the value of personal relationships. You might share my intuition that we form different relationships with a work of art and another person, and that these relationships are valuable for different reasons, but reject my attempt to account for this in terms of complex projection. My solution might seem obscure, but, like Wollheim, "I set out to consider the phenomenon of expression, and our experience of it" and find that one factor of this experience, projection, stands out as offering an explanation "which, for all the obscurity that attaches to it, seems to have support in evidence".[9] If the explanation seems not merely obscure but lacking in evidence, then there is a need to look for something else that can account for the intuition.

Disinterestedness and hedonism

Even assuming that it is only in art that we have a plenary experience of emotion, we must still address the fact that, historically, this has not been identified as the salient feature of our experience of art. Rather, we find a tradition that contains at least two other approaches that offer competing analyses of the experience of art, each pointing to a different way in which we might take pleasure in art. One analysis emphasizes the disinterested nature of the experience; the other, the hedonistic. Neither of these approaches accounts for the kind of value that I have argued that the experience of art has: an experience that is valuable on account of the emotional engagement between what is perceived in the object and what is felt by the subject. If the analysis in terms of emotional engagement is correct, why has it been ignored by the tradition?

The first approach that we can identify in the tradition distinguishes between two ways in which we might attend to an object: the ordinary "interested" attention of practical life, and the special "disinterested" attention that we can take in an object in aesthetic contemplation. The special pleasure of the disinterested experience is then analysed. The idea that a subject might attend to an object without having regard for the subject's own interests was reintroduced into philosophy in the eighteenth century by the third Earl of Shaftesbury, and finds its most sophisticated treatment in Kant's *Third Critique*, although it has remained a persistent approach into the twentieth century.[10] We take disinterested pleasure in an object when we do not have regard for our own interest in the object (e.g. our desire that it exist), but simply take pleasure in the fact that it exists (as opposed to delighting in how its existence gratifies us). Such theorists are concerned with providing an account of how we eliminate our own interest in the object from our engagement with the object and what is pleasurable about engaging with an object in this way.[11] For Kant, this is *Vergnügen ohne Begehren*: the pleasure without desire that we take in the form of an object when we make a judgement without concepts about the form of the object.

The second approach within the tradition concentrates more on the aesthetic state of creation rather than appreciation. This aesthetic state is *Rausch*, a form of rapture that Nietzsche regards as a state of increased force and plenitude. It is continuous with other experiences of excitability, including the original state of *Rausch*, sexual arousal, as well as feasting, victory, cruelty, destruction, springtime and the influence of narcotics.[12] It is a state in which there is teeming of the will, rather than a diminution of the significance of the will. The thrill of such a state is one of gratification. Thus, we might draw a contrast between conceiving of the aesthetic state as *Rausch* and as *Vergnügen ohne Begehren*. On the one conception, it is the pleasure of the artist—hedonist who finds himself in a state that is pleasurable in its magnification of his own willing; on the other conception, the pleasure is one that comes from engaging with the work of art independently of any attempt at, or even contemplation of, satisfying one's own desires.[13]

So we find in this tradition markedly different conceptions of the experience of art. But they share a common preoccupation with pleasure: they differ in their conception of the kind of pleasure we take in art, but they are both interested in establishing what is pleasurable about the experience of art. So we might say that this tradition has been concerned with the pleasures of art. It would hardly be surprising to find that a tradition that is concerned with the pleasures of art has not entertained a theory that emphasizes the value of some aspect of the experience of art other than pleasure.[14] It has been no claim of mine that the plenary experience is pleasurable: it may be, but it might also give rise to unpleasant experiences that are not otherwise possible. So, a tradition concerned with understanding the pleasures offered by the experience of art would not consider the significance of the plenary experience offered by art.

To appreciate the significance of the emotional experience of art, as I have described it, requires a broadening of the interest that we take in the experience of art beyond a preoccupation with pleasure. We ought not to assume that the pleasures offered by the experience of art exhaust the value of the experience offered by art. The theory of plenary experience makes a contribution to our understanding of the values of art, not a contribution to our understanding of the pleasures of art. The pleasures of art, such that they are, might constitute some of the values of art. But I have sought to demonstrate that art has a value independent of the pleasure we might derive from it. At least on my analysis, any pleasure of plenary experience is incidental to its value: what matters is the emotional engagement that it offers. Whatever the correct analysis of the pleasure of art is, it would be wrong to assume that pleasure exhausts artistic value. It would also be wrong to expect that a tradition concerned with understanding the pleasures of art would entertain a theory such as the one developed in this thesis.

One valuable possibility of art

Assuming that the value of the experience of art might be explained in terms of *Rausch* or *Vergnügen ohne Begehren*, how are we to reconcile such accounts with the account in terms of plenary experience of emotion? It might be thought that an advocate of artistic value in terms of emotional engagement must disprove these other value claims in order to ensure that his prevails. However, as I have developed the theory, it is compatible with the possibility that there are other ways in which a work of art might be valuable as art.

In Chapter 4, the plenary experience was introduced as a possibility that might occur in art, but not otherwise. It was asserted neither that such an experience is possible in every work of art, nor that something has to offer the experience in order to count as a work of art. The point was simply that the plenary experience is an experience that is made possible by the special conditions of art, and a possibility that was shown to be a valuable one in the following chapter. The fact that a work of art might realize one valuable possibility does not mean that it might not also offer other valuable possibilities for experience.

Claiming that we achieve emotional engagement in our experience of some works of art does not require us to deny that a disinterested or hedonistic experience of other works of art, or indeed of the same work of art, is also possible. Nor does it require us to deny that some works have artistic value in virtue of the disinterested or hedonistic experience they offer. That would be necessary if it were argued that there can only be one basis for valuing works of art as art. If one were to subscribe to such a view, then it would be necessary to demonstrate why any competing theories of artistic value are incorrect. However, to claim that art is valuable to us because works of art alone have the potential to offer a plenary experience does not require us to argue that this is the exclusive basis for regarding one work of art as finer than another. There may be different kinds of experiences that a single work of art offers, all of which are valuable for different reasons.

We should ultimately want a comprehensive catalogue of all the possible ways that we can experience the properties of a work of art. This would provide us with a catalogue of the different kinds of experiences that count as artistic values. We could then investigate the relationship between these values and determine whether they are compatible with one another. The previous chapters have considered only one variety of experience, which, it has been argued, is an artistic value, and so such a catalogue cannot be compiled without further investigations. Once we have this catalogue, we might be able to argue that part of the value of a fine work of art lies in the susceptibility of its properties to being experienced in a number of valuable ways. If a fine work of art does possess multiple artistic values, we would be able to explain why particular historical circumstances have encouraged theorists to attend to one or other of these values, while failing even to notice other valuable ways of experiencing a work of art, such as the plenary experience.

In addition to explaining the nature of aesthetic experience, the history of aesthetics has also demonstrated an interest in understanding the nature of art. It has been no part of my project to argue that art can be defined in terms of plenary experience. However, the theorists I have been particularly interested in, Tolstoy and Collingwood, have both sought to define art in terms of expression. In both cases, they have been at pains to argue that generating pleasure is no part of the business of genuine artists. Although I have tried to incorporate the insights of their respective theories of expression, I have sought to incorporate them into a theory of the emotional experience of art, not into a new definition of art. Accordingly, I do not feel that I need to be as hostile as they are towards pleasure. If art is, by definition, the expression of emotion (or the plenary experience of emotion), then it cannot also be, by definition, the source of a particular kind of pleasure. But if one valuable experience that art offers is the plenary experience of emotion, that does not preclude the possibility that it also offers other experiences that are valuable on account of their pleasures.

Art, life and human possibilities

When we return to Shih-t'ao's masterpiece, *Returning Home*, we can now appreciate why it is valuable to us as a work of art, and why its value as a work of art contributes to our flourishing. Poetry, calligraphy and painting are all art forms that can offer a plenary experience of emotion. Because he employs the three expressive arts as a single art form, a master of the three perfections creates something that it is possible to experience in a particularly intense way. The special value of the three perfections lies in the possibility for emotional engagement that it realizes: complementary plenary experiences of converging emotions and creative tensions that enable us to feel at home in the world.

Human possibilities have been a theme in this book. It is possible to perceive emotion in the world around us in two different ways. It is possible to experience perceived emotion differently: by feeling what we perceive; by emotionally responding to what we perceive; by comprehending our own feelings. It is also possible to experience art in different ways: disinterestedly, hedonistically, emotionally. That we are able to experience emotion in different ways, and that we are able to perceive different kinds of emotional properties in a work of art, enables us to have plenary experiences of emotion. That the plenary experience is one of a number of possible ways of experiencing art, but a way that makes a special contribution to our flourishing, tells us something about the importance of this possibility for human life and, hence, about the place of art in life as a whole and, ultimately, about how we ought to approach the practice of life.

Notes

Introduction

1. For an introduction to the genre from the perspective of a Western art historian, see M. Sullivan, *The Three Perfections: Chinese Painting, Poetry and Calligraphy (the Sixth Walter Neurath Memorial Lecture, 1974)* (London: Thames & Hudson, 1976).
2. For a recent study of Shih-t'ao's oeuvre and the place of *Returning Home* therein, see J. Hay, *Shitao: Painting and Modernity in Early Qing China* (Cambridge: Cambridge University Press, 2001). For his philosophical writing, see E. J. Coleman, *Philosophy of Painting by Shih-t'ao: A Translation and Exposition of his Hua-P'u (Treatise on the Philosophy of Painting)* (The Hague: Mouton Publishers, 1978).
3. Shih-t'ao, *Returning Home* (*c.*1695): album of twelve paintings, ink and colour on paper, facing pages inscribed by the artist; each painting leaf 16.5 × 10.5 cm; each album leaf 21.1 × 13.5 cm; width of double page 27 cm (Metropolitan Museum of Art, New York).
4. Reproductions of the images and translations of the poems may be found in "Shitao (Zhu Ruoji): Returning Home (1976.280)", in *Heilbrunn Timeline of Art History* (New York: Metropolitan Museum of Art, 2000–), www.metmuseum.org/toah/works-of-art/1976.280 (accessed September 2011).
5. The museum offers the following translation of the poetic component of "Gathering Lotus Flowers" (*ibid.*: leaf 6):

> Fields of flowers and leaves fill
>   Ditches full of water,
> A fragrant breeze lingers
>   By a boat gathering
>   lotus flowers;
> Phrases of a tune mixed
>   with the sound of oars
>   striking the water,
> Stir the white clouds,
>   Setting bits of them afloat.

6. In the "ink plays" of Mi Youren (1074–1151), we find the transformation of painting

from a representational art to an expressive art. The importance of the painter's psychological expression raises painting at this time to the level of poetry and calligraphy in Chinese aesthetics.

7. No less an authority on Western art than E. H. Gombrich writes of the achievement in the artistic traditions of the Far East of subtle calibrations that express nuances so finely calibrated as to make the Western painters appear coarse: E. H. Gombrich, "The Necessity of Tradition: an Interpretation of the Poetics of I. A. Richards", in *The Essential Gombrich* (London: Phaidon, 1996), 186.

8. J. Dewey, *Art as Experience* (London: Allen & Unwin, 1934).

9. Much subsequent aesthetics is a successor to this approach even if the way in which this distinction is drawn varies. For a survey of several more recent attempts to distinguish aesthetic experience from ordinary experience (including disinterested experience and distanced experience), and a criticism of each attempt, see G. Dickie, "All Aesthetic Attitude Theories Fail: The Myth of the Aesthetic Attitude", *American Philosophical Quarterly* **1** (1964), 56–66. For my approach to aesthetic experience, see my "Aesthetic Experience as the Transformation of Pleasure", *Harvard Review of Philosophy* **17** (2010), 56–75.

10. The relationship between the emotional experience of art developed in the following chapters, Kant's disinterested experience of art and Nietzsche's hedonistic experience of art is discussed in the Conclusion.

11. For a biographical memoir of Wollheim's life and work, see M. Budd, "Richard Arthur Wollheim, 1923–2003", *Proceedings of the British Academy* **130** (2005), 227–246.

12. That his philosophy is not intended as an exercise in linguistic analysis is evident from his epigraph to *On the Emotions* (New Haven, CT: Yale University Press, 1999), which he takes from Spinoza's *Ethics* (III.d20): "It is my purpose to explain, not the meaning of words, but the nature of things, and to explain them in such words whose meanings, according to current use, are not debauched by the meaning which I wish to attach to them" (*On the Emotions*, ii).

13. For a justification of Wollheim's approach to the explanation of expression in this way, see his reply to Malcolm Budd's criticism, "A Reply to the Contributors", in *Richard Wollheim on the Art of Painting: Art as Representation and Expression*, R. van Gerwen (ed.), 241–61 (Cambridge: Cambridge University Press, 2001), 255.

14. In *Art and its Objects*, 2nd edn (Cambridge: Cambridge University Press, 1982), §17, Wollheim discusses the need for a more generous conception of mind in order to understand correspondence as the foundation of artistic expression.

15. The idea that aesthetics might involve the redeployment of ordinary faculties in a secondary way has associations with Kant's approach to aesthetics. Having explained the cognitive significance of imagination and understanding in the *First Critique*, he proceeds to explain in the *Third Critique* that judgements of taste involve the free play between imagination and understanding: see I. Kant, *Critique of the Power of Judgment*, P. Guyer & E. Matthews (trans.) (Cambridge: Cambridge University Press, 2000). The basic capacities that Kant and Wollheim think are redeployed are different, but there is a general similarity in the approach that warrants further investigation.

16. For a remarkable application of aspects of this technique to his own self-analysis, see R. Wollheim, *Germs: A Memoir of Childhood* (London: Black Swan, 2004).

17. Wollheim, *On the Emotions*, xi–xii.

18. In the Prelude to *Fear and Trembling* (in *Fear and Trembling and The Book on Adler*, W. Lowrie [trans.] [London: Everyman, 1994]), Kierkegaard demonstrates that the story of Abraham and Isaac can be interpreted in four different ways and that these possibilities are all equally valid.
19. J. Lear, *Radical Hope: Ethics in the Face of Cultural Devastation* (Cambridge, MA: Harvard University Press, 2006).
20. *Ibid.*, 5–6, 104–5.

1. The emotional economy

1. For a discussion of emotion in biblical narrative from a novelist's point of view, see the first endnote and related text in Grossman's retelling of the Samson story in D. Grossman, *Lion's Honey: The Myth of Samson*, S. Schoffman (trans.) (Edinburgh: Canongate, 2006).
2. It might be thought that in addition to providing an account of the object of fear, the fear-disposition/instinct and the fear-state, we also require an account of the fear-thoughts. On the analysis that follows, such thoughts are either mental states that form part of the response to the fear-object (along with bodily feelings, etc.), or they form part of the attitude that is at the core of the fear-disposition that brings about these mental states as appropriate responses to the object. Thus, it is not necessary to have regard to a further category in my analysis.
3. Rembrandt van Rijn, *Belshazzar's Feast* (c. 1606–08): oil on canvas, 167.6 × 209.2 cm (National Gallery, London).
4. My use of this painting as an example does not depend upon its being a particularly expressive painting. I have chosen it because the earlier discussion of the biblical account of the subject matter makes it a neat example. Whether or not the painting succeeds in expressing fear in any sense, we can still ask what it would mean for the painting to succeed or fail in this regard; and that is all that is required for present purposes.
5. Pablo Picasso, *Guernica* (1937): oil on canvas, 349.3 × 776.6 cm (Museo Nacional Centro de Arte Reina Sofía, Madrid).
6. J. Berger, *The Success and Failure of Picasso* (Harmondsworth: Penguin, 1965), 169.
7. W. James, *The Principles of Psychology* (Chicago, IL: Encyclopædia Britannica, 1952), chs 24–5. The theory of emotion in ch. 25 was anticipated in W. James, "What is an Emotion?", *Mind* **9** (1884), 188–205. The theory is often referred to as the James–Lange theory because Lange independently developed a very similar theory which was published a year later in C. G. Lange, *Om sindsbevaegelser: Et psyko-fysiologisk studie* (Copenhagen: Jacob Lunds, 1885).
8. In metaphysics, "disposition" refers to a kind of property that persists even when there is no manifestation of it. A disposition is related to some other phenomenon that the disposition is thought to be the power or capacity to bring about. A disposition may be contrasted with a state, which is the manifestation of the disposition: salt has the dispositional property of solubility; sometimes salt is actually dissolved in water; even when the disposition of solubility is not manifested in the state of being dissolved, we might still want to say that solubility is a dispositional property of salt. Similarly, the disposition of being afraid manifests itself in moments of fear, but will persist even when there is no manifestation.

The distinction between dispositions and states is an important feature of Gilbert Ryle's *The Concept of Mind* (London: Hutchinson, 1949). It is a central claim of Ryle's approach that the mind should be analysed in terms of mental dispositions, which he contrasts with occurrences or events. This gave rise to an important ontological debate about whether dispositional properties exist at all, and a significant literature has developed about the relationship between dispositional properties and categorical properties: see D. H. Mellor, "In Defence of Dispositions", in his *Matters of Metaphysics* (Cambridge: Cambridge University Press, 1991), 104–22; and subsequently the alternative ontological positions of D. M. Armstrong, C. B. Martin and U. T. Place in T. Crane (ed.), *Dispositions: A Debate* (London: Routledge, 1996).

Ryle's analysis of mind, in terms of mental states and mental dispositions, is also the starting point for Wollheim's theory of mental dispositions. However, whereas the ontological debate is concerned with "disposition" as a way of analysing a particular kind of property, Wollheim makes quite a different use of Ryle's "disposition". He is interested in the idea of "manifestation" and the idea that some mental phenomena (mental dispositions) manifest themselves in other mental phenomena (mental states). While there are obviously ontological implications about his theory, it is not primarily a contribution to the established ontological debate. Failure to appreciate this might lead one to conclude that he offers a confused ontological theory, whereas in fact he is not primarily concerned with ontology in the sense that Mellor *et al.* are.

9. James, *The Principles of Psychology*, 743.

10. *Ibid.*, 744.

11. Note, however, that this neuroscientific confirmation does not resolve conceptual debate about what "emotion" refers to. For a recent assessment of James's analysis and its legacy, see J. Robinson, *Deeper than Reason: Emotion and its Role in Literature, Music, and Art* (Oxford: Clarendon Press, 2005), ch. 2.

12. Wollheim, *On the Emotions*, 118–28.

13. That James conceives of the impulse as giving rise to the felt state is apparent from his discussion of the instinct of fear of the supernatural, which clearly involves the kind of bodily changes that he identifies with emotion: "[Fear of the supernatural involves] a vertiginous baffling of the expectation. This last element, which is intellectual, is very important. It produces a strange emotional 'curdle' in our blood to see a process with which we are familiar deliberately taking an unwonted course" (*The Principles of Psychology*, 723).

14. M. Budd, *Music and the Emotions* (London: Routledge & Kegan Paul, 1985).

15. Wollheim, *On the Emotions*, 1.

16. *Ibid.*, 1–2.

17. In Wollheim's system, "phenomenology" refers to the fusing of intentionality and subjectivity. Wollheim is emphatic that mental dispositions lack genuine subjectivity (or "phenomenology", in the sense in which I, and most other theorists, use the term). It may be contentious, however, whether he provides an argument for this claim, or whether he merely stipulates it to be so. The claim is recruited in subsequent chapters of this book, and further research may be required to resolve whether this point is argued for, or merely stipulated; and, if the latter, whether an argument can be advanced to defend the stipulation.

18. Wollheim, *On the Emotions*, 13–15.

19. For a discussion of two different senses in which Wollheim seems to conceive of

emotion colouring experience (as a framework through which we interpret the world in *On the Emotions*; and as the fusing of some pleasure or pain with a sensory perception in his writing on expressive perception, e.g. in "The Sheep and the Ceremony", in *The Mind and its Depths*, 1–21 [Cambridge, MA: Harvard University Press, 1993]), see D. Freeman, "The Lens of Emotions: Wollheim's Two Conceptions of Emotional Colouring", *Literature and Aesthetics* **20**(2) (2010), 74–91.

20. Wollheim, *On the Emotions*, 15–16.
21. *Ibid.*, 10.
22. Ryle, *The Concept of Mind*.
23. The functionalist positions have been discussed in the extensive literature beginning with H. Putnam, "Minds and Machines", in *Dimensions of Mind*, S. Hook (ed.), 136–64 (New York: New York University Press, 1960) and J. A. Fodor, *Psychological Explanation* (New York: Random House, 1968).
24. Wollheim regards Ryle's account as providing the "classical expression" of the kind of depsychologized position in contrast to which he develops his own account: see Wollheim, *On the Emotions*, 4–6. In doing so, he does not address the variations in the later functionalist theories of mind, which might better account for what he regards as the important consequences of the reality of mental dispositions, and this omission is unfortunate. However, even if these theories can account for the reality of mental dispositions, they cannot accommodate his sense of the *psychological* reality of mental dispositions. Such theories still cannot accommodate the diachronic dimension of his account that we shall consider below: they cannot account for how the history of a disposition gives the disposition its role.
25. *Ibid.*
26. I have in mind here various approaches to cave paintings as sympathetic magic, which is defined by Count Bégouën as the idea that the representation of a living being is in some way an emanation of that being; and the more recent and highly influential theory of Lewis-Williams that cave paintings provide a world into which a spectator may enter when in a shamanistic state: for an introduction, see J. Clottes, & D. Lewis-Williams, *The Shamans of Prehistory: Trance and Magic in the Painted Caves*, S. Hawkes (trans.) (New York: Harry N. Abrams, 1998), 35, 66–67. For a comprehensive study, see D. Lewis-Williams, *The Mind in the Cave: Consciousness and the Origins of Art* (London: Thames & Hudson, 2002).
27. In an unpublished conference paper ("Wollheim's Freud and the Extension of Ordinary Psychology", presented at "Mind, Art and Psychoanalysis: Perspectives on Richard Wollheim" conference, Heythrop College, 20 June 2008), Neil Manson offers an evaluation of Wollheim's defence of psychoanalysis as an extension of ordinary psychology in the Supplementary Preface to R. Wollheim, *Freud*, 2nd edn (London: Fontana, 1991). For a more extended account of psychoanalytic theory as the extension of ordinary psychology, see S. Gardner, *Irrationality and the Philosophy of Psychoanalysis* (Cambridge: Cambridge University Press, 1993).
28. This approach is at the core of many of the most fascinating readings in R. Wollheim, *Painting as an Art* (Princeton, NJ: Princeton University Press, 1987). For a critical assessment of this project, see D. Herwitz, "The Work of Art as Psychoanalytical Object: Wollheim on Manet", *Journal of Aesthetics and Art Criticism* **42** (1991), 137–153. Herwitz argues that Wollheim's approach is incorrect, or that if one accepts it, it provides only a partial account.
29. In fact, this is unlikely to present a genuine problem for the behaviourists. The

behaviourist contends that our pre-reflective theory of mind is fundamentally wrong, but that does not prevent folk from employing it effectively in their daily lives. Most behaviourists will admit that their daily lives are lived in terms of the same deluded psychology as the rest of us. It is only in their theorizing that they differ from us. The behaviourist's experience of art must be regarded as part of his ordinary life, not part of his theoretical activity. As long as he brings the deluded theory of mind of his daily life to the experience of art, rather than his reflective depsychologized theory, he will be able to enjoy the authentic experience intended by Rembrandt.

30. Note that the general approach that is advocated in this chapter would be rejected by Jenefer Robinson, who dismisses folk psychology's relevance for a theory of expression in favour of a scientifically informed theory of emotion, which she maintains should be the starting point for understanding art and emotion: see the discussion of her theory of emotion as a process at the end of this chapter.

31. For an account of the distinction between active and passive mental phenomena as a distinction between oneself and not oneself, see R. G. Collingwood, *The New Leviathan* (Oxford: Clarendon Press, 1992), §5.49 (ambiguity of feeling), §§8.17ff. (hunger and love) and §§10.28ff. (passion).

32. There may well be limits, however, as to just how much choice I have; see R. Wollheim, "Imagination and Identification", in his *On Art and the Mind* (London: Allen Lane, 1973), 54–83.

33. Wollheim, *On the Emotions*, 82.

34. B. Spinoza, *Ethics*, E. Curley (trans.) (Harmondsworth: Penguin, 1996), 103, P59S.

35. For the recent literature on Spinoza and the phenomenology of emotion, see E. Marshall, "Spinoza's Cognitive Affects and their Feel", *British Journal for the History of Philosophy* **16** (2008), 1–23.

36. N. Eilan, "Perceptual Intentionality, Attention and Consciousness", in *Current Issues in Philosophy of Mind*, A. O'Hear (ed.), 121–202 (Cambridge: Cambridge University Press, 1998), 193.

37. P. Goldie, "Wollheim on Emotion and Imagination", *Philosophical Studies* **127** (2006), 1–17.

38. For Goldie, passivity evidently has to do with phenomenology; however, he does not explain what he means by activity, although he refers repeatedly to the characteristic mixture of activity and passivity. He does acknowledge that his remarks are of a programmatic nature, which require further development. Although he makes extensive reference to *On the Emotions*, he does not discuss the sense in which Wollheim describes emotion as being active in that work (an idea I have endeavoured to develop in this book).

39. For the various cognitivist accounts of emotion, see the landmark works on emotion in terms of belief and desire: R. C. Solomon, *The Passions: Emotions and the Meaning of Life* (New York: Doubleday, 1976) and R. Gordon, *The Structure of the Emotions: Investigations in Cognitive Science* (Cambridge: Cambridge University Press, 1987); as feeling, see M. Stocker & E. Hegeman, *Valuing Emotions* (Cambridge: Cambridge University Press, 1999) and P. Goldie, *The Emotions: A Philosophical Exploration* (Oxford: Oxford University Press, 2000); and for emotion as evaluative judgement, see M. C. Nussbaum, *Upheavals of Thought: The Intelligence of Emotions* (Cambridge: Cambridge University Press, 2001). A convenient survey of contemporary positions in analytic philosophy may be found in R. C. Solomon (ed.), *Thinking about Feeling: Contemporary Philosophers on Emotions* (Oxford: Oxford University Press, 2004).

40. For the most influential neo-Jamesian defences of emotion as a somatic phenomenon, see Ekman's work on expression of basic emotions, e.g. P. Ekman, "An Argument for Basic Emotions", *Cognition and Emotion* **6** (1992), 169–200, and his *Emotions Revealed* (New York: Henry Holt, 2003); Lazarus's appraisal theory, e.g. R. S. Lazarus, *Emotion and Adaptation* (New York: Oxford University Press, 1991); and Damasio's work in neurology, e.g. A. R. Damasio, *Descartes' Error: Emotion, Reason and the Human Brain* (New York: Putnam, 1994).
41. See P. Griffiths, *What Emotions Really Are* (Chicago, IL: Chicago University Press, 1997) for an account of the deconstruction of emotion through a study of the life sciences; and for a distinct critique of the category of emotion through the history of philosophy, see A. O. Rorty, "Aristotle on the Metaphysical Status of Pathe", *Review of Metaphysics* **38** (1984), 521–46, and A. O. Rorty (ed.), *Explaining Emotions* (Berkeley, CA: University of California Press, 1980).
42. Aristotle, *De Anima*, 403a2–403b19. A translation may be found in J. Barnes (ed.), *The Complete Works of Aristotle: The Revised Oxford Translation* (Princeton, NJ: Princeton University Press, 1984), vol. 1, 641–92.
43. Aristotle's treatment of the emotions is spread across the *Rhetoric* (see 1378a20–1380a4), *De Anima*, and *Nicomachean Ethics* (e.g. 1125b26–1126b9). Translations of these texts may be found in Barnes, *The Complete Works of Aristotle*, vol. 2, 2152ff. and 1729ff., respectively.
44. Robinson, *Deeper than Reason*, 59.
45. For a similar proposal that combines cognitive and non-cognitive components in the form of an embodied appraisal rather than a process, see J. J. Prinz, *Gut Reactions: A Perceptual Theory of Emotion* (Oxford: Oxford University Press, 2004).
46. Robinson, *Deeper than Reason*, 61–70.
47. E.g. R. B. Zajonc, "Feeling and Thinking: Preferences Need no Inferences", *American Psychologist* **39** (1984), 117–29; S. T. Murphy & R. B. Zajonc, "Affect, Cognition, and Awareness: Affective Priming with Suboptimal and Optimal Stimulus", *Journal of Personality and Social Psychology* **64** (1993), 723–39.
48. K. R. Scherer, *Facets of Emotion: Recent Research* (Hillsdale, NJ: Erlbaum, 1988).
49. Lazarus, *Emotion and Adaptation*.

2. Perception of emotion in the world

1. E. Dickinson, *Selected Poems of Emily Dickinson*, J. Reeves (ed.) (Oxford: Heinemann Educational, 1957), 19–20.
2. The question might be one that admits of a range of answers in response, but, beyond the range of legitimate answers, there will also be pseudo-answers that are not really answers at all because they do not address the question.
3. The term "communication" might seem misleading if it is thought to suggest either intentional transfer of emotion or communication in the non-intentional sense of motion. In settling upon this term, I seek to draw attention to the sense of communication as interchange of emotion; of one person feeling one emotion in place of, and in response to, another emotion that he perceives in his interlocutor.
4. A translation of the *Poetics* may be found in Barnes, *The Complete Works of Aristotle*, vol. 2, 2316–40.
5. M. C. Nussbaum, "Tragedy and Self-Sufficiency: Plato and Aristotle on Fear and

Pity", in *Essays on Aristotle's Poetics*, A. Oksenberg Rorty (ed.), 261–90 (Princeton, NJ: Princeton University Press, 1992).

6. J. Lear, "Katharsis", in Oksenberg Rorty, *Essays on Aristotle's Poetics*, 315–40.
7. For Plato's repudiation of emotion, see Plato, *Republic*, G. M. A. Grube (trans.) (Indianapolis, IN: Hackett, 1974), 606d1–5.
8. Nussbaum, "Tragedy and Self-Sufficiency", 282.
9. After discussing various examples, Nussbaum concludes: "Forgetfulness, ignorance, self-preoccupation, military passion – all these things are obstacles (fully compatible with general goodness of character) that are "cleared up" by the sharp experience of pity and fear. Is there anyone so good as not to need such reminders, such an emotional house-cleaning? I do not think so, and I do not think that Aristotle thought so" (*ibid.*: 282–3).

   Note, however, that many commentators have rejected this interpretation. Lear, for example, argues in "Katharsis" that this interpretation cannot be correct because κάθαρσις is meant to be beneficial to good people and thus cannot be a matter of moral improvement. As the previous quotation demonstrates, however, Nussbaum takes Aristotle to believe that even virtuous people are not beyond further self-improvement. Despite the objections to Nussbaum's specific formulation, Alexander Nehamas ("Pity and Fear in the *Rhetoric* and the *Poetics*", in Oksenberg Rorty, *Essays on Aristotle's Poetics*, 307), concludes that the approach is a generally acceptable one, and that the concept should be understood as some form of "clarification", "resolution" or "explanation".

10. A. Bennett, *The History Boys* (London: Faber, 2004).
11. This suggests that a sequence of affects can in some sense be a unified experience. For a more sophisticated study of what it would mean for a sequence of affects to constitute a unified experience, and for a criticism thereof, see G. Dickie, "Beardsley's Phantom Aesthetic Experience", *Journal of Philosophy* **62** (1958), 129–36; and for reply to this criticism, see M. C. Beardsley, "Aesthetic Experience Regained" and "Aesthetic Experience", in his *The Aesthetic Point of View: Selected Essays* (Ithaca, NY: Cornell University Press, 1982), 77–92 and 285–97, respectively.
12. We might, of course, use emotion words to describe the physical world without intending to ascribe emotional properties to it: see R. Wollheim, "Correspondence, Projective Properties, and Expression in the Arts", in his *The Mind and Its Depths*, 148–9. My interest, however, is in what it would mean actually to perceive emotion in the physical world. Wollheim, for one, believes that there are some instances in which we genuinely claim to perceive emotion in the world.
13. R. Mistry, *Tales from Firozsha Baag* (London: Faber, 1992), 144–5.
14. W. P. Alston, "Expressing", in *Philosophy in America*, M. Black (ed.), 15–34 (London: Allen & Unwin, 1965).
15. For a discussion of the possibility that physiognomy might reveal something about a person's state of mind, see S. Hampshire, "Feeling and Expression", in his *Freedom of Mind* (Princeton, NJ: Princeton University Press, 1971), 143–59.
16. R. Wollheim, "Expression", in his *On Art and the Mind*, 84–100.
17. Paul Ekman, "An Argument for Basic Emotions", argues that in the case of what he calls "basic emotions" (anger, fear, enjoyment, sadness and disgust), there are universally recognized facial expressions. He has shown that there are appropriate similarities and differences between expression of closely related emotions, as well as between spontaneous and deliberate expressions of the same emotion. A

universal capacity to perceive basic emotions might be thought to support the claim that there is an affinity between a facial expression and a particular emotion, but it might also support the constant-conjunction relationship discussed in the following paragraph.

18. After considerable success in establishing universal ability to interpret facial expressions in literate cultures subject to mass media, Ekman *et al.* proceeded to carry out the same experiments with the isolated South Fore people of Papua New Guinea. Their results were very encouraging, as the South Fore were able to identify the basic emotions of anger, sadness, happiness and disgust. However, they could not distinguish fear and surprise from one another (although they could distinguish these from the other four basic emotions): see P. Ekman, E. R. Sorenson & W. V. Friesen, "Pan-Cultural Elements in Facial Displays of Emotion", *Science* **164** (1969), 86–8.

19. That a marked canvas can be the trace of a manual activity through which an emotion is pressed out is central to Harold Rosenberg's conception of "action painting", in which the artist engages in painting as an exploratory process, and this activity terminates in a marked surface which serves as a record of that manual activity; see H. Rosenberg, *The Tradition of the New* (New York: Horizon Press, 1959).

20. I am inclined to think that "innocence" is probably not a particularly helpful label for what we perceive in a smile, even in a rough-and-ready way. I have retained the term, however, out of respect for the integrity of the Rohinton Mistry story that has informed my thinking on this point.

21. Wollheim's considered position on this topic is to be found in "Correspondence, Projective Properties". Earlier accounts are found in "The Sheep and the Ceremony", "Expression" and *Painting as an Art* (Princeton, NJ: Princeton University Press, 1987). An extended discussion of projection may also be found in his *The Thread of Life* (New Haven, CT: Yale University Press, 1984).

22. M. Budd, "Wollheim on Correspondence, Projective Properties, and Expressive Perception", in Gerwen, *Richard Wollheim on the Art of Painting*, 101–11.

23. The ability to perceive a *projective* property without having first *projected* it might seem a bit tricky. At this point, I want only to suggest that it is appropriate to refer to this kind of perceptual property as a "projective property" because our capacity to perceive such properties in the world is bound up with our capacity for projection. How it is bound up must be investigated below. I shall explain why I believe that, although we owe our ability to perceive this kind of perceptual property to our capacity for projection, we develop the capacity to perceive such properties independently of our having actually projected them.

24. Although Wollheim works with the psychoanalytic concept of projection, his idea of "complex projection" would not appear to have its origin in the standard psychoanalytic literature. Its connection to mainstream psychoanalytic theory seems, at most, to be a gloss by Wollheim on the published psychoanalytic literature, the point not being made explicitly by Freud or Klein, the analysts who most influenced Wollheim.

25. It is central to Wollheim's theory that the property that we project onto other people is the same as the property we subsequently perceive in them, whereas the property we project onto the landscape is different from the property we perceive in it: "The core difference [between simple and complex projection], is this: In the case of simple projection the property that the person ends up believing some figure to

have is the same as the property that he started off by having himself and then pro-jected ... However in the case of complex projection the property that the person ends up experiencing the world as having is not the same as the property that he started off by having himself. It is not the property that he projected" (*Painting as an Art*, 83).

26. Wollheim writes of our deep desire for the world to mirror our own feelings: "And that there is a tendency, operative in us (we are to believe) from the earliest experi-ences, to find objects in the outer world that seem to match, or correspond with, what we experience inwardly. This tendency is particularly sharp or poignant for us when we are in the grip of a strong feeling, but it is never long out of operation" ("Expression", 94–5).

27. W. Wordsworth, *The Poems*, J. O. Hayden (ed.) (Harmondsworth: Penguin, 1977), vol. 1, 619.

28. Correspondence has a long history in Wollheim's thought. For the most extended discussion, which develops and revises some earlier positions (including the account in *Painting as an Art*), see Wollheim, "Correspondence, Projective Properties".

29. For an introduction to the psychological study of synaesthesia, see S. Baron-Cohen & J. Harrison (eds), *Synaesthesia: Classic and Contemporary Readings* (Oxford: Blackwell, 1997).

30. Composers including Messiaen, Rimsky-Korsakov, Scriabin and Arthur Bliss reported experiencing coloured-hearing synaesthesia. However, the experience is rarely consistent between different synaesthetes: whereas Rimsky-Korsakov saw white when he heard C major and a greyish-green when he heard F-sharp major chord, Scriabin saw red and bright blue when he heard these same chords. In *Couleurs de la cité céleste*, Messiaen provides annotations in the score so that the conductor knows the particular colours that he visualized at each point in the score, e.g. brass instructed to "play red" and woodwind to "play blue". See M. Hall, *Leaving Home* (London: Faber, 1996), 107.

31. C. Baudelaire, *The Complete Verse*, F. Scarfe (trans.) (London: Anvil Press Poetry, 1986), vol. 1, 61. This is translated by Scarfe as: "There are perfumes fresh and cool as the flesh of children, / Mellow as oboes, green as fields".

32. This much is not intended to establish any role – let alone a necessary one – for projection in an account of the match between different sense perceptions, or a sense perception and emotion. Mitchell Green, for instance, offers an account that makes no reference to projection. He argues that emotions and sense perceptions may be plotted on at least three dimensions – intense/mild, pleasant/unpleas-ant and dynamic/static – and that we can then speak of "intermodal congruence" when two or more experiences are located in the same position within this three-dimensional space. For example, the experiences of a certain colour, the timbre of a certain musical instrument and a certain emotion might all be similarly intense, pleasant and dynamic. See M. S. Green, *Self-Expression* (Oxford: Clarendon Press, 2007), 178–82. As an account of the congruence between different sense modalities, this might be acceptable. However, when it comes to emotion, the point of such an account is to suggest that we can account for the similarity between perceptions and emotions without claiming that we actually perceive the emotions in the world. I am interested, however, in experiences in which we do perceive emotion in the world. Something more is required in order to explain not just congruence with, but per-ception of, emotion. It is at this point that I suggest that there is a role for projection.

33. It is hardly surprising that correspondence should seem like a somewhat mystical phenomenon given that Wollheim attributes its genealogy to Swedenborg. For Swedenborg's conception of correspondence, and its application in his commentaries on Genesis and Exodus, see E. Swedenborg, *Heavenly Secrets (Arcana coelestia)*, J. F. Potts (trans.) (New York: Swedenborg Foundation, 1978), 12 vols. For an intellectual biography, see S. Toksvig, *Emanuel Swedenborg* (New Haven, CT: Yale University Press, 1948).

34. Wollheim, *On the Emotions*, 78–9. The application of the analysis to this example is mine, not Wollheim's.

35. Note that in the case of the daffodils – unlike that of the children's flesh – the perception is not an ordinary sense perception: it is a more complex form of perception – the perception of a projective property. Whereas Baudelaire's claim is that an ordinary aural perception can match an ordinary visual perception, Wollheim introduces the idea that there is a special kind of projective property that Wordsworth perceives in the daffodils. It might be the case that the sound of oboes, the smell of children's flesh and the colour of meadows all have the same projective property, but such a claim is more than is suggested by the poem, which is closer to the account of synaesthesia. It was for this reason that I introduced the example of *correspondance* before that of correspondence.

36. For Wollheim's discussion of the relation of "fit" in belief and desire, see *On the Emotions*, 46–8.

37. Although Wollheim emphasizes the significance of deeply personal associations formed through one's psychosexual development, he does not preclude the relevance of other associations. For a discussion of the relevance of the other extreme, see the literature on aesthetic appeal of landscapes in evolutionary psychology, e.g. J. H. Heerwagen & G. H. Orians, "Humans, Habitats, and Aesthetics", in *The Biophilia Hypothesis*, S. R. Kellert & E. O. Wilson (eds), 138–72 (Washington, DC: Island Press, 1993).

38. I have concentrated here on illustrating how the object of projection might also be the object of a personal association. One could equally illustrate how, in addition to being an object of projection, a cloud or daffodil might be the object of a cultural or universal association, as well as a personal association, and these might reinforce one another.

39. If I were interested in the conceptual analysis of expression, it might be important to eliminate the possibility that this kind of experience of emotion can be achieved through the introduction of emotion by any means other than projection. However, that is not my project. I am interested in investigating the kind of experiences that might be possible when we engage in projection, an activity Wollheim claims we engage in from the earliest age.

40. Stendhal, *De l'amour* (Paris: P. Mongie l'Aîné, 1822), ch. 2, and the appendix "Le Rameau de Salzbourg". See also Wollheim's discussion of Stendhal in *On the Emotions*, 80–81.

41. Note that, in "The Sheep and the Ceremony", Wollheim anticipates my approach when he suggests that typically the landscape corresponds to a "constellation of mental states" rather than an individual one: "Characteristically a multiplicity of internal states is projected, and along with these states their structure is also projected. A landscape corresponds not to this or that mental state but to what may be called a constellation of mental states" (*ibid.*: 7).

42. This does not establish anything about what I feel when I perceive the fine-grained projective property. For an appreciation of the sense in which I experience melancholy when I perceive this fine-grained projective property in the estuary, we must wait until the account of correspondence in Chapter 3.

43. W. Kandinsky, *Concerning the Spiritual in Art*, M. T. H. Sadler (trans.) (London: Tate Publishing, 2006).

44. Wollheim acknowledges that a theory of expressive perception that confines the perception of emotion to "perceptions which occur in the immediate aftermath of projection" is "uselessly narrow", and, in order to widen the account to accommodate perceptions that are not in the immediate aftermath, he invokes the intimation thesis ("Correspondence, Projective Properties", 153). Earlier in the same essay (*ibid.*: 149–50), the intimation thesis is introduced, in a more general way, as a partial explanation of the special complexity that experiences of expressive perception have, which other related experiences – such as experience of secondary qualities – do not have. In this respect, they are said to share a similarity with the formative experiences of life. However, it seems that the purpose of the intimation thesis truly becomes apparent in the later passage (*ibid.*: 153). It is significant that Wollheim does not invoke this thesis in earlier discussions of expressive projection, and it seems that he introduces it into this essay specifically in order to address the objection that the account would be "uselessly narrow" without it. However, even if this is the reason that he introduces it, we should acknowledge that it is broadly consistent with his psychoanalytical approach, which emphasizes the fact that some other experiences (in particular, formative psychosexual experiences) can intimate their origins

45. Budd, "Wollheim on Correspondence", 105–7. Budd also raises other criticisms of Wollheim's account of expression which will be addressed in the following chapter.

46. In Chapter 4, I shall introduce the analysis of experiences of expressive perception. Such experiences involve two aspects: a perceptual aspect and an affective aspect. The perceptual aspect, I shall suggest, might involve perceiving externalized or projective properties. Or it might be a "perceptual hybrid" that involves both externalized and projective properties. This perceptual hybrid is only one aspect of such an emotional experience. So the reference to a perceptual hybrid here should not be read as being inconsistent with the reference earlier in this chapter to an emotional experience consisting of parts, the sum of which is greater than its parts. That experience, the plenary experience of emotion, it will be seen, involves two aspects, one of which is a perceptual hybrid.

47. L. Carroll, "The Garden of Live Flowers", in *Alice's Adventures in Wonderland and Through the Looking-Glass* (Harmondsworth: Penguin, 1998).

48. As the following discussion explains, this also prevents her from perceiving projective properties in the flowers: they are now things that are ripe for simple projection, rather than complex projection.

49. It is beyond the scope of this book to discuss such matters. However, we might distinguish two kinds of theological positions. If the natural world is the product of a divine creator, it is a creation. But theists who hold this view might still be divided as to whether God creates the world as an externalizing activity, i.e. in order to press out His inner condition. Then there are other spiritual beliefs, such as those held by the Australian Aborigines, who maintain that parts of nature possess their own spirit. If a tree or a mountain is regarded as possessing something approaching a

NOTES

psychology, then it is possible that one might perceive the appearance of that part of nature as a pressing out, or externalizing, of its inner spirit.

50. The aesthetic appreciation of nature *as nature*, and as the natural object that it actually is, is a corollary of the aesthetic appreciation of a work of art *as art*, and as the particular work that it is. The significance of appreciating nature as nature, rather than as art or in some other way, is a central theme of M. Budd, *The Aesthetic Appreciation of Nature* (Oxford: Clarendon Press, 2002), esp. 119–21, 147.

51. D. Hume, *A Treatise of Human Nature*, D. F. Norton & M. J. Norton (eds) (Oxford: Oxford University Press, 2000), bk 1, pt 3, § xiv, 112.

52. For an introduction to the use of projection in the history of philosophy, see S. Blackburn, "Projectivism", in *Routledge Encyclopedia of Philosophy*, E. Craig (ed.) (London: Routledge, 1998).

53. Although projection is perhaps the single most important idea in Wollheim's mature philosophy, he employs it in a number of different ways, without explicitly acknowledging this. The sense in which projection can affect our perceptions of the world through Wollheim's *complex projection* is extensively discussed in this book.

When projection affects our beliefs about the world, it does so through *simple projection*, a capacity that Wollheim hypothesizes, drawing on Freud's discussion of the archaic mind's defence mechanisms. For Freud's account of projection, first as a defence mechanism in paranoia, see S. Freud, *Psycho-Analytic Notes on an Autobiographical Account of a Case of Paranoia*, in *The Standard Edition of the Complete Psychological Works of Sigmund Freud*, vol. 12, J. Strachey (ed. & trans.) (London: Hogarth Press & Institute of Psycho-Analysis, [1911] 1958), 66; and subsequently as a defence mechanism for coping with bereavement, see Freud, *Totem and Taboo*, in *The Standard Edition*, vol. 13, 61–5. For its origin (together with that of introjection) in the oral stage in the development of archaic mental functioning, see Freud, "Negation", in the *Standard Edition*, vol. 19, 236–7.

Projection can also affect our evaluations, and Wollheim's moral theory contrasts the concept of value, which has its origin in projection, with obligation, which has its origin in internalization or introjection. See Wollheim, *The Thread of Life*, ch. 7, "From Voices to Values: The Growth of the Moral Sense" for Wollheim's account of simple and complex projection, and their relation to belief and evaluation; see also the discussion in D. Matravers, "Wollheim on the Origins of Value" (paper presented at "Mind, Art and Psychoanalysis: Perspectives on Richard Wollheim" conference, Heythrop College, 20 June 2008). A discussion of Wollheim's theory of projection in relation to ethics may also be found in A. W. Price, "Three Types of Projection", in *Psychoanalysis, Mind and Art: Perspectives on Richard Wollheim*, J. Hopkins & A. Savile (eds), 110–28 (Oxford: Blackwell, 1992). The difficulty with this paper is that it fails to acknowledge the different senses in which projection is employed by Wollheim with respect to beliefs, evaluations and perceptions of the world. A proper understanding of Wollheim's position requires us to understand that there are a number of different ways in which the mind spreads itself on the world, and the situation is further complicated when different kinds of projections interact with one another.

54. O. K. Bouwsma, "The Expression Theory of Art", in *Aesthetics and Language*, W. Elton (ed.), 73–99 (Oxford: Blackwell, 1954).

55. This debate is structured such that the defence of musical expression as involving the arousal of the audience's emotion is defended at the exclusion of musical expression as awareness of emotion that inheres in the music. For an account of musical

expression of an emotion as resembling the natural expression of the emotion, see P. Kivy, *Sound Sentiment* (Philadelphia, PA: Temple University Press, 1989), and S. Davies, *Musical Meaning and Expression* (Ithaca, NY: Cornell University Press, 1994); and for expression as awareness of a *sui generis* musical manner of expressing the emotion, see J. Levinson, "Musical Expressiveness", in his *The Pleasures of Aesthetics*, 90–126 (Ithaca, NY: Cornell University Press, 1996). For an account of musical expression of an emotion as the actual arousal of the emotion in the listener, see D. Matravers, *Art and Emotion* (Oxford: Clarendon Press, 1998). For an account of musical expression of an emotion as the imaginative arousal of the emotion in the listener, see K. Walton, "What is Abstract about the Art of Music?", *Journal of Aesthetics and Art Criticism* **46** (1988), 351–64, and "Listening with Imagination: Is Music Representational?", *Journal of Aesthetics and Art Criticism* **52** (1994), 47–61.

56. If it is possible, as I suggest, to have plenary experiences of emotion when listening to music, an account of this experience might be thought to displace the existing debate about musical expression. However, it might also be thought to supplement the existing debate by introducing a further kind of experience not considered in that debate. It is sufficient for us to accept that it supplements the existing debate. Even if it does only supplement the debate, its significance is still far greater because this experience is valuable in a way that the others are not: it makes a contribution to human flourishing that neither of the experiences described in the contemporary debate can offer. This value will be considered in Chapter V.

57. F. Sibley, "Aesthetic Concepts", *Philosophical Review* **68** (1959), 421–50.

58. E.g. T. Cohen, "Aesthetic/Non-Aesthetic and the Concept of Taste: A Critique of Sibley's Position", *Theoria* **39** (1973), 113–252.

59. See J. Levinson, "Aesthetic Properties, Evaluative Force, and Differences of Sensibility" and "What Are Aesthetic Properties?", in his *Contemplating Art: Essays in Aesthetics* (Oxford: Clarendon Press, 2006), 315–35, 236–351, respectively.

60. D. Matravers, "Aesthetic Properties", *Proceedings of the Aristotelian Society* **79** (supplement) (2005), 191–210.

61. Although we might note that Wollheim does seem to suppose answers to such questions based on introspection and the hypotheses of psychoanalysis.

62. It might be argued that I am not clear about whether the higher-order ways of appearing and the responses that I discuss are object-dependent or subject-dependent. Such a concern would strike someone coming out of the established debate as a weakness of my work. However, (i) I do not think that it is necessary for me to resolve the question in order to study the encounters between higher-order ways of appearing and responses that interest me; (ii) as it happens, these are not, I suspect, matters that admit of convenient distinction into subject-dependent and object-dependent categories as epistemological concepts might (Levinson's remarks on the topic might be read as gesturing towards such a position); and (iii) the fact that my claims might have particular consequences in other metaphysical debates, or seem inadequate for the purposes of those debates, is not a relevant criticism given that I do not purport to enter into those debates.

63. For an analysis of these issues in the contemporary debate in terms of realism versus anti-realism, objectivism versus subjectivism, and cognitivism versus non-cognitivism, see E. Schellekens, "Three Debates in Meta-Aesthetics", in *New Waves in Aesthetics*, K. Stock & K. Thomson-Jones (eds), 170–87 (Basingstoke: Palgrave Macmillan, 2008).

3. The varieties of emotional experience

1. Some theorists might prefer the more technical term, "contagion". I retain "infection" as this is regularly used to translate Tolstoy's idea, which has been the dominant influence on my thinking about this interaction.
2. For a social history of this phenomenon see B. Ehrenreich, *Dancing in the Streets: A History of Collective Joy* (New York: Metropolitan Books, 2006).
3. L. Tolstoy, *What is Art?*, R. Pevear & L. Volokhonsky (trans.) (Harmondsworth: Penguin, 1995), ch. 5.
4. E. Véron, *Aesthetics*, W. H. Armstrong (trans.) (London: Chapman & Hall, 1879).
5. For an explanation of Tolstoy's use of the concept of "feeling" and its relationship to "thought", see G. R. Jahn, "The Aesthetic Theory of Leo Tolstoy's *What Is Art?*", *Journal of Aesthetics and Art Criticism* **34**(1) (1975), 61. Tolstoy uses the Russian word чувство (*chuvstvo*) in the context of his own theory and эмоция (*emotsiia*) when discussing Véron's theory. Jahn, a scholar of Russian, explains that эмоция is a word of foreign origin that has the same denotation as the English word "emotion" and is more precise than чувство, which is translated into English as "feeling". Thus, the word Tolstoy uses to describe the subject matter in his own theory, чувство, or "feeling", is broader in meaning than "emotion".

   According to Jahn, we might understand the range of meaning that "feeling" has for Tolstoy by first understanding what he means by мысль (*mysl'*, "thought"). He suggests that, for Tolstoy, "thought" should be understood as "anything which may be objectively the same for all persons", and this would commonly include "mathematical calculations, geometric theorems, matters of accepted historical fact, observable natural occurrences and the like" (*ibid.*: 62). On the basis that Tolstoy by implication draws a mutually exclusive and all-encompassing dichotomy between thought and чувство, Jahn concludes that "*chuvstvo* subsumes all human experience which does not fall into the category of thought and includes emotions, feelings, impressions, sensations, intuitions, and … any conclusions derived from any source other than objective reason" (*ibid.*). Something that would usually be regarded as the subject of a thought could also be the subject of a feeling. Jahn gives as an example the statement "2 + 2 = 4". This would usually be regarded as a thought. But he suggests that if it were to become the object of hatred, as it does for Dostoevsky's Underground Man, then it could be regarded as a feeling. He says that as used in *What Is Art?*, "feeling" may include "all human experience, for it is not an entity or a list, however long, of entities, but rather the subjective mode of regarding any entity" (*ibid.*).
6. For the classical criticism of the expression theory of art, see A. Tormey, *The Concept of Expression* (Princeton, NJ: Princeton University Press, 1971).
7. A. Tennyson, *In Memoriam, Maud and Other Poems* (London: J. M. Dent, 1974), 81.
8. D. F. Tovey, *Essays in Musical Analysis: Symphonies and Other Orchestral Works* (Oxford: Oxford University Press, 1981), 75.
9. Budd, "Wollheim on Correspondence", 108.
10. Wollheim, "A Reply to the Contributors", 255.
11. Wollheim, *Art and Its Objects*, 28–9.
12. S. Freud, *Notes Upon a Case of Obsessional Neurosis*, in *The Standard Edition*, vol. 10.
13. See J. D. Velleman, "Identification and Identity", in his *Self to Self*, 330–60 (Cambridge: Cambridge University Press, 2006), 343.

14. Budd, "Wollheim on Correspondence", 108.
15. Wollheim, *Art and Its Objects*, 29.
16. Velleman, "Identification and Identity", 343.
17. *Ibid.*
18. *Ibid.*
19. *Ibid.*, 344.
20. Freud, *Notes Upon a Case of Obsessional Neurosis*, 184.
21. Velleman, "Identification and Identity", 44.
22. Obviously, further work is required to establish the nature of the connection between dissociated experiences generally and secondary experience of emotion. However, given Wollheim's commitment to the hypotheses of psychoanalysis, I believe that Freud's analysis of the Rat Man affirms the reality of the kind of non-dispositional experience of emotion that does not involve a primary experience of emotion, which Budd argues Wollheim's account requires.
23. It is our capacity for complex projection that enables us to perceive projective properties that might infect us through correspondence. According to Wollheim, complex projection also enables us to make assignments of value, which are central to our experience of love. For present purposes, I am interested in the contribution of complex projection to our perception of the world in correspondence, rather than the contribution complex projection makes to our value judgements about the world. Accordingly, the variety of emotions that we might feel in response to the projective activity through which we make assignments of value is not relevant to this discussion. For Wollheim's discussion of the different ways in which complex projection can affect perception and evaluation, see Wollheim, *The Thread of Life*, 215.
24. I shall argue later in this chapter that emotional response to projective properties through the interaction of communication is not possible.
25. In Chapter 2, we considered Wollheim's claim that the difference between simple projection and complex projection originates in the fact that, whereas the archaic mind can project a psychological condition onto something that it regards as another psychological agent, it cannot project the psychological condition onto something that is not regarded as possessing a psychology, and so it projects a projective property that is of a piece with a psychological property, without actually being psychological.
26. John Constable, *Hadleigh Castle, the Mouth of the Thames – Morning After a Stormy Night* (1829): oil on canvas; 121.9 × 164.5 cm (Yale Center for British Art, Paul Mellon Collection).
27. See Venning's discussion in *Constable*: "The wildness of the landscape, together with the turbulence of the sky (more marked in the sketch) are often taken to be an expression of his state of mind after his wife's death in November 1828 ... In fact he seems to have begun the picture before Maria died, and may have resumed work on it in 1829, when the desolation of the scene was consistent with his mind" (B. Venning, *Constable*, rev. edn [London: Studio Editions, 1993], 118).
28. If I talk about the painting being harrowing, "harrowing" is only a placeholder for a far more fine-grained feeling. So I might just as well refer to loss/grief/harrowing/distress, or even the more remote feeling of melancholy. My project is not to offer a justification for the most appropriate label in this context.
29. Wollheim, *The Thread of Life*, 67–9.

30. W. Shakespeare, *The Tragedy of King Lear*, III.vii.
31. The distinction between voluntary and involuntary experience constitutes a crude use of terminology that is useful in so far as it gestures at a relevant distinction, but should not be read as carrying any significant theoretical weight.
32. R. Scruton, *Beauty* (Oxford: Oxford University Press, 2009), 47.
33. Meta-response has been advanced by Feagin as a way of understanding the paradox of tragedy in terms of a pleasurable response to the painful response to the tragedy: see S. L. Feagin, "The Pleasures of Tragedy", *American Philosophical Quarterly* **20** (1983), 95–104. This might get us out of the paradox; however, it does so at the price of arguing that the pleasurable response is not actually a response to the tragedy itself. Just as the pleasurable response that Feagin describes is a response to the painful response to the tragedy, so too, I argue, is the emotional response to the emotion that is aroused in us through correspondence with a projective property in the landscape a meta-response rather than a direct engagement with the landscape.
34. J. M. W. Turner, *Staffa, Fingal's Cave* (1831–32): oil on canvas; 90.8 × 121.3 cm (Yale Center for British Art, Paul Mellon Collection).
35. Turner's quotation from Scott's *Lord of the Isles*, canto IV, section X, in the catalogue of the 1832 Royal Academy exhibition is quoted in M. Butlin & E. Joll, *The Paintings of J. M. W. Turner* (New Haven, CT: Yale University Press, 1984), 198. For Gage's suggestion of an alternative quotation from *Lord of the Isles*, see J. Gage, "The Distinctness of Turner", *Journal of the Royal Society of Arts* **123** (1974–75), 450.
36. See J. Ziff, "J. M. W. Turner on Poetry and Painting", *Studies in Romanticism* **3** (1964), 198.
37. Turner's letter to James Lennox is quoted in Butlin & Joll, *The Paintings of J. M. W. Turner*, 198; and also J. Hamilton, *Turner: A Life* (London: Hodder & Stoughton, 1997), 257.
38. In a letter from Leslie to Colonel Lennox, dated 4 November 1845, it has long been thought that Leslie quotes Turner's famous remark, "indistinctness is my *forte*". However, A. M. Holcomb, who studied the manuscript in the Manuscript Division of the New York Public Library, has established that there is no doubt that the text in fact reads, "indistinctness is my *fault*" ("'Indistinctness is my Fault'. A Letter about Turner from C. R. Leslie to James Lennox", *Burlington Magazine* **114** [1972], 557–8).
39. Gage, "The Distinctness of Turner", 449.
40. *Ibid.*, 454.
41. J. Lear, *Love and its Place in Nature* (New York: Farrar, Straus & Giroux, 1990).
42. For Lear's discussion of reasons as causes for mental events, see *ibid.*, 49.
43. Lear's approach to attitude is closely related to Wollheim's. See Wollheim, *On the Emotions*, 74 n.7.
44. It will be apparent that there is a similarity between my claim that Turner explores his emotional experience of the waves through his painting and Collingwood's claim that Cézanne explores his emotional experience of Mont Saint-Victoire through his painting: for the latter, see R. G. Collingwood, *The Principles of Art* (London: Oxford University Press, 1938), 144ff. I have endeavoured to draw out the basic similarities between Collingwood's theory and Wollheim's. Thus, I have tried to reinterpret Collingwood's insight in a way that locates it in my version of Wollheim's theory of emotion: through art, we can become aware of the mental disposition that Wollheim claims we are not otherwise aware of, and in doing so we comprehend our emotional activity. For something closer to an apologist interpretation,

see A. Ridley, "Not Ideal: Collingwood's Expression Theory", *Journal of Aesthetics and Art Criticism* **55** (1997), 263–72, and R. G. *Collingwood: A Philosophy of Art* (London: Orion, 1998). For an idealist critic's objection to this realist defence, see C. R. Hausman, "Aaron Ridley's Defense of Collingwood Pursued", *Journal of Aesthetics and Art Criticism* **56** (1998), 391–3; J. Dilworth, "Is Ridley Charitable to Collingwood?", *Journal of Aesthetics and Art Criticism* **56** (1998), 393–6; and A. Ridley, "Collingwood's Commitments: A Reply to Hausman and Dilworth", *Journal of Aesthetics and Art Criticism* **56** (1998), 396–8.

45. It will now be apparent that the third example at the beginning of Chapter 2, in which a man grasps his previously incomprehensible emotions through the experience of the landscape, is not strictly an instance of articulation. It was introduced merely in order to direct the reader to a certain possibility without unnecessary complication.

4. Art and the plenary experience of emotion

1. The concept of expressive perception is found in much of Wollheim's writing, including *Painting as an Art*, esp. 80–89, and "Correspondence, Projective Properties". He uses the term in a narrower sense than I do. For him, it is not a paradigm for the different ways in which the two aspects of the experience might interact. Rather, it describes one particular way in which they interact. That interaction is what I have described as correspondence (again, Wollheim uses the term "correspondence" in a narrower sense, to describe the relation that holds between the two terms in the interaction).

2. The importance of adopting an approach that treats expressiveness both in terms of the audience's awareness of emotion and experience of emotion is discussed in Chapter 2 and the Conclusion.

3. This makes good the promise, mentioned in the Introduction,to understand the nature of our experience of art by studying the sense in which it is continuous with other kinds of emotional experiences. This will also be seen to have significance for the subsequent discussion of the relative value of different works of art depending upon the different kinds of emotional experiences that they offer (in the discussion about intrinsic and instrumental values of art and the plenary experience as an intrinsic value of art in Chapter 5).

4. Wollheim, *Art and its Objects*, §18.

5. E. H. Gombrich, *Art and Illusion* (Princeton, NJ: Princeton University Press, 1960); see ch. 11, "From Representation to Expression".

6. For Wollheim's criticism of Gombrich, see Wollheim, *Art and its Objects*, §§28–31.

7. Wollheim's views on the nature of artistic expression shift over time. Here, I am interested in his early position, as represented by *Art and its Objects*, in which he writes: "I shall argue that the concept of expression, at any rate as this applies to the arts, is indeed complex, in that it lies at the intersection of two constituent notions of expression" (*ibid.*: 30). These two constituent notions are natural expression and correspondence (or the perception of externalized properties and projective properties, as I have described them). This suggests that he regards artistic expression as involving both our ability to perceive externalized properties and our ability to perceive projective properties. Over time, the significance of externalized properties

diminishes in Wollheim's thinking, and, in his mature thought, the problem is resolved exclusively in terms of projective properties, with little more than a nod to a possible role for externalized properties; see Wollheim, *Painting as an Art*, 88–89, and *On the Emotions*, 178.

8. I. A. Richards, *Principles of Literary Criticism* (London: Kegan Paul, Trench, Trubner, 1925).

9. The distinction between projection and externalization only maps the distinction between Richards and Tolstoy much more roughly than Wollheim suggests.

10. Note that other theorists have also identified the desirability of reconciling these two positions, but have sought to do so in other ways. Ducasse, for instance, proposes a resolution between these two positions, but not in terms of the different perceptual properties that they involve: see C. J. Ducasse, *The Philosophy of Art* (London: George Allen & Unwin, 1929).

11. Wollheim, *Art and its Objects*, 32–3.

12. In the case of the sublime, it is the very inappropriateness of trying to draw an analogy between nature and humanity that might be thought to give rise to the distinctive aesthetic experience: that a natural phenomenon's size and/or force can be of a magnitude that overwhelms our faculties is central to Kant's concept of the sublime: see Kant, *Critique of the Power of Judgment*. For a critical evaluation of the mathematical and dynamical sublime, see Budd, *The Aesthetic Appreciation of Nature*.

13. Budd, "Wollheim on Correspondence", 108.

14. For a discussion of the freedom that we enjoy in the expressive perception of nature because of the absence of a standard of correctness that determines how we are meant to perceive a natural object or scene, see the last chapter of Budd, *Aesthetic Appreciation of Nature*. This is contrasted with the experience of art where knowledge of the artist's intention limits our freedom by dictating a correct way to perceive a work of art.

15. We should note here a difference between trying to explain two kinds of aesthetic experience in the same way, and trying to explain one kind of aesthetic experience in terms of another. Savile, for instance, argues that aesthetic experience of nature is a matter of attending to nature *as if* it were a work of art. Even though we know there is no artistic intention, we can appreciate it as the realization of an imaginary intention: see A. Savile, *The Test of Time* (Oxford: Clarendon Press, 1982), ch. 8. Wollheim's position here is slightly ambiguous. He rejects the claim that he has subjugated the expressive perception of nature to the expressive perception of art. For him, the capacity to perceive expressive properties is refined through our experience of the natural world. The expressive perception of nature forms the foundation for the theory of the expressive perception of art, the only addition being that in art there is a standard of correctness. However, his analysis of aesthetic attitude in *Art and its Objects*, §§41–4, is very close to Savile's in that he regards aesthetic experience as a matter of engaging with something as a work of art. So the experience of nature is primitive to the experience of art for the purpose of Wollheim's theory of expressive perception, but the experience of art is primitive to the experience of nature for the purpose of his theory of aesthetic attitude.

16. In Chapter 1, we considered an experience in which the affective aspect gives rise to the perceptual aspect; an experience in which how we feel colours the way we perceive the world. This is important for understanding the nature and development of

our emotions, but it is not what interests us when we consider the expressive perception of art. What is remarkable about our experience of art is that our perception of the world can give rise to affective experiences that we did not previously have. This involves our capacity to have experiences in which the perceptual aspect gives rise to the affective aspect.

17. In doing so, we must remember that these concepts of activity and passivity are more rudimentary than the concepts of voluntary and involuntary that were introduced in Chapter 3.

18. We noted that a mental state can, in Wollheim's system, be the manifestation of a mental disposition, but it need not be. In this case, the perception initiates a mental state in the baby that might, in other circumstances, also be initiated by an emotion-disposition that manifests itself in the mental state.

19. See the treatment of the relationship between the roles of artist and spectator in Wollheim, *Painting as an Art*, 36–40.

20. Hall, *Leaving Home*, 1–2.

21. *Ibid.*, 35.

22. D. McVeagh, "Preface", in E. Elgar, *Concerto for Violoncello and Orchestra, E minor, Op. 85* (London: Eulenburg, 1986), iv.

23. Wollheim lists examples of emotions that might be expressively perceived in art, but then points out that what is perceived is really too fine-grained for words: "But note that melancholy, turbulence, serenity, are textbook objects of expression, and they are deeply misleading if they suggest that, whenever a picture is expressively perceived, it is perceived as expressing something as simple as these examples. If I continue to use these examples for the sake of convenience, it is only for the sake of convenience, and it has to be remembered that they stand in for something that eludes the grasp of language. It is unwarranted to think that, as has often been thought, a painting cannot express an emotion or feeling unless that emotion or feeling can also be caught in language" (*Painting as an Art*, 80).

24. Budd, *Music and the Emotions*, ch. 7.

25. See *ibid.*, 127–31, for Budd's application of Walton's theory of make-believe to Elliott's idea that we can imagine hearing a voice in the music; for Elliot's position, see R. K. Elliott, "Aesthetic Theory and the Experience of Art", reprinted in *Aesthetics*, H. Osborne (ed.), 145–57 (Oxford: Oxford University Press, 1972).

26. See J. Levinson, "Musical Expressiveness as Hearability-As-Expression", in his *Contemplating Art*, 91–108 (Oxford: Oxford University Press, 2006).

27. It is unclear whether Wollheim regards projective properties as a distinctively visual phenomenon. In certain places, he seems to suggest that, although it might occur in other forms of sensory experience, he is interested in developing an account in the context of visual experience. In other places, he might be suggesting that it is a distinctively visual experience, or perhaps that there is a distinctively visual way of experiencing projective properties. Either way, it should be noted that my application to aural experience develops the idea in a way that is either an extension of, or departure from, the theory that Wollheim presents.

28. Édouard Manet, *Young Lady in 1866* (1866): oil on canvas; 185.1 × 128.6 cm (Metropolitan Museum of Art, New York). The picture is commonly known as *Woman with a Parrot*.

29. I am indebted to Professor Geuss for pointing out that a characterization of *Woman with a Parrot* as a single-figure painting assumes that the parrot does not count as

a figure. I had noticed this myself. Wollheim evidently regards the parrot as a non-psychological entity, or at least one with which the woman cannot engage. The earlier discussion about psychological agents and non-psychological objects explained that what matters is how we regard the object when we perceive it. We shall persist with this example of Wollheim's in the spirit that he does, noting that others might regard it otherwise, even if a safer course would see us choose a picture in which there is clearly only one figure. Wollheim's treatment of the picture might afford some insight into the artist's project, however; perhaps if Manet had selected a cat rather than a parrot for the composition, we would be required to engage with it as a multi-figure painting.

30. See Wollheim, *Painting as an Art*, lecture III.

31. *Ibid.*, 141.

32. Édouard Manet, *Le Balcon* (1866): oil on canvas; 170 × 124.5 cm (Musée d'Orsay, Paris).

33. For a criticism of Wollheim's approach to the spectator in the picture and its application to Manet, see R. Hopkins, "The Spectator in the Picture", in Gerwen, *Richard Wollheim on the Art of Painting*, 215–31.

34. For Wollheim's seminal contribution to the debate about the nature of representational properties of paintings, see R. Wollheim, "Seeing-as, Seeing-in, and Pictorial Representation", in his *Art and its Objects*, 205–26; and for a criticism of this position, see M. Budd, "On Looking at a Picture", in *Psychoanalysis, Mind and Art*, J. Hopkins & A. Savile (eds), 259–80 (Oxford: Oxford University Press, 1992). I do not propose to enter into that debate. Whatever account is to be given of representation, if it is possible for us to perceive the representation of the features of a face in a two-dimensional surface, then I see no reason why we cannot also perceive the representation of the physiognomy of a face. Accordingly, it is perfectly conceivable that we perceive the trace of an externalizing activity in the woman that Manet has painted.

35. Cf. Robinson's discussion of the way in which the reader responds emotionally both to the characters in *The Reef* and to the (implied) novelist, Edith Wharton, in *Deeper than Reason*, "Part Two: Emotion in Literature".

36. That an externalized property might be perceived both in the depiction of a trace of an externalizing activity and in the trace of the artist's own externalizing activity that terminates in this representation is similar to the sense in which we might hear externalized properties in the concerto both as the trace of the composer's externalizing activity (which terminates in the composition) and as the trace of the soloist's externalizing activity (which terminates in the performance). The traces of Elgar and du Pré's externalizing activities are mutually reinforcing, just as the traces of Manet and the woman's externalizing activities are. Furthermore, the mutually reinforcing externalized properties need not be identical: my perception of Manet's trace of externalized emotion might be reinforced by the perception of a different (albeit related) emotion in his subject.

37. Cf. Wollheim's account of imaginative identification in the theatre in *The Thread of Life*, which was discussed as a possible mechanism for effecting an emotional response in Chapter 3 above.

38. Wollheim, *Painting as an Art*, 160.

39. These issues are considered in the investigation of the physical object hypothesis in Wollheim, *Art and Its Objects*.

5. The value of art and the practice of life

1. When I assert that the plenary experience of emotion's contribution to the good life is the alleviation of emotional isolation, I have in mind a very specific sense of emotional isolation, one that involves the relationship between our emotions and our *perception* of emotion in the world. It may be that there are other forms of emotional isolation, such as one that involves the relationship between our emotions and our *belief* about the emotions of others (rather than our perception of emotion). The good life might be one that ensures a proper engagement between our emotions and our beliefs about the emotions of others as well as an engagement between our emotions and our perception of emotion in the world. Even if this is the case, and it is not possible to achieve both of these through the plenary experience of emotion offered by art, art might still make a valuable contribution to the good life by overcoming one of these, albeit a contribution that needs to be supplemented by other kinds of experiences. For a discussion of personal relationships and the emotional isolation they overcome, and the relationship between escaping emotional isolation through art and through personal relationships, see the discussion below in the Conclusion.
2. The value of the hedonistic and disinterested experiences of art is considered in the Conclusion, as is the relationship between hedonism, disinterestedness and plenary experience of emotion.
3. See L. Wittgenstein, *Tractatus Logico-Philosophicus*, D. F. Pears & B. F. McGuinness (trans.) (London: Routledge, 1961).
4. See A. J. Ayer, *Language, Truth, and Logic* (New York: Dover, 1962).
5. E. Schellekens, "Art, Emotion, Ethics: Conceptual Boundaries and Kinds of Value", *Philosophical Books* **50**(3) (2009), 159.
6. B. Gaut, *Art, Emotion and Ethics* (Oxford: Oxford University Press, 2007).
7. *Ibid.*, 6–9.
8. See L. Tolstoy, *What is Art?*, R. Pevear & L. Volokhonsky (trans.) (Harmondsworth: Penguin, 1995).
9. See M. C. Beardsley, *Aesthetics: Problems in the Philosophy of Criticism*, 2nd edn (Indianapolis, IN: Hackett, 1981).
10. See O. Wilde, "The Decay of Lying", in *The Works of Oscar Wilde*, 909–31 (London: Collins, 1948).
11. N. Carroll, "Art and Ethical Criticism: An Overview of Recent Directions of Research", *Ethics* **110** (2000), 350–87.
12. Gaut, *Art, Emotion and Ethics*, 8.
13. E.g. Schellekens, "Art, Emotion, Ethics".
14. *Ibid.*, 160.
15. *Ibid.*, 160–61.
16. *Ibid.*, 161.
17. For Hegel, the supreme achievement of Greek civilization was that the Greeks were able to be at home in the world because "they made their world their home": G. W. F. Hegel, *Lectures on the History of Philosophy*, E. S. Haldane & F. H. Simon (trans.) (London: Kegan Paul, 1892), vol. I, 150. It is this achievement, Hegel believes, that enables us to feel at home with the Greeks, and more particularly in philosophy (*ibid.*: 151–2). For a discussion of the Hegelian sense in which we have a fundamental (or "absolute") need to be at home in the world, and how art might address

this need, see R. Geuss, "Art and Theodicy", in his *Morality, Culture, and History*, 78–115 (Cambridge: Cambridge University Press, 1999), 80ff.

For Hegel, we are only at home in the world when we are able to reconcile ourselves to all aspects of our world, including "physical, corporate, legal, moral and political existence" (Hegel, *Lectures on the History of Philosophy*, 151). I am interested in something narrower: our ability to reconcile ourselves to one aspect of the world, namely our perception of emotion in the world. Whatever else might be required for reconciling ourselves to the world, and hence being at home in the world, I shall suggest that we must be able to reconcile ourselves with the emotion we perceive in the world. Through some form of emotional engagement, I shall argue, we might overcome emotional isolation, and hence meet (at least one aspect of) the fundamental need to be at home in the world.

18. On this occasion, I am using "response" in a more general sense than the technical one which I assigned to "emotional response" in the discussion of responding to perceived emotions in Chapter 3.

19. Scruton, *Beauty*.

20. *Ibid.*, 65.

21. *Ibid.*, 67.

22. *Ibid.*, 168. For "The Waste Land", see T. S. Eliot, *Collected Poems 1909–1962* (London: Faber, 2002), 51–76.

23. Scruton, *Beauty*, 174–5.

24. Ovid, *Metamorphoses*, D. Raeburn (trans.) (London: Penguin, 2004), bk III, ll. 131–250, 102.

25. It is not that Actaeon perceives the dogs as a hunter does, but engages emotionally with them as a stag does: we are told that his feelings remain unchanged; they are the feelings of a hunter, but he can only act upon them as a stag (presumably he has the hunter's emotional experience but can only act on the emotional experience in the way that a stag can).

26. Mistry, *Tales from Firozsha Baag*.

27. *Ibid.*, 136.

28. This assumes that we are all equally capable of perceiving emotion in the world, and so we each have an equally great need for engagement between perception of emotion and our own emotions. However, it might be the case that, although some people have a particularly acute ability to perceive emotion in the world, others do not. Richard Wollheim, it seems, was an example of a person who was highly sensitive to perception of emotion in the world around him. If other people do not perceive emotion in the way that he did, then these other people might bear a closer resemblance to the first creature than to the second or third. This suggests that although emotional engagement will be a real issue for the Wollheimian character, it might not be a pressing one for less sensitive characters.

If, as I shall suggest, the emotional engagement offered by art is necessary in order to be at home in the world, then it seems that no philistine is ever at home in the world. However, some philistines do seem to feel at home in the world. Perhaps we can accommodate this: people who do not readily perceive emotion in the world might be at home in the world without the emotional engagement offered by the plenary experience of emotion that occurs in the experience of art. This would explain why some people have not valued the emotional experience of art. I shall continue to assume, however, that, like Wollheim, most people resemble the second or third creatures. (That the peculiarities of Wollheim's personality might shed light on human nature is hardly surprising given the insights that he believed were revealed by studying the Rat Man's pathologies.)

29. For Tolstoy, the significance of the experience of art lies in the repetition of an earlier experience, for example: "Art begins when a man, with the purpose of communicating to other people a feeling he once experienced, calls it up again within himself and expresses it by external signs ... so that listeners are infected by them and experience them *in the same way* as he has experienced them" (Tolstoy, *What is Art?*, 38–9, emphasis added).

30. For Collingwood, Tolstoy's arousal theory provides an account of what Collingwood calls "art as magic" or "art as amusement", which are concerned with arousing emotion to different ends (for Collingwood's accounts of these experiences see *The Principles of Art*, chs 4 and 5, respectively), rather than an account of "art proper". He regards "art proper" as a matter of "expressing" rather than "arousing" emotion (see *ibid.*, ch. 6). Note that Tolstoy's "expression" of emotion is Collingwood's "arousal/betrayal" of emotion, which is roughly my "infection" of emotion. Collingwood's "expression" of emotion is roughly my "articulation" of emotion. It should now be apparent why I have avoided the term "expression" of emotion, which has ceased to be helpful.

31. Robinson proposes an account of expression that can be formulated either as an account of what it means for an artist to express emotion in a work of art, or as an account of what it means for a work to constitute an expression of emotion. In either case, there is evidence in the work that a persona (not necessarily the artist) experiences the emotion, and that this evidence is put there intentionally by the artist; that this emotion can be perceived in the work; that the work "articulates and individuates" the emotion; and that the audience is able to get clear about the emotion through this articulation and individuation: Robinson, *Deeper than Reason*, 270–71.

32. *Ibid.*, 272; Levinson, *The Pleasures of Aesthetics*, 106.

33. Robinson, *Deeper than Reason*, 413.

34. M. Budd, *Values of Art* (Harmondsworth: Penguin, 1995), 4–8.

35. *Ibid.*, 4.

36. Carroll, *Alice's Adventures in Wonderland*, 134.

37. E. M. Forster, *Maurice* (Harmondsworth: Penguin, 1972), 122.

38. In addition to this intrinsically valuable consequence, it is possible that some aspect of reading was intrinsically valuable (perhaps he too had his head filled with ideas). For the purpose of this discussion, I shall ignore that possibility.

39. I shall return to the plenary experience's relationship to other valuable experiences of art in the Conclusion.

40. For Wollheim's conception of individual style, see *Painting as an Art*, 26–36. Much more work would be required to establish the relationship between my idea and Wollheim's. It would, however, be a fruitful exercise.

41. Baudelaire, *The Complete Verse*, vol. 1, 91.

42. For a defence of immoral content as a possible aesthetic value, see M. Kieran, "Forbidden Knowledge: The Challenge of Immoralism", in *Art and Morality*, S. Gardner & J. Bermudez (eds), 56–73 (London: Routledge, 2002).

43. For Collingwood, art is a mental entity; it is a matter of expressing emotion through the total imaginative experience. Something that is not such an expression does not count as a work of art. So, for Collingwood, the distinction between a successful work of art and an unsuccessful work of art collapses into a distinction between art

and non-art: there cannot be a work of art that is less successful than another work of art. Thus we might object that Collingwood cannot account for the fact that we regularly regard some works of art as less successful than others without asserting that the less successful works are, in fact, non-art. This objection, though important, has perhaps been overshadowed by a criticism of his idealist definition of art. For the criticism of the idealist theory, see Wollheim, *Art and its Objects*, §§21–3.

44. That the value of a work of art might be tied to its relationship to the history of art, or the social commentary that it offers, is central to the approach of art historians such as T. J. Clark; see, for example, T. J. Clark, *The Painting of Modern Life: Paris in the Art of Manet and his Followers* (Princeton, NJ: Princeton University Press, 1999). On the other hand, the same works might be valued exclusively for their formal properties; for example, Bell's account of significant form: C. Bell, *Art* (London: Chatto & Windus, 1913). Unlike Herwitz's interpretation of Wollheim's approach in *Painting as an Art*, I do not seek to deny that formal and historical considerations might have artistic relevance. The plenary experience is put forward as a valuable possibility, not as the only artistic value. Thus, I avoid the kind of objection that Herwitz raises against Wollheim.

Conclusion

1. Prinz, *Gut Reactions*, 1–19.
2. Collingwood, *The Principles of Art*, 161.
3. *Ibid.*, 162.
4. J. Levinson, "Music and Negative Emotions", *Pacific Philosophical Quarterly* **63** (1982), 335.
5. The reader who has heard Levinson sing jazz, as he did after dinner one evening in my rooms at Magdalene College, Cambridge, will quickly dismiss the uncharitable explanation.
6. Scruton, for instance, has noted the similarity between the pleasure of art and the pleasure of friendship: Scruton, *Beauty*, 31. Gaut, though acknowledging the long tradition of connecting literature and friendship, concludes that the connection is not as useful as some have thought: Gaut, *Art, Emotion and Ethics*, 109–14.
7. E. M. Forster, *Howards End* (London: Softback Preview, 1995), 196.
8. A house, as a piece of architecture, might offer a plenary experience. Likewise, the gardens around a house might offer a plenary experience. For a discussion of the aesthetic appreciation of gardens as art and/or nature, see A. Carlson, *Aesthetics and the Environment: The Appreciation of Nature, Art and Architecture* (London: Routledge, 2002). If Forster's "place" is something in which we can perceive both projective and externalized properties, it might be the object of plenary experience, and hence offer emotional engagement.
9. Wollheim, "A Reply to the Contributors", 255.
10. Stolnitz provides a detailed account of how the third Earl of Shaftesbury's interest in ancient philosophy led him to develop an account of disinterested attention in aesthetic experience via his study of the disinterested attention to the good and God that is commended by ethics and religion: J. Stolnitz, "On the Origins of 'Aesthetic Disinterestedness'", *Journal of Aesthetics and Art Criticism* **20** (1961), 131–43. It becomes an important feature of a number of theories, most notably Kant's: see

Kant, *Critique of the Power of Judgment*, and Budd, *The Aesthetic Appreciation of Nature*, esp. 29–34 on the distinctive pleasure of the beautiful in the *Third Critique*. For an example of the persisting attraction of disinterestedness, see Stolnitz's own theory, in J. Stolnitz, *Aesthetics and Art Criticism* (Boston, MA: Houghton Mifflin: 1960). For a criticism of this particular theory and the whole approach to aesthetic experience as disinterested experience, see Dickie, "All Aesthetic Attitude Theories Fail".

11. An important variation on this approach is found in Bullough's theory of psychical distance: see E. Bullough, "'Psychical Distance' as a Factor in Art and an Aesthetic Principle", *British Journal of Psychology* 5 (1912), 87–98. Bullough observes that we can characterize our ordinary practical experiences as "personal experiences" and distinguish them from "impersonal experiences" in which the subject seeks to eliminate any personal interest, so that he is attending to the objective properties of the object unencumbered by self-interest. His suggestion is that in addition to eliminating self-interest, we can retain it, but put it out of gear by inserting psychical distance between the subject and his interests when engaging with the object. This is not an impersonal experience, but a special kind of personal experience.

There is a connection here with the plenary experience of emotion. The plenary experience is not a claim about whether we experience emotion when we engage with a work of art, but *how* we experience emotion. It is a claim that there is a special (plenary) way of experiencing emotion that intensifies the experience. Bullough's claim about distanced experience argues that what intensifies experience is not the presence or absence of personal interest, but the way in which it is present. Similarly, I have argued that the value of art is not the presence or absence of emotion, but the special way in which it might attend the experience. Unlike Bullough, I have not contrasted the plenary experience with ordinary experience by arguing that the former involves an activity that is not found in ordinary emotional experiences. Rather, I have argued that it combines ordinary experiences in a way that gives rise to a special kind of experience.

12. See various references to the aesthetic state in F. Nietzsche, "Toward the Physiology of Art", in M. Heidegger, *Nietzsche: Volume I: The Will to Power as Art*, D. F. Krell (trans.) (London: Routledge, 1981) (originally published in Nietzsche's *Grossoktavausgabe*, vol. 16, 432–4 [Leipzig: Naumann, 1905]), *The Will to Power*, W. Kaufmann & R. J. Hollingdale (trans.) (London: Weidenfeld & Nicolson, 1968), §§794–853, and *Twilight of the Idols*, D. Large (trans.) (Oxford: Oxford University Press, 1998).

13. Note that Heidegger offers an analysis of *Rausch* that suggests Nietzsche's conception of the aesthetic state should not be contrasted with Kant's conception, which can be read as being consistent with Nietzsche, but rather it should be contrasted with misinterpretations of Kant, most notably by Schopenhauer, upon whose guidance Nietzsche relies for an understanding of Kant (M. Heidegger, *Nietzsche: Volume I: The Will to Power as Art*, D. F. Krell [trans.] [London: Routledge, 1981], lectures 14, "Rapture as Aesthetic State", and 15, "Kant's Doctrine of the Beautiful: Its Misinterpretation by Schopenhauer and Nietzsche"). For present purposes, the correct analysis of Nietzsche is not germane. What matters is that the tradition has – for better or worse – been dominated by two ways of thinking about the aesthetic state.

14. That aesthetic value is concerned with truth, rather than the pleasure of the aesthetic state, is a matter that Hegel stressed when explaining how art allows us to

reconcile ourselves to our world (later developed by Adorno, who argues that art's aesthetic value is concerned with truth, but for him it is the truth that we cannot reconcile ourselves to our world), and in response to eighteenth-century theories of taste: G. W. F. Hegel, *Introductory Lectures on Aesthetics*, B. Bosanquet (trans.) (Harmondsworth: Penguin, 1993).

Bibliography

Alston, W. P. "Expressing". In *Philosophy in America,* M. Black (ed.), 15–34 (London: Allen & Unwin, 1965).

Aristotle. *De Anima.* In *The Complete Works of Aristotle: The Revised Oxford Translation,* vol. 1, J. Barnes (ed.) (Princeton, NJ: Princeton University Press, 1984).

Aristotle. *Nicomachean Ethics.* In *The Complete Works of Aristotle: The Revised Oxford Translation,* vol. 2, J. Barnes (ed.) (Princeton, NJ: Princeton University Press, 1984).

Aristotle. *Poetics.* In *The Complete Works of Aristotle: The Revised Oxford Translation,* vol. 2, J. Barnes (ed.) (Princeton, NJ: Princeton University Press, 1984).

Aristotle. *Rhetoric.* In *The Complete Works of Aristotle: The Revised Oxford Translation,* vol. 2, J. Barnes (ed.) (Princeton, NJ: Princeton University Press, 1984).

Ayer, A. J. *Language, Truth, and Logic* (New York: Dover, 1962).

Baron-Cohen, S. & J. Harrison (eds). *Synaesthesia: Classic and Contemporary Readings* (Oxford: Blackwell, 1977).

Baudelaire, C. *The Complete Verse,* F. Scarfe (trans.) (London: Anvil Press Poetry, 1986).

Beardsley, M. C. *Aesthetics: Problems in the Philosophy of Criticism,* 2nd edn (Indianapolis, IN: Hackett, 1981).

Beardsley, M. C. *The Aesthetic Point of View: Selected Essays* (Ithaca, NY: Cornell University Press, 1982).

Bell, C. *Art* (London: Chatto & Windus, 1913).

Bennett, A. *The History Boys* (London: Faber, 2004).

Berger, J. *The Success and Failure of Picasso* (Harmondsworth: Penguin, 1965).

Blackburn, S. "Projectivism". In *Routledge Encyclopedia of Philosophy,* E. Craig (ed.) (London: Routledge, 1998).

Bouwsma, O. K. "The Expression Theory of Art". In *Aesthetics and Language,* W. Elton (ed.), 73–99 (Oxford: Blackwell, 1954).

Budd, M. *The Aesthetic Appreciation of Nature: Essays on the Aesthetics of Nature* (Oxford: Clarendon Press, 2002).

Budd, M. "On Looking at a Picture". In *Psychoanalysis, Mind and Art,* J. Hopkins & A. Savile (eds), 259–80 (Oxford: Oxford University Press, 1992).

Budd, M. *Music and the Emotions* (London: Routledge & Kegan Paul, 1985).

Budd, M. "Richard Arthur Wollheim 1923–2003". *Proceedings of the British Academy* **130** (2005): 227–46.

Budd, M. *Values of Art* (Harmondsworth: Penguin, 1995).

Budd, M. "Wollheim on Correspondence, Projective Properties, and Expressive Perception". See Gerwen, *Richard Wollheim on the Art of Painting*, 101–11.

Bullough, E. "'Psychical Distance' as a Factor in Art and an Aesthetic Principle". *British Journal of Psychology* **5** (1912): 87–98.

Butlin, M. & E. Joll. *The Paintings of J. M. W. Turner* (New Haven, CT: Yale University Press, 1984).

Carlson, A. *Aesthetics and the Environment: The Appreciation of Nature, Art and Architecture* (London: Routledge, 2002).

Carroll, L. *Alice's Adventures in Wonderland and Through the Looking-Glass* (Harmondsworth: Penguin, 1998).

Carroll, N. "Art and Ethical Criticism: An Overview of Recent Directions of Research". *Ethics* **110** (2000): 350–87.

Clark, T. J. *The Painting of Modern Life: Paris in the Art of Manet and his Followers* (Princeton, NJ: Princeton University Press, 1999).

Clottes, J. & D. Lewis-Williams. *The Shamans of Prehistory: Trance and Magic in the Painted Caves*, S. Hawkes (trans.) (New York: Abrams, 1998).

Cohen, T. "Aesthetic/Non-Aesthetic and the Concept of Taste: A Critique of Sibley's Position". *Theoria* **39** (1973): 113–252.

Coleman, E. J. *Philosophy of Painting by Shih-t'ao: A Translation and Exposition of his Hua-P'u (Treatise on the Philosophy of Painting)* (The Hague: Mouton, 1978).

Collingwood, R. G. *The Principles of Art* (Oxford: Oxford University Press, 1938).

Collingwood, R. G. *The New Leviathan* (Oxford: Clarendon Press, 1992).

Crane, T. (ed.). *Dispositions: A Debate* (London: Routledge, 1996).

Damasio, A. R. *Descartes' Error: Emotion, Reason and the Human Brain* (New York: Putnam, 1994).

Davies, S. *Musical Meaning and Expression* (Ithaca, NY: Cornell University Press, 1994).

Dewey, J. *Art as Experience* (London: Allen & Unwin, 1934).

Dickie, G. "All Aesthetic Attitude Theories Fail: The Myth of the Aesthetic Attitude". *American Philosophical Quarterly* **1** (1964): 56–66.

Dickie, G. 1958. "Beardsley's Phantom Aesthetic Experience". *Journal of Philosophy* **62** (1958): 129–36.

Dickinson, E. *Selected Poems of Emily Dickinson*, J. Reeves (ed.) (Oxford: Heinemann Educational, 1957).

Dilworth, J. "Is Ridley Charitable to Collingwood?" *Journal of Aesthetics and Art Criticism* **56** (1998): 393–6.

Ducasse, C. J. *The Philosophy of Art* (London: Allen & Unwin, 1929).

Ehrenreich, B. *Dancing in the Streets: A History of Collective Joy* (New York: Metropolitan, 2006).

Eilan, N. "Perceptual Intentionality, Attention and Consciousness". In *Current Issues in Philosophy of Mind*, A. O'Hear (ed.), 121–202 (Cambridge: Cambridge University Press, 1998).

Ekman, P. "An Argument for Basic Emotions". *Cognition and Emotion* **6** (1992): 169–200.

Ekman, P. *Emotions Revealed* (New York: Henry Holt, 2003).

Ekman, P., E. R. Sorenson & W. V. Friesen. "Pan-Cultural Elements in Facial Displays of Emotion". *Science* **164** (1969): 86–8.

Eliot, T. S. *Collected Poems 1909–1962* (London: Faber, 2002).

Elliott, R. K. "Aesthetic Theory and the Experience of Art". Reprinted in *Aesthetics*, H. Osborne (ed.), 145–57 (Oxford: Oxford University Press, 1972).

Feagin, S. L. "The Pleasures of Tragedy". *American Philosophical Quarterly* **20** (1983): 95–104.

Fodor, J. A. *Psychological Explanation* (New York: Random House, 1968).

Forster, E. M. *Howards End* (London: Softback Preview, 1995).

Forster, E. M. *Maurice* (Harmondsworth: Penguin, 1972).

Freeman, D. "Aesthetic Experience as the Transformation of Pleasure". *Harvard Review of Philosophy* **17** (2010): 56–75.

Freeman, D. "The Lens of Emotions: Wollheim's Two Conceptions of Emotional Colouring". *Literature and Aesthetics* **20**(2) (2010): 74–91.

Freud, S. "Negation". In *The Standard Edition of the Complete Psychological Works of Sigmund Freud*, vol. 19, J. Strachey (ed. & trans.) (London: Hogarth Press & Institute of Psycho-Analysis, [1925] 1961).

Freud, S. *Notes Upon a Case of Obsessional Neurosis*. In *The Standard Edition of the Complete Psychological Works of Sigmund Freud*, vol. 10, J. Strachey (ed. & trans.) (London: Hogarth Press & Institute of Psycho-Analysis, [1909] 1955).

Freud, S. *Psycho-Analytic Notes on an Autobiographical Account of a Case of Paranoia*. In *The Standard Edition of the Complete Psychological Works of Sigmund Freud*, vol. 12, J. Strachey (ed. & trans.) (London: Hogarth Press & Institute of Psycho-Analysis, [1911] 1958).

Freud, S. 1953–74. *Totem and Taboo*. In *The Standard Edition of the Complete Psychological Works of Sigmund Freud*, vol. 13, J. Strachey (ed. & trans.) (London: Hogarth Press & Institute of Psycho-Analysis, [1912–13] 1955).

Gage, J. "The Distinctness of Turner". *Journal of the Royal Society of Arts* **123** (1974–75): 448–54.

Gardner, S. *Irrationality and the Philosophy of Psychoanalysis* (Cambridge: Cambridge University Press, 1993).

Gaut, B. *Art, Emotion and Ethics* (Oxford: Oxford University Press, 2007).

Gerwen, R. van (ed.). *Richard Wollheim on the Art of Painting: Art as Representation and Expression* (Cambridge: Cambridge University Press, 2001).

Geuss, R. "Art and Theodicy". In his *Morality, Culture, and History*, 78–115 (Cambridge: Cambridge University Press, 1999).

Goldie, P. *The Emotions: A Philosophical Exploration* (Oxford: Oxford University Press, 2000).

Goldie, P. "Wollheim on Emotion and Imagination". *Philosophical Studies* **127** (2006): 1–17.

Gombrich, E. H. *Art and Illusion* (Princeton, NJ: Princeton University Press, 1960).

Gombrich, E. H. *The Essential Gombrich* (London: Phaidon, 1996).

Gordon, R. *The Structure of the Emotions: Investigations in Cognitive Science* (Cambridge: Cambridge University Press, 1987).

Green, M. S. *Self-Expression* (Oxford: Clarendon Press, 2007).

Griffiths, P. *What Emotions Really Are* (Chicago, IL: Chicago University Press, 1997).

Grossman, D. *Lion's Honey: The Myth of Samson*, S. Schoffman (trans.) (Edinburgh: Canongate, 2006).

Hall, M. *Leaving Home* (London: Faber, 1996).

Hamilton, J. *Turner: A Life* (London: Hodder & Stoughton, 1997).

Hampshire, S. *Freedom of Mind* (Princeton. NJ: Princeton University Press, 1971).

Hausman, C. R. "Aaron Ridley's Defense of Collingwood Pursued". *Journal of Aesthetics and Art Criticism* **56** (1998): 391–3.

Hay, J. *Shitao: Painting and Modernity in Early Qing China* (Cambridge: Cambridge University Press, 2001).

Heerwagen, J. H. & G. H. Orians. "Humans, Habitats, and Aesthetics". In *The Biophilia Hypothesis*, S. R. Kellert & E. O. Wilson (eds), 138–72 (Washington, DC: Island Press, 1993).

Hegel, G. W. F. *Lectures on the History of Philosophy*, E. S. Haldane & F. H. Simon (trans.) (London: Kegan Paul, 1892).

Hegel, G. W. F. *Introductory Lectures on Aesthetics*, B. Bosanquet (trans.) (Harmondsworth: Penguin, 1993).

Heidegger, M. *Nietzsche: Volume I: The Will to Power as Art*, D. F. Krell (trans.) (London: Routledge, 1981).

Herwitz, D. "The Work of Art as Psychoanalytical Object: Wollheim on Manet". *Journal of Aesthetics and Art Criticism* **42** (1991): 137–53.

Holcomb, A. M. "'Indistinctness is My Fault'. A letter about Turner from C. R. Leslie to James Lennox". *Burlington Magazine* **114** (1972): 557–8.

Hopkins, R. "The Spectator in the Picture". See Gerwen, *Richard Wollheim on the Art of Painting*, 215–31.

Hume, D. *A Treatise of Human Nature*, D. F. Norton & M. J. Norton (eds) (Oxford: Oxford University Press, 2000).

Jahn, G. R. "The Aesthetic Theory of Leo Tolstoy's *What Is Art?*" *Journal of Aesthetics and Art Criticism* **34**(1) (1975): 59–65.

James, W. "What Is an Emotion?" *Mind* **9** (1884): 188–205.

James, W. *The Principles of Psychology* (Chicago. IL: Encyclopædia Britannica, 1952).

Kandinsky, W. *Concerning the Spiritual in Art*, M. T. H. Sadler (trans.) (London: Tate Publishing, 2006).

Kant, I. *Critique of the Power of Judgment*, P. Guyer & E. Matthews (trans.) (Cambridge: Cambridge University Press, 2000).

Kieran, M. "Forbidden Knowledge: The Challenge of Immoralism". In *Art and Morality*, S. Gardner & J. Bermudez (eds), 56–73 (London: Routledge, 2002).

Kierkegaard, S. *Fear and Trembling, and The Book on Adler*, W. Lowrie (trans.) (London: Everyman, 1994).

Kivy, P. *Sound Sentiment* (Philadelphia, PA: Temple University Press, 1989).

Lange, C. G. *Om sindsbevaegelser: Et psyko-fysiologisk studie* (Copenhagen: Jacob Lunds, 1885).

Lazarus, R. S. *Emotion and Adaptation* (New York: Oxford University Press, 1991).

Lear, J. "Katharsis". In *Essays on Aristotle's Poetics*, A. Oksenberg Rorty (ed.), 315–40 (Princeton, NJ: Princeton University Press, 1992).

Lear, J. *Love and its Place in Nature* (New York: Farrar, Straus & Giroux, 1990).

Lear, J. *Radical Hope: Ethics in the Face of Cultural Devastation* (Cambridge, MA: Harvard University Press, 2006).

Levinson, J. *Contemplating Art: Essays in Aesthetics* (Oxford: Clarendon Press, 2006).

Levinson, J. "Music and Negative Emotions". *Pacific Philosophical Quarterly* **63** (1982): 327–46.

Levinson, J. *The Pleasures of Aesthetics* (Ithaca, NY: Cornell University Press, 1996).

Lewis-Williams, D. *The Mind in the Cave: Consciousness and the Origins of Art* (London: Thames & Hudson, 2002).

Manson, N. C. "Wollheim's Freud and the Extension of Ordinary Psychology". Paper presented at "Mind, Art and Psychoanalysis: Perspectives on Richard Wollheim" conference, Heythrop College, 20 June 2008.

Marshall, E. "Spinoza's Cognitive Affects and their Feel". *British Journal for the History of Philosophy* **16** (2008): 1–23.

Matravers, D. "Aesthetic Properties". *Proceedings of the Aristotelian Society Supplement* **79** (2005): 191–210.

Matravers, D. *Art and Emotion* (Oxford: Clarendon Press, 1998).

Matravers, D. "Wollheim on the Origins of Value". Unpublished paper delivered at "Mind, Art and Psychoanalysis: Perspectives on Richard Wollheim" conference, Heythrop College, 20 June 2008.

McVeagh, D. "Preface". In Elgar, *Concerto for Violoncello and Orchestra, E minor, Op. 85* (London: Eulenburg, 1986).

Mellor, D. H. *Matters of Metaphysics* (Cambridge: Cambridge University Press, 1991).

Mistry, R. *Tales from Firozsha Baag* (London: Faber, 1992).

Murphy, S. T. & R. B. Zajonc. "Affect, Cognition, and Awareness: Affective Priming with Suboptimal and Optimal Stimulus". *Journal of Personality and Social Psychology* **64** (1993): 723–39.

Nehamas, A. "Pity and Fear in the *Rhetoric* and the *Poetics*". In *Essays on Aristotle's Poetics*, A. Oksenberg Rorty (ed.), 291–314 (Princeton, NJ: Princeton University Press, 1992).

Nietzsche, F. "Toward the Physiology of Art". In M. Heidegger, *Nietzsche: Volume I: The Will to Power as Art*, D. F. Krell (trans.) (London: Routledge, 1981). Originally published in Nietzsche's *Grossoktavausgabe*, vol. 16, 432–4 (Leipzig: Naumann, 1905).

Nietzsche, F. *Twilight of the Idols*, D. Large (trans.) (Oxford: Oxford University Press, 1998).

Nietzsche, F. *The Will to Power*, W. Kaufmann & R. J. Hollingdale (trans.) (London: Weidenfeld & Nicolson, 1968).

Nussbaum, M. C. "Tragedy and Self-Sufficiency: Plato and Aristotle on Fear and Pity". In *Essays on Aristotle's Poetics*, A. Oksenberg Rorty (ed.), 261–90 (Princeton, NJ: Princeton University Press, 1992).

Nussbaum, M. C. *Upheavals of Thought: The Intelligence of Emotions* (Cambridge: Cambridge University Press, 2001).

Ovid. *Metamorphoses*, D. Raeburn (trans.) (London: Penguin, 2004).

Plato. *Republic*, G. M. A. Grube (trans.) (Indianapolis, IN: Hackett, 1974).

Price, A. W. "Three Types of Projection". In *Psychoanalysis, Mind and Art: Perspectives on Richard Wollheim*, J. Hopkins & A. Savile (eds), 110–28 (Oxford: Blackwell, 1992).

Prinz, J. J. *Gut Reactions: A Perceptual Theory of Emotion* (Oxford: Oxford University Press, 2004).

Putnam, H. "Minds and Machines". In *Dimensions of Mind*, S. Hook (ed.), 136–64 (New York: New York University Press, 1960).

Richards, I. A. *Principles of Literary Criticism* (London: Kegan Paul, Trench, Trubner, 1925).

Ridley, A. "Collingwood's Commitments: A Reply to Hausman and Dilworth". *Journal of Aesthetics and Art Criticism* **56** (1998): 396–8.

Ridley, A. "Not Ideal: Collingwood's Expression Theory". *Journal of Aesthetics and Art Criticism* **55** (1997): 263–72.

Ridley, A. *R. G. Collingwood: A Philosophy of Art* (London: Orion, 1998).

Robinson, J. *Deeper than Reason: Emotion and its Role in Literature, Music, and Art* (Oxford: Clarendon Press, 2005).

Rorty, A. O. (ed.). *Explaining Emotions* (Berkeley, CA: University of California Press, 1980).

Rorty, A. O. "Aristotle on the Metaphysical Status of Pathe". *Review of Metaphysics* **38** (1984): 521–46.

Rosenberg, H. *The Tradition of the New* (New York: Horizon, 1959).

Ryle, G. *The Concept of Mind* (London: Hutchinson, 1949).

Savile, A. *The Test of Time* (Oxford: Clarendon Press, 1982).

Schellekens, E. "Art, Emotion, Ethics: Conceptual Boundaries and Kinds of Value". *Philosophical Books* **50**(3) (2009): 158–71.

Schellekens, E. "Three Debates in Meta-Aesthetics". In *New Waves in Aesthetics*, K. Stock & K. Thomson-Jones (eds), 170–87 (Basingstoke: Palgrave Macmillan, 2008).

Scherer, K. R. *Facets of Emotion: Recent Research* (Hillsdale, NJ: Erlbaum, 1988).

Scruton, R. *Beauty* (Oxford: Oxford University Press, 2009).

Shakespeare, W. *Tragedy of King Lear* (London: Nathaniel Butter, 1608).

Shih-t'ao. "Shitao (Zhu Ruoji): Returning Home (1976.280)". In *Heilbrunn Timeline of Art History* (New York: Metropolitan Museum of Art, 2000). www.metmuseum.org/toah/works-of-art/1976.280 (accessed September 2011).

Sibley, F. "Aesthetic Concepts". *Philosophical Review* **68** (1959): 421–50.

Solomon, R. C. *The Passions: Emotions and the Meaning of Life* (New York: Doubleday, 1976).

Solomon, R. C. (ed.). *Thinking about Feeling: Contemporary Philosophers on Emotions* (Oxford: Oxford University Press, 2004).

Spinoza, B. *Ethics*, E. Curley (trans.) (Harmondsworth: Penguin, 1996).

Stendhal. *De l'amour* (Paris: P. Mongie l'Aîné, 1822).

Stocker, M. & E. Hegeman. *Valuing Emotions* (Cambridge: Cambridge University Press, 1999).

Stolnitz, J. *Aesthetics and Art Criticism* (Boston, MA: Houghton Mifflin, 1960).

Stolnitz, J. "On the Origins of 'Aesthetic Disinterestedness'". *Journal of Aesthetics and Art Criticism* **20** (1961): 131–43.

Sullivan, M. *The Three Perfections: Chinese Painting, Poetry and Calligraphy (The Sixth Walter Neurath Memorial Lecture 1974)* (London: Thames & Hudson, 1976).

Swedenborg, E. *Heavenly Secrets (Arcana coelestia)*, J. F. Potts (trans.) (New York: Swedenborg Foundation, 1978).

Tennyson, A. *In Memoriam, Maud and Other Poems* (London: J. M. Dent, 1974).

Toksvig, S. *Emanuel Swedenborg* (New Haven, CT: Yale University Press, 1948).

Tolstoy, L. *What is Art?*, R. Pevear & L. Volokhonsky (trans.) (Harmondsworth: Penguin, 1995).

Tormey, A. *The Concept of Expression* (Princeton, NJ: Princeton University Press, 1971).

Tovey, D. F. *Essays in Musical Analysis: Symphonies and Other Orchestral Works* (Oxford: Oxford University Press, 1981).

Velleman, J. D. "Identification and Identity". In his *Self to Self*, 330–60 (Cambridge: Cambridge University Press, 2006).

Venning, B. *Constable*, rev. edn (London: Studio Editions, 1993).

Véron, E. *Aesthetics*, W. H. Armstrong (trans.) (London: Chapman & Hall, 1879).

Walton, K. "Listening with Imagination: Is Music Representational?" *Journal of Aesthetics and Art Criticism* **52** (1994): 47–61.

Walton, K. "What is Abstract about the Art of Music?" *Journal of Aesthetics and Art Criticism* **46** (1988): 351–64.

Wilde, O. "The Decay of Lying". In *The Works of Oscar Wilde*, 909–31 (London: Collins, 1948).

Wittgenstein, L. *Tractatus Logico-Philosophicus*, D. F. Pears & B. F. McGuinness (trans.) (London: Routledge, 1961).

Wollheim, R. *Art and its Objects*, 2nd edn (Cambridge: Cambridge University Press, 1980).

Wollheim, R. *On Art and the Mind* (London: Allen Lane, 1973).

Wollheim, R. "Correspondence, Projective Properties, and Expression in the Arts". In his *The Mind and Its Depths*, 144–58 (Cambridge, MA: Harvard University Press, 1993).

Wollheim, R. *On the Emotions* (New Haven, CT: Yale University Press, 1999).

Wollheim, R. "Expression". In his *On Art and the Mind*, 84–100 (London: Allen Lane, 1973).

Wollheim, R. *Freud*, 2nd edn (London: Fontana, 1991).

Wollheim, R. *Germs: A Memoir of Childhood* (London: Black Swan, 2004).

Wollheim, R. *The Mind and Its Depths* (Cambridge, MA: Harvard University Press, 1993).

Wollheim, R. *Painting as an Art* (Princeton, NJ: Princeton University Press, 1987).

Wollheim, R. "A Reply to the Contributors". See Gerwen, *Richard Wollheim on the Art of Painting*, 241–61.

Wollheim, R. "The Sheep and the Ceremony". In his *The Mind and Its Depths*, 1–21 (Cambridge, MA: Harvard University Press, 1993).

Wollheim, R. *The Thread of Life* (New Haven, CT: Yale University Press, 1984).

Wordsworth, W. *The Poems*, vol. 1, J. O. Hayden (ed.) (Harmondsworth: Penguin, 1977).

Zajonc, R. B. "Feeling and Thinking: Preferences Need no Inferences". *American Psychologist* **39** (1984): 117–29.

Ziff, J. "J. M. W. Turner on Poetry and Painting". *Studies in Romanticism* **3** (1964): 198.

Index

Dewey, J. 4–5
Dickinson, E. 39, 42
disinterestedness 167
dispositions 173—4; *see also* mind,
  philosophy of
Ducasse, C. J. 189

Eilan, N. 35
Ekman, P. 178–9
Elgar, E. 122–9, 152–4, 156–7
Eliot, T. S. 137
emotion
  and attitude 24, 94, 98
  cognitive theory and non-cognitive
    theory 37
  emotional disposition as framework
    94–5, 98
  emotional economy theory 26–7, 160
  and feeling 17–19
  and instinct 17, 19–20
  as mental state or mental disposition
    16, 26–7
  process theory 37–8
  psychological reality of emotion 27–9
  theory of 16–20, 24–5, 36–8, 160–62
  see also art and emotion; emotional
    engagement; mind, philosophy
    of; perceptual properties; plenary
    experience of emotion
emotional economy *see* emotion; *see
  also* emotional engagement, plenary
  experience of emotion
emotional engagement 39–41, 47–8,
  169, 193–4
  and being at home in the world
    192–3
  and emotional articulation 94–103,
    177
  and emotional communication 86–93
  and emotional infection through
    correspondence 79–85
  and emotional infection through
    resonance 76–9, 84, 86
  and emotional isolation 192
  as fulfilment of human need 136,
    138–41, 157
  with the landscape 80, 84, 92–3
  with other people 49, 85, 91

and other ways of experiencing
  emotion 75
and personal relationships 163, 165
and plenary experience of emotion
  184
with works of art 84–5, 93, 106,
  143–6
see also expressive perception
emotional experience *see* emotional
  engagement
emotional interaction *see* emotional
  engagement
expressive perception 106
  affective aspect 114
  and art 107–8, 113–15
  interaction between aspects 107, 115
  perceptual aspect 108–14
  see also plenary experience of emotion
empathy 88
expression
  and music 71, 80, 124–5, 183–4
  theory of 70, 109–11, 180
  see also expressive perception
externalized properties *see* perceptual
  properties

Feagin, S. L. 187
fear 13–15, 19, 43–5, 86
feeling *see* emotion
folk psychology 30–31
Forster, E. M. 149, 165
framework *see* interpretative framework
Freud, S. 68, 82–3, 97, 186
functionalism 28

Gage, J. 96–7
Gaut, B. 134–6
Geuss, R. and cats 190
Gibbons, G. 147
Gloucester (Shakespearian character)
  88–9, 91
Goldie, P. 35, 176
Gombrich, E. H. 109, 172
Gogh, V. van 130–31
Green, M. S. 180
Guernica (painting) *see* Picasso

Hadleigh Castle (painting) *see* Constable